*Trading in Lives?*

Operations of the Jewish Relief and Rescue Committee
in Budapest, 1944–1945

# Trading in Lives?

## Operations of the Jewish Relief and Rescue Committee in Budapest, 1944–1945

by

SZABOLCS SZITA

CEU PRESS

Central European University Press
Budapest • New York

©2005 by Szabolcs Szita
English translation © by Sean Lambert

Published in 2005 by

*Central European University Press*
An imprint of the
Central European University Share Company
Nádor utca 11, H-1051 Budapest, Hungary
*Tel:* +36-1-327-3138 or 327-3000
*Fax:* +36-1-327-3183
*E-mail:* ceupress@ceu.hu
*Website:* www.ceupress.com

400 West 59th Street, New York NY 10019, USA
*Tel:* +1-212-547-6932
*Fax:* +1-646-557-2416
*E-mail:* mgreenwald@sorosny.org

Translated by Sean Lambert

ISBN 963 7326 30 8 cloth


Library of Congress Cataloging-in-Publication Data

Szita, Szabolcs.
  [Aki egy embert megment—a világot menti meg. English]
  Trading in lives? : operations of the Jewish Relief and Rescue Committee in Budapest, 1944–
1945 / by Szabolcs Szita ; [translated by Sean Lambert]. – 1st ed.
    p. cm.
  Includes index.
  ISBN 9637326308
  1. Va'adat ha-'ezrah veha-hatsalah be-Budapesht. 2. World War, 1939–1945–Jews–Rescue–
Hungary–Budapest. 3. Holocaust, Jewish (1939-1945)–Hungary–Budapest. 4. Jews–
Persecutions–Hungary–Budapest. I. Lambert, Sean. II. Title.

  DS135.H92S9335 2005
  940.53'1835'0943912–dc22

                                        2005014583


Printed in Hungary by
Akaprint Kft., Budapest

# Contents

# 1. Operations of the Budapest Relief and Rescue Committee from 1941 to 1944

From the fall of 1941 on, the persecution of Jews intensified in the countries surrounding the Kingdom of Hungary. Thousands of refugees fled from systematic looting, ghettoization and deportation to Hungarian territory. The Jewish charity organizations in Hungary were faced with a new challenge. They were compelled to broaden the scope of their activities in order to provide assistance to the forlorn, defenseless multitudes.

The territorial revisions and the re-expansion of the country that took place between 1938 and 1941 brought a palpable strengthening in the Hungarian Zionist movement. (With hardly more than 4,000–5,000 members, Zionism had little influence over the lives of Hungarian Jews before 1938.)[1] The growing popularity of Zionism was also due to the effect of a several rounds of anti-Jewish legislation and widespread, institutionalized discrimination directed against Hungarian Jews.

In Budapest and several provincial towns, Jews, both young and old, began to take notice of the Zionists, whose role, until that time, had been marginal in Hungarian Jewish society. Heavily pressed, indeed, driven against the wall, Hungarian Jews began to realize that the traditional spirit of Hungarian–Jewish coexistence was a thing of the past, and that rapid "Magyarization" was no longer a viable alternative. "Official" Hungarian Jewry had failed to stand its ground, adopting a wait-and-see attitude that merely aggravated the plight of all Jews. Zionism, by contrast, confronted Hungarian Jews with alternate patterns of identification and strategies, essentially offering them the prospect of deliverance.

---

[1] Attila Novák, *Átmenetben. A cionista mozgalom négy éve Magyarországon* [In Transition. Four Years of the Hungarian Zionist Movement] (Múlt és Jövő Kiadó, 2000), p. 17. Zionist-inspired emigration was continually low. For example, only 306 Jews emigrated from Hungary in 1931; in 1936 this number increased to 416, then fell again to a mere 318 in 1941.

Zionist leaders perceived correctly that the rising tide of National Socialism, the change of climate brought upon by the war, the ceaseless hate-mongering, and the hysterical upsurge of anti-Semitism were strengthening the appeal of their ideas. Legalized discrimination, existential insecurity and impoverishment, and the humiliating experience of enlistment of Jewish men into unarmed forced labor battalions in the Hungarian Army afflicted hundreds of thousands of Hungarian Jews. These phenomena were evidence of a profound change in the status of Hungarian Jewry, one that brought it closer to the frequently maligned Hungarian Zionist movement which had taken root in response to social ostracism and offered an alternative to the assimilationist tenets of the Jewish religious establishment.

The upswing in the movement was, if anything, dramatic, though this did not entail unity. The movement continued to encompass several groups espousing diverse principles. Still, compared to the earlier state of affairs, the sheer fact that representatives of the barely tolerated, only semi-legal Zionist groups at least managed to establish a joint framework for future cooperation marked true progress.

Cooperation between Zionists in Northern Transylvania and the Budapest Relief and Rescue Committee (*Va'adat ha-Ezra ve-ha-Hatzala be-Budapest,* known as *the Va'ada*) took years to develop. Operating as the Hungarian arm of the Palestine-based *Va'adat Ezra ve-ha Hatzala,* the Budapest team was a dynamic group, highly committed to Zionism. Its leaders were Ottó Komoly, an engineer and the president of the Hungarian Zionist Association (*Magyar Cionista Szövetség,* or MCSz), legalized in 1927, and Dr. Rezső Kasztner, a journalist from Kolozsvár (Cluj). Working with them at various times were Joel Brand and his wife Hansi, Sámuel Springmann, Sándor (Shalom) Offenbach, Endre Biss, Dr. Miklós (Moshe) Schweiziger, Ernő (Tzvi) Szilágyi from the Pro-Palestine League of Hungarian Jews[2] and others.

Members of the Budapest Relief and Rescue Committee (to be referred to from now on as the Rescue Committee) represented various trends within the Zionist movement. Komoly was affiliated to the General Zionists, Kasztner and Joel Brand to the *Ichud,*[3] while Miklós (Moshe) Krausz, who later worked with them, was a member of the *Mizrachi.*[4]

---

[2] This organization was founded with the aim of recruiting prominent Jews to the cause of promoting Zionism in Hungary.

[3] A union of the Zionist groups *Hanoar Hatzioni, Dror,* and *Maccabi Hatzair.*

[4] This *portmanteau* was the name of an organization working to realize Zionist ideals based on religious ideals. From 1934, Krausz served as an agent for the immigration division of the

Following the German occupation of Hungary, Zionist activity in Budapest crystallized around the Budapest Palestine Office[5] (*Palamt*), led by Krausz, and the *Chalutz* Movement.[6] These groups were forced to deal with the most pressing issues of the day: emigration to Palestine (*aliyah* in Hebrew), organization of Jewish self-defense and support of refugees. Necessity increasingly dictated the utilization of both legal and illegal methods of dealing with these matters.

The head of the Rescue Committee, the construction engineer Ottó Komoly, was born in Kolozsvár (Cluj) in 1892. He had been raised in a Zionist spirit since his early youth.[7] He began his work with the Hungarian Zionist Association following World War I as an editor for *Zsidó Szemle* [Jewish Review]. In 1940, he became president of the League. His study "The Zionist View of Life" as well as a series of well-argued appeals he submitted to the government probably contributed to the Kállay cabinet's partial authorization of Zionist activity in Hungary in 1943.[8] At this time, Komoly was linked closely to parties, politicians and journalists working to promote democratic political transformation and the interests of the "other Hungary." He considered prompt withdrawal from the war to be in Hungary's national interest, utilizing the Zionist News Service to advocate this position.

Komoly took a deep interest in issues regarding the future of Hungarian Jewry and the creation of a Jewish homeland. On several occasions he exchanged views with Hungarian diplomats, including Aladár Szegedy-Maszák, the head of the political department of the Foreign Ministry, about the treatment of the "Jewish problem." Szegedy-Maszák was a highly respected liberal politician who espoused bourgeois ideals.

---

Hungarian branch of the Jewish Agency for Palestine. Working with him at the agency was fellow *Mizrachist* Mihály Salamon, who became president of the Hungarian Zionist Association following the war.

[5] This office administered emigration to Palestine, disseminated the so-called *Zertifikat* issued by the British government and distributed with assistance from the Jewish Agency (*Sochnut*). Between World War I and 1938, between 200 and 300 Jews emigrated annually from Hungary to Palestine, mainly through legal channels.

[6] *Chalutzim* was a term used to designate young, prospective immigrants who had been trained to do agricultural work in Palestine. There were approximately 500 such immigrants in Hungary between 1942 and 1944—eighty came from the *B'nai Akiba* (religious), thirty from the *Betar* (Revisionist), seventy from the *Dror Habonim* (Social Democratic), forty from the *Ichud* (also Social Democratic) as well as ninety from the *Maccabi Hatzair* (Socialist) organizations.

[7] The son of the Zionist David Kohen translated Theodore Herzl's seminal work, *Altneuland*, into Hungarian in 1916.

[8] Dr. Alexander Emed, *A magyarországi cionista mozgalom története* [History of the Hungarian Zionist Movement], (Bethlen Téri Oneg Sábbát Klub, s.a.), p. 102.

Dr. Rezső Kasztner was born in 1906. After graduating from the Jewish High School in Kolozsvár he took a degree in law. Between 1929 and 1931 he worked at the Jewish Agency in Bucharest, after which he returned to Kolozsvár where he worked for the newspaper *Új Kelet* [New East], first as a sports reporter, then as a political correspondent. In the meantime he edited several standard Zionist works. Kasztner subsequently joined the staff of the Pro-Palestine Association in Budapest, where he was an employee. According to some evidence his primary job was to collect donations for the Association. His own financial situation however, was seen by many as pretty unstable.

From July to December 1942, Kasztner served in a forced labor battalion along with some 440 other Jewish intellectuals, constructing military fortifications on the revised Hungarian–Romanian border in Northern Transylvania, a duty from which he was relieved, according to some allegations, through German intercession.[9] He also maintained contacts with Hungarian counterintelligence, primarily with Staff Lieutenant-Colonel József Garzoly, Head of the Southeast Europe Division.

In his capacity as leader of the Rescue Committee, Ottó Komoly capitalized on the experience Kasztner had gained as a member of northern Transylvania's well-developed Zionist movement. He was decisive, flexible and competent. Kasztner's skills and gifts became particularly obvious following the German occupation of Hungary in the spring of 1944. If necessary, he took great risks without hesitation in order to achieve the association's objectives. A workaholic, he cared little about his own well-being. Kasztner made good use of his vast network of personal connections to promote Jewish rescue operations in Europe.

Joel (also known as Jenő) Brand was born in 1906 in Naszód, Transylvania. He finished grammar school in Erfurt, then sought his fortune in America. In 1927, Brand returned to Erfurt, where he worked in his father's factory until his arrest, in March 1933, for alleged Communist activity.[10] After spending a year in prison, Brand took up residence in Kolozsvár, Romania before moving

---

[9] Historical Office (henceforth referred to as the HO), V-129355, p. 2. According to testimony given in 1946, the Kolozsvár Jewish community sent financial aid to Kasztner's forced-labor battalion. The money disappeared, prompting an investigation of Kasztner. (The leader of Kolozsvár's Neologue Jewish community was Kasztner's father-in-law Dr. József Fischer, a former member of the Romanian Parliament.) Though the inquiry resulted in a verdict of not guilty, the Pro-Palestine Association dismissed Kasztner. For a detailed biography see Randolph L. Braham, ed., *The Destruction of Hungarian Jewry* vol. II, (New York, 1963), pp. 907–908.

[10] Brand was considered to be the *enfant terrible* of his family. Even in his father's factory he incited workers to rebel against "exploitation."

to Hungary at the end of 1936. While in Hungary, he made plans to emigrate to Palestine. During his preparatory agricultural training he met his future wife, Hajnalka (known commonly as Hansi) Hartmann, who was five years his junior. Soon a marriage of convenience took place between the two.

With an improvement in their financial situation the pair dropped their plan to emigrate. They gradually became a genuine couple and started a family. Starting with a single sewing machine, they soon employed outside help to manufacture gloves and other hand-made products. Their business became stable by 1942, and a year later they prospered.[11] The Brands' home—first in Bulyovszky Street, then, from the summer of 1944 on, at 15 Andor Semsey Street—became a hub of Budapest social life. Proficient in several languages and self-confident, Brand took Hungarian citizenship, avoiding conscription into a Jewish forced labor battalion by feigning diabetes.

By 1943, Brand was better known and had more influence within the Budapest social élite than Kasztner, due mainly to his extensive connections with the *demimonde*. He did a great deal of business, mostly shady dealings, in the city's night life, and was involved in everything from the black market to human smuggling. Brand seemed to be oblivious to the potentially lethal risks he was taking.

On several occasions, Brand bragged openly of having connections that reached all the way to the White House; thus German agents saw him as an embodiment and an influential representative of the imagined "Jewish world power" *(Weltmacht)*, and the *de facto* leader of the Rescue Committee. It should be noted that these agents, being realistic and therefore considering also the likely consequences of a German defeat in the war, presumably sought to obtain "good marks" with the Allies through their connections with Brand.

It is certain that by that time Brand was already on good terms with some German military officers, and maintained contacts with the Hungarian network of Admiral Canaris' *Abwehr*,[12] specifically with the agents Josef Winninger[13] and Bandi (Andreas) Grosz.[14] He also established ties with several

---

[11] Testimony from the niece of Mrs. Jenő Brand, HO V-129355/a, p. 35.

[12] The *Abwehr* was the intelligence unit of the German military, operating both at home and abroad.

[13] There exist some indirect references to Winninger's half-Jewish ancestry.

[14] Grosz was born in Beregszász (today Beregovo, Ukraine). He earned his living as a rug dealer, then smuggler. In 1930, he was convicted of customs violations, in 1934 for rug smuggling. Following the Anschluss he sold passports to Jewish refugees from Austria, for which he was condemned to a year and a half in a Hungarian prison. Grosz volunteered his services to the *Abwehr* in order to avoid serving his sentence, working with the Germans first in Switzerland,

paid informants of Hungarian Counterintelligence, VKF 2 (the 2nd Department of the Chiefs-of-Staff).[15]

The watchmaker and jeweler Sámuel Springmann was born in 1900. This colorful character working for the Rescue Committee established and operated the critically important courier network. Springmann was able to recruit diplomatic couriers to forward messages and letters as well as double agents who were prepared to undertake any mission for the right price. The courier network extended as far as Będzin and Warsaw.[16] Its reach stretched South as well, as far as Istanbul, where it maintained invaluable links to the Zionist Rescue Committee and the Jewish Agency based in that city. The financial support that arrived regularly from Istanbul was vital to the operations of the Budapest Rescue Committee and the Hungarian Zionist Movement.

Springmann gained extensive experience dealing with the extremely complex affairs involving refugees in the early 1940s. As far as it can be concluded from the scanty evidence, Springmann worked primarily with the Brands on matters pertaining to international transit and the establishment of contacts. Sick and exhausted, Springmann emigrated before the German occupation of Hungary.

Shalom (known also as Sándor) Offenbach was born in Łodz, Poland in 1896. He became involved with the Rescue Committee through his work assisting Polish refugees in 1943. Offenbach was responsible for oversight of monies donated to the Polish Committee, assuming more responsible tasks during Brand's trips to Turkey. He helped lay the financial groundwork for the first *aliyah*,[17] which *Obersturmbannführer* Adolf Eichmann referred to as the "sample train," appraising and transferring to the SS the jewels, gems and other valuables collected in exchange for a permission to emigrate. He also took part

---

then in Sofia. This enabled him to return to Hungary. However, because his prison sentence was still in force, he felt compelled to establish contacts with Hungarian military intelligence while continuing to serve as an agent of the *Abwehr.* Grosz operated as a Balkan courier for both intelligence agencies, travelling to Turkey eight times between March and May 1944. (In the meantime he was also transmitting information to the Budapest Zionists.) He also worked for the Poles, the Japanese and even the Americans. After the war Grosz served as a witness in Adolf Eichmann's Jerusalem trial. He died in Munich in 1970.

[15] István Ujszászy's memorandum regarding the proceedings of the 2nd Department of the Chiefs-of-Staff (HO A 414/3) is published in Szabolcs Szita's *A Gestapo Magyarországon* [The Gestapo in Hungary], (Korona Kiadó, 2002), pp. 60–63.

[16] Springmann employed couriers of various nationalities, from Austrians and Swedes to Poles and Japanese. Following the occupation of Hungary it became evident that several of them had been working "full-time" with the Germans.

[17] The literal meaning of this word is "ascension." In practice it meant emigration to Palestine.

in the financial committee that collected resources for the second *aliyah*. His wife was also engaged in rescue operations.

Little information survives regarding the Zionist activities of the Zionist lawyer Dr. Miklós Schweiger (Moshe, as he was called in the movement). The 39-year-old lawyer from Szabadka was a member of the *Ichud*. In compliance with orders received from Palestine in February 1944, Schweiger was appointed head of the nascent Jewish Defense Committee in Budapest.[18]

Following the German occupation, Schweiger wanted to return to Szabadka, but then he stayed on in Budapest. The *Geheime Staatspolizei*[19] (Gestapo) took him into custody during the summer of 1944, sending him to the Mauthausen concentration camp, where he was registered as prisoner No. 79,500 on July 14. Schweiger was fortunate enough to be released from Mauthausen on account of "higher" German interests, because his health deteriorated greatly as a result of hard labor in the camp quarries.[20]

Ernő Szilágyi was born in Kaposvár in 1898. By 1939 he had become one of the leaders of the Marxist–Zionist *Ha-Shomer ha-Tza'ir* Party, playing an important role in the work of the Palestine Office. He took pleasure in teaching the precepts of Zionism to young Jews, gradually assembling a steady circle of pupils around him. In April 1944, following the German occupation of Hungary, he was arrested and held briefly on suspicion of organizing illegal emigration and maintaining contacts with Tito's Yugoslav Partisans. His doubts about collaboration made him resign from the Rescue Committee when it began to negotiate with the SS in serious. He left the country as one of the passengers of the "Kasztner Train."

Though not a member herself, Baroness Edit Weisz unselfishly gave substantial fianancial contributions to the committee from her own private fortune.[21]

The roots of cooperation among the members of the Relief and Rescue Committee can be traced back to the early summer of 1941. The rapidly dete-

[18] The *Haganah* (literally, "Defense") Committee was established in accordance with this plan, though Schweiger never did assume much authority within this body. Due to Schweiger's poor health, Móse Rosenberg assumed leadership of the committee. The Palestinian *Haganah* had been founded in 1920 to organize defense of Jewish settlements. It also played an important role in the organization of illegal immigration.

[19] German State Secret Police. One of the terror organizations of the German National Socialist state.

[20] Szabolcs Szita, *Magyarok az SS ausztriai lágerbirodalmában* [Hungarians in the Austrian SS Camps], (MAZSÖK, 2000), pp. 71–72.

[21] Mrs. Weisz was a member of the oversight committee of the Palestine Office. Her multifaceted humanitarian work has not yet been sufficiently explored.

riorating positon of European Jewry and the arrival of refugees required improvisation and spontaneity. The crisis reached new dimensions when several thousand Jews—relatives, business associates, friends and acquaintances of many people throughout the Kingdom of Hungary—were caught up in the deadly net of the national authority for the control of foreigners, KEOKH, because of their "unsettled citizenship."[22] These people were in immediate danger and had to be rescued without delay from internment camps in Budapest and the provinces. An ominous future awaited them: they were destined for the first wave of deportations from Hungary, when thousands of Jews who had been deemed "homeless" were transported by the Hungarian authorities to Podolia via Kőrösmező.[23]

The Brands and Springmann got hold of critical information from their contacts within Hungarian counterintelligence during the summer of 1941. They used counterintelligence agents to liberate family members who had been seized in "lighting raids" by the KEOKH, in unexpected identity checks and nighttime arrests, in order to save them from certain death.[24] (Those who had been rescued went through terrible trials. After struggling back to Hungary, they met a nearly universal sense of denial and self-deception. Most Budapest Jews considered accounts of their deportation to be nothing more than panic mongering.)

One of Mrs. Brand's sisters and her husband were located and successfully smuggled home from the theater of military operations by a Hungarian counterintelligence agent named József Krem.[25] Several sources indicate that Brand made a handsome profit by collaborating with Krem and liberating captive Jews.

Jewish refugees had to be smuggled home, a venture fraught with deadly risks, through forests and mountain passes with the help of Polish and Ruthenian peasants, couriers, innkeepers, local officials and, on more than one occasion, soldiers. The rescue of every single Jew represented an uncommonly exciting and exhausting operation of its own.

---

[22] Hungarian-language acronym for the National Central Authority for Alien Control. This organization established internment camps in several Budapest synagogues: at Dohány Street, Aréna Road, Rumbach Sebestyén Street and Páva Street in Ferencváros.

[23] For detailed documentation of this incident see Zoltán Szirtes, *Temetetlen halottaink, 1941 Kőrösmező, Kamenyec-Podolszk* [Our Unburied Dead, 1941 Kőrösmező, Kamenyec-Podolszk (Budapest, 1996).

[24] Those who could not produce documentation verifying their Hungarian nationality, which the authorities had never before requested, were taken into legal custody, often along with their families. The authorities subsequently decided who qualified as a Hungarian citizen.

[25] Andreas Biss, *Der Stopp der Endlösung. Kampf gegen Himmler und Eichmann in Budapest* (Seewald Verlag: Stuttgart–Degerloch, 1966), p. 46.

Establishing legitimacy for the rescued Jews and the continually arriving refugees faced members of the Rescue Committee once again with a new set of tasks and responsibilities. They learned how to obtain suitable temporary living quarters and official residential registration forms. At the same time they had to find ways to feed and cloth the ragged fugitives and refugees, help them to regain some strength, and then to assist them on their way toward their desired destination at the right time and through the appropriate channels.

Sámuel Springmann accomplished a great deal in this endeavor. He was a veteran Zionist, skilled in hiding and adept at harboring fugitives, and he had a broad network of contacts extending from the KEOKH to agents of the *Abwehr*. One of Springmann's close contacts was the already mentioned Bandi Grosz, who served as a highly active agent under a variety of aliases. Depending on the job at hand, Grosz enlisted the help of his many friends and associates to establish a courier network that covered most of Europe. Intermediaries typically received a ten-percent commission when handling Zionist financial issues, though higher compensation was not unknown.[26] Springmann used his liaisons to obtain transit permits for several hundred refugees.

Oskar Schindler, the German industrialist from Cracow, whose rescuing of Jews during World War II inspired the internationally acclaimed film *Schindler's List*, came into contact with Dr. Rezső Kasztner and others involved in the rescue operations in 1942. Even many years after the war, Schindler described the former journalist from Kolozsvár as "dauntless" and his acts "unparalleled." Serving as a liaison between Schindler and Kasztner was the Viennese dentist Dr. Rudolf Sedlatschek, who traveled regularly between Cracow and Budapest. Sedlatschek's primary functions were to transmit messages and large sums of money.

The dentist also maintained contacts with other Polish and Czech Jewish groups. There are some indications that he worked for the Zionists in Turkey as well.

Schindler and Kasztner first met while the latter served as an emissary for the U.S.-based Jewish aid organization called The American Jewish Joint Distribution Committee (often referred to simply as the Joint).[27] Schindler had

---

[26] Information from Hansi Brand's October 22, 1998 lecture at the Yad Vashem Institute in Jerusalem. Video footage of this presentation is in the possession of the author. Grosz served primarily as a German agent, though his "cooperation" extended to many directions.

[27] This organization was established in October 1914 by Felix Warburg and others in order to provide assistance for impoverished Jews who had sought refuge on the territory of what is now Israel at the beginning of World War I. The Joint continued to utilize contributions to support

been introduced to Sedlatschek by Major Franz von Korab, head of the Cracow *Abwehr*, who was Austrian-born.[28] During their subsequent meeting Sedlatschek confided to Schindler that he was the Joint's Budapest representative. He asked for Schindler's help in finding a way to somehow forward letters sent from Palestine via Turkey to Polish Jews who were being held in concentration camps. After comprehensively and thoroughly checking the matter, Schindler decided to help, then established a new, secure postal route. Schindler introduced Dr. Sedlatschek to the SS commander of the Plaszow concentration camp who invited the dentist to visit the camp. *"He was certainly the only person affiliated with the Joint to whom the SS bragged of the horrors of the concentration camps."*[29]

Thereafter a new avenue of cooperation existed between them that was both secure and efficient. Schindler accepted invitations to visit Budapest on several occasions, each time staying for a period of three or four days. During these visits he provided Hungarian Zionists with *detailed information regarding the secret, though undeniable mass murder of Jews that was going on.*

> "I gave Dr. Kasztner a precise description of what was happening to the Jews, the increasingly ruthless actions of the SS, the primary threats, the most effective forms of aid and possible escape routes. Kasztner brought another representative of the relief organization along with him to the hotel where we met. If I remember correctly he was the son of a Budapest jeweler."[30]

According to Schindler the Budapest meetings resulted in the establishing of a series of escape routes. He saw Kasztner's role in this achievement as decisive, and confirmed that their informants had quickly apprised them of the plots and intrigues of the Gestapo. Their losses were insignificant because "Dr. Kasztner's sources of information and intelligence were always *exceptionally good, positively first-rate.*"[31]

---

Jews living in Palestine and Europe during the interwar period. During World War II it donated $78 million to Jews who had been persecuted by the Nazis.

[28] After it became clear that he had Jewish relatives, von Korab was released from service.

[29] Erika Rosenberg, ed., Én, Oskar Schindler. Személyes feljegyzések, levelek és dokumentumok. [*I, Oskar Schindler. Personal notes, letters and documents*] (Canissa Publishing, 2001.), p. 79. (Originally published as *Ich, Oskar Schindler* (F. A. Herbig Verlagsbuchhandlung GmbH: Munich). According to Schindler, Dr. Sedlatschek delivered 125,000 Reichmarks in general aid for Jews confined to concentration camps. He also brought smaller sums for specific prisoners.

[30] Ibid., pp. 79–80. The person in question was presumably Sámuel Springmann.

[31] Ibid., p. 80.

Schindler opened a new chapter in his collaboration with Kasztner when he began making cash advances on money required for urgent rescue operations, and he occasionally also provided assistance to groups designated by the dentist. Dr. Kasztner repeatedly encouraged Schindler to "hire out" as many Jewish prisoners as possible from the SS concentration camp where he had connections, and to shelter them in his "private camp" located next to his factory. (Schindler had to use his own funds to construct and maintain this camp, and run it in accordance with SS security specifications.)

Schindler agreed to Kasztner's request to travel to Istanbul in order to provide several Joint leaders with first-hand information. However, the SD (*Sicherheitzdienst*)[32] prevented him from travelling, confiscating the passport he had submitted in order to obtain the proper transit visas, which he never got back. Schindler consequently made his last visit to Budapest illegally, traveling in a railway coach reserved for daily transport of the Viennese National Socialist newspaper *Völkischer Beobachter*, thus escaping passport checks. According to Schindler, Kasztner and the Viennese dentist also exploited this opportunity to travel clandestinely.

They took advantage of the newspaper-delivery route to help *U-Boots*, as Jews living underground in Vienna were nicknamed. The route was used by the Rescue Committee to provide food to these refugees.[33]

The Budapest rescue team maintained contacts with the Bratislava Rescue Committee as well. The self-defense action group served as a link between Poland, Silesia, Romania and Bulgaria as well as Switzerland. Its members came to the conclusion that their only hope lay in contacts with corrupt officers of the SS or the Gestapo who could be bribed and perhaps persuaded to stop the deportations or at least to protect Jews "for the right fee."

Information from the Bratislava self-defense action group indicated that certain officers attached to special SS deportation units were amenable to negotiations regarding a "ransom" for Jews.[34] SS *Hauptsturmführer* (Captain) Dieter

---

[32] The National Socialist German régime established its security service in 1931. Under the command of Reinhard Heydrich, it monitored the activities of opposing parties and organizations as well as the internal opposition of the Nazi Party.

[33] *Haladás*, March 20, 1947, p. 6. *U-Boot* (submarine) was the nickname given at that time to Jews who "submerged," i. e. went underground, in order to survive.

[34] Negotiations were being started over and over again, but were often frustrated by a lack of financial support from abroad. In 1943, for example, the engineer Endre Steiner discussed a deal that would have saved one thousand Jewish children from Poland from the gas chambers; however, the deal fell through when Swiss sources failed to provide him the aid they promised (delay and procrastination were all it was good for). The Germans also proved receptive to the possibility of releasing interned Jews in exchange for raw materials, such as light metals, and

Wisliceny was one such officer. (Following the deportation of 55,000 Slovak Jews in March 1942, Wisliceny appeared ready to halt the removal of the remaining 25,000 members of Slovakia's Jewish community in exchange for $50,000).

Few were aware that Wisliceny's "magnanimity," temporarily sparing the lives of Slovak Jews, was owed to the intercession of the Papal Nuncio, who had protested against the deportations to leading Slovak political figures, and also informed them of the fact that Jews were being gassed in the German concentration camps. When Slovak officials questioned the SS *Hauptsturmführer* about the gas chambers, he vigorously denied their existence as sheer rumor. At the same time, Wisliceny recommended to Berlin that the deportations be temporarily suspended, because "this might be turned into economic gain with the Jews."

Thus the SS had already begun to view Jewish lives as a source of commercial profit by 1942. This human trade took on new dimensions beginning in 1943. The Germans were talking of a new "Europe Plan" (*Europaplan*). They announced that they were willing to cease deportations from every occupied or Axis country with the exception of Poland, for which they demanded two million dollars in compensation. However, this "deal" collapsed after several months of negotiation and correspondence.

The Budapest Relief and Rescue Committee became solidified by the beginning of 1943. Called into being by sheer necessity, it stood on a foundation of friendly and informal ties between individuals who wanted to support Jews seeking refuge from German persecution. Connections between the Budapest group and the Gizi Fleischmann-led Bratislava Rescue Committee as well as several underground Jewish organizations working abroad became increasingly close. The widening network extended as far as Istanbul, where a delegation of Jews from Palestine began operating in 1942. They were collecting evidence of the persecution and the fate of European Jewry, organized relief and rescue operations, and raised and coordinated financial assistance.

Collaboration between Brand and József Krem proved effective in maintaining contacts inside the occupied territories in Poland and the Ukraine, suffering from Nazi terror, particularly where the smuggling out of refugees was concerned. In September 1943, for example, five young Polish Jews arrived almost like "castaways." Tusia Herzberg remembered Brand's work this way:

---

medicine. Negotiations were soon halted due to opposition from the Allied powers, which did not sanction export of materials and supplies that could strengthen the fighting capacity of the German army.

The only address that we got in Slovakia was Joel Brand's. In order to find him on Yom Kippur,[35] we looked for him in several synagogues in Budapest. There we found out that the war had not yet reached Hungary, and people there didn't even want to hear about it ... Joel Brand and Dr. Szigfrid Roth were the first to smile at us in Budapest... [T]hey helped us from the very first moment that we arrived in the city without identification, knowledge of the language or even money.

During the first days after their arrival the young Budapest Zionists taught them a few key Hungarian words and expressions and took care of hiding places for them. The Polish refugees talked of their concerns and expressed worry at the expected arrival of the Germans. They also discussed the situation in Poland. They spoke of their own ordeals, persecution, armed struggle and escape. These experiences seemed distant, viewed from the peaceful atmosphere predominant in Hungary at the time. The Hungarians "said or thought that it couldn't happen to them."[36]

The Palestinian organizations recognized Joel and Hansi Brand for their successful deliverance (*aliyah*) of Jewish children and families. The couple also occasionally assisted French and British prisoners of war who had escaped to Hungary.[37]

Zionist leaders published bulletins regarding news of the Germans' mass murder of Jews in the East, and also took care of delivering these to as many people as possible. This successful Zionist bulletin and news service also assisted Jews in locating long-lost family members, relatives and Jewish leaders.

From the middle of 1942 on, the Rescue Committee transmitted countless reports and testimonies taken from refugees regarding the ongoing extermination of European Jewry. However, there exists almost no record of the reception and effect of these desperate calls for help. It seems that the world *did not want to be informed* of the facts, that it *was not willing to lend credence* to the appalling news emanating from the German-occupied territories. This frame of mind predominated in Hungary as well.

---

[35] The Day of Atonement. It was on this day that Moses descended from the mountain, where he had spent forty days pleading for the people of Israel. The promise of absolution was given on the Day of Atonement.

[36] Dr. Hava Eichler, ed., *A halál árnyékában. A nagy megpróbáltatások kora* [In the Shadow of Death. A Time of Great Affliction]. (Kibbutz Tel Yitzhak: 1991), pp. 13–14.

[37] *Haladás,* March 13, 1947, p. 7

The information that the Zionist activists were collecting and disseminating throughout the Jewish world really seemed almost unbelievable. Still, evidence of the true scale of murder and destruction was growing. Accounts from Springmann's Polish couriers and the staggering testimony of refugees all provided proof that the Germans were conducting a comprehensive campaign of persecution and murder against the Jews, that they were actually carrying out a plan of organized genocide. The refugees told of the extermination of the entire Jewish population of a multitude of cities and villages. News of the Warsaw Ghetto uprising and the information that not a single Jewish community in Poland had survived spread to other countries via Budapest. We agree with the conclusion of the Israeli scholar Asher Cohen: *there is no doubt that by the end of 1943 there was a broad awareness of the catastrophe.*[38]

Several channels of direct and indirect communication were open, either constantly or intermittently, until the German occupation of Hungary. One of them operated under the auspices of the official courier service of the Hungarian Foreign Ministry; the other through the aforementioned network of counterintelligence agents and the "collaboration" of well-paid, though doubtful, informants. Kasztner also mentioned the involvement of diplomatic couriers from a certain neutral European state, whose identity we have not yet been able to pinpoint.[39]

Jews arrived from Poland, Slovakia and other countries, in clusters of various sizes that swelled with time into groups of several hundred. Others helped besides the Rescue Committee. Many Hungarian Jews living under the pressure of the Jewish Laws came to view support for these refugees as their irrefutable responsibility. Numerous provincial Jewish communities not only sheltered but also employed and supported refugee Jews, both young and old.

Beginning in the early 1940s, the hungry and defenseless refugees began to benefit from more attention and solidarity at the religious community

---

[38] Asher Cohen, *Soá* (Shoah), (Cserépfalvi, Múlt és Jövő: Budapest, 1994), p. 88.

[39] *Haladás,* March 20, 1947, P. 6. Ernő Szilágyi wrote the following of Kasztner in his mémoirs: "This Jewish political figure had managed to gather all the strands that connected the various obscure and illegal Jewish rescue operations in his own hands. Decisive negotiations took place in his small room in a second-class Budapest boarding house ... [where] ... he even maintained secret archives kept in a gigantic travel chest, which was stuffed with documents, transcriptions, memoranda ... distress calls and reports that indicated whether aid had been beneficial or had arrived too late to prevent doom's arrival." Attila Novák: *Egy "ismeretlen" a magyar vészkorszak nyitányáról* [An "unknown" aspect of the preface to the Hungarian calamity], (*Beszélő,* volume IX, no. 6, June, 2004), pp. 49–50.

level as well. This included various Zionist groups, which established the Sponsor Office. Led by Dr. Nison Kahane, its executive committee was called the National Hungarian Jewish Relief Action (known by its Hungarian acronym OMZSA). It had several subcommittees functioning in the provinces.

Upon experiencing the consequences of the flood of refugees, Orthodox Jews also established their own relief committee in response to it. In November 1943, they came to an agreement with the Relief Committee regarding collaboration between them. Lipót Blau, Miksa Brick, Adolf Deutsch, Fülöp Freudiger and other leaders decided on joint action with the Zionists in the handling of refugee affairs and the raising of necessary funds.

The Hungarian Zionist Alliance could also rely on the experience of the Transylvanian and Slovak Zionists in the administration of refugee affairs. The Kállay government shut up some of those Jews who had entered Hungary illegally in internment camps. (The primary collection point for captured Jews was in northern Hungary, close to the Slovak border, in the community of Garany.) At the same time, though, the Prime Minister also permitted that the Hungarian police establish refugee camps deep inside the country and in Szabolcs Street in Budapest. OMZSA provided food and medical care for Jews confined to the refugee camps.

The Rescue Committee established contacts with Jean de Bavier with regard to foreign nationals interned in Hungary. The International Red Cross emissary to Hungary did much to help both interned Jews and prisoners of war during World War II. (Though he was unable to intervene in the matter of the escalating persecution of Hungarian Jews, he nevertheless took great concern for their well-being and remained well informed of their circumstances). Having a good view of the international picture, he clearly saw the grave danger that Hungarian Jews were in.

In addition to Kasztner, de Bavier held talks with Samu Stern, president of the Pest Israelite Synagogue and head of the National Office of Hungarian Israelites (known by its Hungarian-language acronym as MIOI), with Baroness Edit Weiss, well-known for her support of humanitarian causes, and others.[40] (The Zionists, like the members of other, pro-democracy Jewish organizations,

---

[40] Jean-Claude Favez, *Das Internationale Rote Kreuz und das Dritte Reich. War das Holocaust aufzuhalten?*, (Verlag Neue Züricher Zeitung: Zürich, 1989), pp. 440–441. Following the German occupation of Hungary, de Bavier was called back to Switzerland, though there would have been a great need for his experience and resolve at this time.

did not think highly of the "bank Jew" Stern. These groups were convinced that the leadership of the Jewish community, consisting of wealthy members, will not be able, by its very nature, to represent the interests of Hungarian Jewry as a whole.)

Envoy de Bavier sent a report to the Red Cross headquarters in Geneva regarding a November 13, 1945 conversation that he had held with Kasztner on the prospects for Jewish emigration. It is worth noting that on this very same day de Bavier had also met with Prime Minister Kállay, whom he described as "very obliging" and supportive of Jewish emigration plans. The Hungarian prime minister also gave voice to his opinion that the emigrants should leave the country by sea, because the railways were already overcrowded.[41]

A clear division of labor within the Budapest Rescue Committee evolved by the end of 1943 and beginning of 1944: the Brands dealt primarily with illegal border crossings and issues pertaining to support of refugees during their (temporary) stay in Hungary; Kasztner maintained the foreign contacts necessary to conduct rescue operations; and Springmann ran the courier network and handled financial affairs (foreign currency exchange).

The helpers of the refugees in Hungary became convinced that the fanatics of deportations, the SS officers in the service of the genocidal operations, had been increasingly influenced by money. Thereafter money became the primary means of rescuing Jews from the concentration camps. However, the procurement, transfer and expenditure of money for this purpose was a risky and delicate business. Relief organizations, headed by Chaim Barlas, affiliated with the Jewish Agency in Istanbul, the *Halutz* emissary in Switzerland, Nathan Schwalb, and later—through Schwalb's mediation—the Swiss representative of the American Joint Jewish Distribution Committee, Saly Mayer, provided the financial resources required for rescue operations.

More often than not the allocated funds ended up in the hands of the enemy. If, on the other hand, the money arrived too late (as happened in Slovakia, for example) the loss of life could no longer be prevented.[42] The Zionist leadership in Budapest arrived at the opinion that where the choice was between life and death, there was no room for compromise.

---

[41] Arieh Ben-Tov, *Holocaust. A Nemzetközi Vöröskereszt és a magyar zsidóság a második világháború alatt* [Holocaust. The International Red Cross and Hungarian Jewry during World War II], (Dunakönyv Kiadó: Budapest, 1992). p. 63.

[42] The Slovak Karel Hochberg helped SS *Hauptsturmführer* conduct his machinations. Slovak partisans captured this Jewish engineer near the end of the war and executed him.

By 1944 the Rescue Committee had gained significant experience in the employment of illegal tactics. Zionist principles lay at the root of the committee's resolve and performance; its operations were signified by several forms of resistance to persecution. Its primary resources could be identified as the cohesion and secrecy of its clandestine network of connections, its growing experience and prominence, and the financial support it received via Istanbul and Switzerland.

# 2. The German Occupation of Hungary, March 19, 1944

From the second half of 1943 on, Adolf Hitler viewed the Kingdom of Hungary's reluctance in fulfilling his demands with increasing suspicion. In the middle of March 1944, Hitler summoned Hungary's regent, Admiral Miklós Horthy, to his headquarters in Klessheim Castle. The tense discussions had hardly concluded when the German army, the *Wehrmacht*, began its operations to occupy Hungary, an ally.

The March 19 invasion of the country by German troops caught Hungary off guard. The political, economic and military repercussions of the invasion were catastrophic. German security forces immediately began to take hostages and prisoners. After some wrangling, Horthy appointed Hungary's former ambassador to Berlin, Döme Sztójay, as prime minister. At the same time he authorized the formation of what the Third Reich's Hungarian plenipotentiary, Dr. Edmund Veesenmayer, qualified as a "national government under German protectorate."

Veesenmayer, who had been promoted to the rank of SS *Brigadführer* (major-general) before the invasion of Hungary, was an economic expert, an experienced foreign ministry official and a committed proponent of National Socialism.[1] He was well-versed in Hungarian affairs, of which he had previously written summaries and analyses. Though Veesenmayer was an advocate of Germany's use of terror and oppression, he believed that his objectives vis-à-vis Hungary could best be obtained through diplomatic maneuvering. He viewed his mission in Hungary to be the establishment of an occupational structure that would relieve Germany of direct administrative and police re-

---

[1] Following a long series of hearings and interrogations at Nuremberg, Veesenmayer was sentenced to twenty years in prison on April 11, 1949. He was released from Landsberg Prison in September 1951. Facts in the present work regarding members of the German occupying forces come from the book Robert Wistrich, *Wer war wer im Dritten Reich? Ein biografisches Lexicon* (München, 1993).

sponsibility by allowing Hungarian authorities and institutions a modicum of autonomy. Veesenmayer's policies contributed to the success of the occupation and allowed the Wehrmacht to maintain control over the country with a relatively small contingent of German troops.

Total economic subjugation of the country followed. Hungary was compelled to provide Hitler's Reich with agricultural products of "twice the usual amount, or more." Industrial output and exploitation of natural resources had to be increased and transportation, communications and shipping capacity had to be utilized "to a significantly greater degree" in order to satisfy German needs.

The German occupation spelled ultimate tragedy for the approximately 850,000 Jews living in Hungary. Germany's armed intervention was intended, in part, to ensure implementation of the "final solution" (*Endlösung*) to the Jewish question in Hungary too. Regent Miklós Horthy, who had previously withstood German pressure to deport Hungarian Jews, gave the Sztójay government free reign to handle this affair as it chose.

## a. Special Units Strike Immediately

Units of the SS, the police and "special forces" all operating under the command of the Security Service (SD) moved into Hungary after nearly a week spent in a state of readiness following the invasion. The Chief Office of Reich Security (*Reichs-Sicherheits-Hauptamt*, or RSHA) dictated the duties and *modus operandi* of these organizations. On March 17, Ernst Kaltenbrunner, head of both the security police (*Sicherheitspolizei*, or Sipo) and the secret service outlined what needed to be done to "establish order" in Hungary.[2]

The security units arrived to Hungary combined into an operational action group (*Einsatzgruppe*), a proven German military procedure. At the head of the group was SS *Obergruppenführer* and *Waffen SS* General Otto Winkelmann, whose military classification was "Superior SS and Police Chief." Among his subordinates were SS *Standartenführer* Dr. Hans-Ulrich Geschke, commander[3] of the German security police and secret services in Hungary; a

---

[2] Péter Bokor, *Végjáték a Duna mentén* [End Game along the Danube]. Interview with Dr. Trenker, (Budapest, 1982), p. 86. Tranker had a staff of thirty-two and a list of 300–400 names of people to be arrested.

[3] The thirty-seven-year-old Gestapo officer reached the pinnacle of his carrier while serving in Hungary in April 1944. His primary duties in Budapest were intelligence and counterintelli-

police battalion; locally deployed members of the Gestapo,[4] SS *Sturmbann-führer* (Major) Wilhelm Höttl's political security service; the Gestapo command post with jurisdiction over Budapest and its environs (headed by SS Captain Alfred Trenker); and other German agencies. The head of the Vienna Gestapo, Sipo and the SD superintendent, Franz-Josef Huber, also appeared in the country.[5]

Höttl wrote in his memoirs that SS Reich Commander Heinrich Himmler was already asking for reports on the initial operations and general situation in Hungary by noon on the day of the invasion. Himmler caught Geschke off guard during a telephone conversation when the SS Reich Commander inquired about the number of Jews taken prisoner thus far. Geschke solved his predicament with a Budapest telephone book from which he obtained the addresses of two hundred doctors and lawyers with "Jewish-sounding" names. These people were promptly arrested. That evening he proudly informed Berlin that *2,000 leading members of the Hungarian Jewish community* had been taken into custody.[6]

Kaltenbrunner soon arrived in Budapest to evaluate the security situation there. His Hungarian associates were Jenő Ruszkay, László Baky and other far-right political figures whom the Germans considered to be fully reliable.

Following the country's smooth and systematic occupation, Winkelmann's new objectives were to liquidate anti-German groups and Polish military organizations and to oversee the ongoing fight against partisans and Communists. He had an indirect role in the deportation of Jews as well. Among Winkelmann's subordinates was SS *Obersturmbannführer* (Lieutenant-Colonel) Adolf Eichmann, head of the special commando unit (*Sonderkommando* or *Judenkommando*) in charge of operations directed against Jews, though he did not exercise direct authority over him.

Orders from the Superior SS and Police Chief were being carried out by eight operational task forces. Preliminary plans called for these forces to be deployed in cities of strategic interest to the Germans. The official name given to the security police (Sipo) units was *Kommandeur der Sicherheitspolizei und*

---

gence. His official title of his military appointment was Sipo and SD commander (*Befehlshaber der Sicherheitspolizei*/SD. BdS).

[4] Beginning on February 19, 1944, the Gestapo carried out the military counterintelligence duties of the Abwehr as well.

[5] Friedrich Wilhelm, *Die Polizei im NS-Staat*, (Ferdinand Schöningh: Padernborn, Munich, Vienna, 1999), p. 45.

[6] Wilhelm Höttl, *Einsatz für das Reich*, (Verlag Siegfried Bublies: Koblenz, 1997), pp. 247–248.

*des SD* (acronym KdS). There were between 300 and 400 men attached to these units, though Sipo's extensive network of informants made its effective strength much greater than its number of personnel would indicate. German or German-associated companies, legations, services and several shipping firms provided safe cover for these agents.

Members of the German security organs wore uniforms during the initial weeks of the occupation, after which most switched to civilian clothing. An official of the SD or Gestapo took direct control over most towns and villages in Hungary. (The SD demanded immediate notification of any anti-government activity as well as current information regarding all important political movements.) The German network of informants extended into the provinces as well. These organizations also engaged in extensive telephone wire-tapping, for which they had both the staff and the up-to-date technology at their disposal.

At the same time as these arrests, the Gestapo occupied and ransacked the headquarters of the remaining political parties of the Left and the editorial offices of the newspapers that were sympathetic to these as well as several premises belonging to trade unions and social organizations. The German occupation resulted in the banning of 126 newspapers.

Hostage-taking was a proven method of intimidation with which the Germans had plenty of prior experience. Informants prepared lists of people to be apprehended in advance. It is quite certain that German authorities used lists drawn up beforehand in their arrests of people in Budapest as well as in Western and Southern Hungary. They took into custody many Hungarian civil servants and other public officials who were considered hostile to the interests of the German Reich; these included Liberals, Loyalists, political figures sympathetic to the Smallholders' Party or the Social Democrats, many well-known journalists, several prominent capitalists and some scientists and scholars as well.[7]

A large number of Poles, Germans, Austrians and Italians were also arrested (soldiers and civilians whom the German authorities knew to have taken refuge in Hungary, and occasionally even diplomats.) They hunted for French, for escaped POW's as well as American and British pilots who, their planes shot down, landed on Hungarian soil, and had either been arrested or escaped.

---

[7] Jenő Vida, Director of the General Coal Mine Company, Miklós Halmi, President of the Hungarian–Italian Bank, Baron Marcell Madarassy-Beck, CEO, Frigyes Tályai-Roth, hospital director and chief physician, Antal Goldberger, industrialist, Lajos Ádám, surgeon and university professor.

The German occupying forces immediately assumed all police functions in Budapest. Following the invasion they immediately took twenty-eight members of the upper and lower houses of Parliament and about fifty other prominent public figures into custody. (They characterized their detention as "protective custody" [*Schutzhaft*], an established legal status in the National Socialist state.) The Germans arrested Minister of the Interior Ferenc Keresztes-Fischer, Minister of Agriculture Dániel Bánffy, József Sombor-Schweinitzer, the head of the political police, as well as several members of his staff. They arrested people who had assisted military personnel and civilians who had fled to Hungary to escape National Socialist terror. Several of their charges were so distraught at Hungary's occupation that they committed suicide.

The Gestapo did not, however, infiltrate Buda Castle. Though there was no immediate German presence in the regent's residence, he was aware of what was going on in the country. Already on March 19 the minutes of the daily crown council read as follows: "*The Gestapo is engaging in autonomous action in disregard of the country's sovereignty.*"

Most people did not flee, choosing instead to await their fate. Arrests were completed in a matter of minutes. In some instances arrests were accompanied by house searches, ransacking of rooms and confiscation of documents deemed of value. If the sought-after individual was not found at home, or had hidden, Gestapo officers left threatening letters. They often took family members into custody instead. A gun-battle erupted during the arrest of Endre Bajcsy-Zsilinszky, a Member of Parliament of the opposition Smallholder Party who seized a pistol and tried to resist. He was carried away with bullet wounds. On April 19, he was put into a Gestapo prison.

The Germans immediately removed valuables and documents from the homes of those imprisoned. Both in Budapest and the provinces, it became customary for them to return for plunder days after the arrests had been made. Furniture and household goods were hauled away in trucks.

Upon learning of the German invasion, political prisoners in Sátoraljaújhely made a heroic breakout attempt, based on a previously devised escape plan. The fourth item in a telegram sent from the general staff of Operation Margarethe to *Wehrmacht* headquarters reported that an "extraordinary event" had taken place:

Uprising of 400 captives at Sátoraljaújhely prison on the afternoon of March 22, 1944. Forty-four prisoners escaped after overpowering the Hungarian guards. At the request of the Hungarian commander, and because soldiers were being fired upon from inside the prison, an additional company deployed. Thirteen escapees executed, six returned to prison. Around twenty-four on the loose. Transfer of the prisoners to the authority of the SD underway.[8]

When using the word "uprising," the Germans were acknowledging the significance of armed resistance

In the week following the invasion, the Germans arrested ten thousand people, including 3,076 Jews, for the sake of intimidation.[9] All these arrests, during which the Germans suffered no casualty, were looked upon with indifference by the populace in general.

For years, German security organizations had been monitoring the political, military and intelligence activities of Polish refugees in Hungary and their support of the anti-German resistance in their own country. The occupation provided the Germans with the opportunity to settle accounts with the Polish exiles. Himmler instructed Gestapo officials from Warsaw and Cracow to move their operations to Hungary. (Several officers and investigators had arrived earlier to do reconnaissance work in Budapest.)

The Gestapo obtained the security files and copies of forged residency permits and identity papers belonging to leaders of the polish émigré community. With these documents in their possession, the Germans were able to apprehend them within a matter of hours. Major-general Dr. Jan Kołłątaj, the head of the Polish Medical and Public Health Service and his secretary, the forty-two-year-old medical second-lieutenant Dr. Teofil Kandefer, were killed in a gun-battle in a Buda street close to the Danube.[10] Several of the Poles on the arrest list were summarily executed on the spot when they were captured.

A manhunt began for Polish couriers who had long been on the wanted list of the Gestapo. The majority of these detainees were sent to the court prison in Buda, which had been turned into a Gestapo jail. Following a series of ruthless interrogations, most of these prisoners ended up in German concentration

[8] Dr. Klára Székely, ed., *Börtönfelkelés. Sátoraljaújhely 1944. március 22* [Prison Uprising. Sátoraljaújhely, March 22, 1944] (Budapest: 1994), p. 207. In May, some of the survivors of the prison uprising were sent to join a forced-labor battalion. The others were deported to the Dachau and Buchenwald concentration camps in November.

[9] *Kriegstagebuch des Oberkommandos der Wehrmacht, Erster Halbband,* (Frankfurt-am-Main, 1961), p. 189.

[10] *Menekült rapszódia. Lengyelek Magyarországon, 1939–1945* [Refugee Rhapsody. Poles in Hungary, 1939–1945] (Széphalom Könyvműhely, 2000), pp. 472–473. On several occasions the wives of wanted Poles were arrested in their place. Henryk Slawik, head of the Polish Citizens' Committee, turned himself in to the Gestapo for this reason. Both husband and wife were then sent to a concentration camp.

camps. The twenty Polish officers interned in the small town of Siklós in southern Hungary were transported by the Germans to Serbia, to the fortress of Belgrade. Their fate is unknown.

The acclaimed landscape artist and a member of the Polish Citizens' Committee, Stefan Filipkiewicz, was brutally tortured following his capture. He died of his injuries in Vienna, en route to a concentration camp.[11]

According to Louis Bargés, a French professor and an escaped prisoner of war, the Gestapo agents who went about in civilian clothing were the most dangerous. Until the occupation, the French émigrés living in Hungary felt free to speak their mother tongue in public. Following the occupation anybody heard speaking French on the street risked immediate arrest. In a period of just a few days the Gestapo detained forty French citizens; after two weeks the number had grown to seventy. The Gestapo even imprisoned the French nationals teaching at the prestigious *Eötvös Kollégium* (a special elite training institute belonging to the University of Budapest where the brightest students were being taught).[12] These arrests were most likely part of a Gestapo campaign of intimidation, since they affected only about ten percent of the approximately one thousand French exiles living in Hungary.

In addition to the aforementioned relocation center at the court prison, captives were held first at a detention center set up on the first floor of the Astoria Hotel in central Budapest. On March 20, the Gestapo, along with armed SS personnel, took over the Jewish Teacher and Rabbi Training Institute on Rökk Szilárd Street. By the next day the institute had been transformed into an internment camp with 240 Jewish prisoners.[13] Jews of all ages were arrested in even greater numbers in the course of routine identity checks at train stations and in the streets. These detainees were sent to the notorious vagrants' detention center. Due to overcrowding, many of these Jews were transferred to an internment camp in Kistarcsa, on the outskirts of Budapest.

The Gestapo categorized its detainees. If possible, Jews and Aryans were separated and the former subjected to more brutal treatment. In the provinces

---

[11] *Barátok a bajban. Lengyel menekültek Magyarországon 1939–1945* [Friends in Need. Polish Refugees in Hungary 1939–1945], (Európa Könyvkiadó: 1985), p. 88.

[12] László Antal, ed., *Ego sum gallicus captivus. Francia menekültek Magyarországon* [Ego Sum Gallicus Captivus. French Refugees in Hungary], (Európa Könyvkiadó: 1980), p. 77.

[13] Records from the Holocaust Documentation Center and Deportee Commemoration Collection Committee (henceforth the HDC and DCCC) no. 3606. Account from Dr. István Hahn, seminary teacher. Adolf Eichmann inspected the institute's library, removing 3,000, mostly German-language, books from its collection. *Almanac of the National Rabbi Training Institute, 1985–1991*, (Budapest, 1991), p. 392.

Jews were often arrested with the help of Gestapo collaborators recruited from the local *Volksbund*, the organization of ethnic Germans, and transported to police jails or abandoned Jewish-owned buildings. It seems the arrests were made according to some kind of lists, but people were never informed of the reason for their detention.

All the time while this was going on, Hungary's public administration and political apparatus, with Regent Miklós Horthy at its head, remained in place, acting as if nothing out of the ordinary had happened. The humiliating occupation and its consequences were passively tolerated by the Hungarian army and its largely pro-German officers' corps.

# 3. The *Sonderkommando* and the *Ungarnaktion*

The highly skilled and experienced *Sonderkommando* that had entered Hungary along with the occupational forces launched the so-called "Hungary Action" (*Ungarnaktion*), the Hungarian chapter of the *Endlösung*, with great expertise. Its chief, SS *Obersturmbannführer* Adolf Eichmann, was determined that the "relocation" of Hungarian Jewry to the Reich should take place as quickly and thoroughly as possible, without provoking a repeat of the Warsaw ghetto uprising.

At their postwar trials, the SS officers who had served in Hungary defended themselves by claiming that they had played a purely "advisory" role. Be it as it may, their mission was to dispatch the still nearly intact Hungarian Jewish population of 825,000 people as quickly as was possible.

Horthy's concessions to Hitler undoubtedly played a part in the unfolding tragedy. These concessions resulted in governmental authorities turning Hungarian citizens "to be regarded as Jewish" over to the Germans. Deportations on such a massive scale, however, could never have been implemented without the coordinated assistance and willing cooperation of Hungarians.

Eichmann, highly experienced as he was, made use of all the skill and trickery that he had perfected in the course of earlier "de-Jewification" operations. The carrot-and-stick strategy of the Germans involved exposing Jewish leaders to a calculated sequence of threats and promises, intimidation and reassurance. On April 13, Prime Minister Sztójay and Veesenmayer agreed that Hungary would deliver 50,000 Jewish workers to the Reich by the end of the month. They also engaged to accelerate conscription into the Hungarian military of Jews between the ages of thirty-six and forty-eight to serve in unarmed labor battalions; they also agreed to simultaneously increase the head count of these Jewish forced-labor battalions to a total of between 100,000 and 150,000 men.[1]

---

[1] György Ránki, Ervin Pamlényi, Loránt Tilkovszky, Gyula Juhász eds., *Wilhelmstrasse és Magyarország. Német diplomáciai iratok Magyarországról 1933-1944* [Wilhelmstrasse and

## a. Eichmann on the Move Again

The SS *Sonderkommando* acted decisively and effectively. Serving in its ranks were: SS *Obersturmbannführer* Hermann Krumey; SS *Sturmbannführer* Rolf Günther; SS *Hauptsturmführer* (Captains) Franz Abromeit, Bethke, Anton Burger, Theodor Dannecker, Franz Novak, Otto Hunsche, Wilhelm Schmidtsiefen, Siegfried Seidl and Dieter Wisliceny, in order of seniority; SS *Obersturmführer* (First Lieutenant) Ernst Girczik; SS *Untersturmführer* (Second-Lieutenant) Richard Hartenberger; SS Hauptscharfüher (Sergeant Major) Werner Lemke; *Oberscharführer* (Sergeants First Class) Eduard Neumann, Leopold Richter and Wilhelm Vrtoch; and an additional fifty junior SS men and auxiliary forces.[2]

The *Sonderkommando* ordered the establishment in Budapest of a Jewish Council, which the Germans employed as a body carrying out its orders. SS directives issued via the Council, whose members were granted special protection and other privileges, actually served to paralyze communications between Budapest and provincial towns and villages. The consequent lack of information made the organization of any Jewish self-defense impossible. The SS was thus able to exploit the Council and Samu Stern in order to demoralize Jews, and to act as an instrument of the *Endlösung*.

Though Hungarian Jews had apparently been left to their own devices, they continued to believe in Hungarian "lawfulness." Many Jews regarded the Council leadership as a crucial source of stability and continuity. Amid the changed circumstances people regarded the Council leaders as stable points of reference, whereas in reality they did nothing but served the Germans "of their own will." They were incapable of doing anything else.[3]

The memoirs of Ernő Szilágyi are characteristically ironic and derisive, but nonetheless paint an accurate picture of the situation as it existed following the occupation. At two Jewish religious community meetings, SS officers successfully manipulated the assembled leaders into believing that the Ger-

---

Hungary. German Diplomatic Documents Pertaining to Hungary 1933–1944], (Kossuth Könyvkiadó: 1986), p. 823.

   [2] Dokumentationsarchiv des österrechischen Widerstandes (henceforth DÖW), E 20 952/3; Hans Safrian, *Die Eichmann-Männer* (Europa Verlag GesmbH: 1993), pp. 295–307. The precise number of SS officers serving in Hungary is still uncertain. An analysis of the organization's operations does not substantiate the estimate of between 150 and 200.

   [3] Prior to the occupation, Ottó Komoly asked permission to deliver a lecture on the tragedy of the Polish Jews and the dangers threatening Hungarian Jewry to the Jewish WW I veteran association. They did not even listen to what he had to say.

mans' reputation was "worse" than their true conduct and demeanor. One Jewish participant at the Council declared that "I've been saying for two years that the Zionist rumors are exaggerated. Naturally I wouldn't deny that some unfortunate things happened in Poland, for instance. But it will certainly be not so bad here. All we have to do is make sure that nobody undermines discipline."

"'There is just one thing I would like to know,' said another court counselor (the polite German speaker—*author's note*):[4] 'What did he mean when he spoke of "certain restrictions"? A half an hour later all Budapest knew what had happened. They aren't going to do anything to us.'"[5]

In truth, most people *were unwilling to face* the changes that the occupation had produced, taking refuge in silent suffering, fatalism and passivity. Most of all, they refused to believe that what the Germans had done to Jews in the neighboring countries could possibly happen to them.

Though German officers consistently denied it, they had quickly implemented their well-thought-out campaign against Hungarian citizens classified as Jews. Thereafter large numbers of detainees were sent to Kistarcsa and Csepel, on the periphery of Budapest, to Nagykanizsa and Sárvár in western Hungary, and to Topolya in southern Hungary. Forty or fifty Jewish citizens were arrested and held in separate detention facilities in most cities and towns as a means of intimidation.

German garrison headquarters acted with great expertise. A hopeless situation ensued: Jews in most larger towns and cities were forced to pay large "security deposits." The Germans then turned the tens of thousands of *pengős* collected in this way to their own purposes.

Based on German "recommendations," Hungarian state administrators initiated a vigorous and large-scale effort (an element of the *Ungarnaktion*) to segregate the large number of Jews living on the eastern borderlands known as Sub-Carpathia. As a consequence, on April 8, the offices of the Jewish Council in the region's most important city, Munkács (Mukacevo, Ukraine), announced that as of that date "the competent authorities will issue their instruc-

[4] The assembly was enchanted by Wisliceny on March 20 and Krumey, Eichmann's deputy, on March 28. For more detail see Ernő Munkácsi, *Hogyan történt? Adatok és okmányok a magyar zsidóság tragédiájához* [How did it happen? Data and Documents Pertaining to the Tragedy of Hungarian Jewry], (Renaissance: Budapest, 1947), pp. 19–22.

[5] Attila Novák: *Egy "ismeretlen" a magyar vészkorszak nyitányáról* [An "Unknown" Aspect of the Preface to the Hungarian Holocaust], (*Beszélő*, volume IX, no. 6, June, 2004), pp. 49–50.

tions through the Jewish Council." At the same time, the Council, which had been established based on "orders from above," reassured everybody that "there is no cause for concern." The Council transmitted the deceitful German promises because "if all brethren in faith follow our instructions they will come to no harm ... [and nobody should forget] that ... *only through strict compliance with our orders can one spare both oneself and our entire community from misfortune.*"

The misled Council apparently disregarded all stories of deportation and mass-murder that refugee Jews had been telling for years, just as it turned a blind eye to the dark clouds that had appeared over the heads of Jews living in Sub-Carpathia. Instead of falling into despair, the Council admonished Jews to act in "strict compliance" with its declarations. Yet just one week later, on April 16, the Council transmitted additional restrictive measures to the Sub-Carpathian Jews, who had already been compelled to wear yellow stars on their outer clothing. *Ghettoization had begun.* The expertise of the SS and the complete submission of the Jews played into the hands of the stewards of this well-planned and well-disguised operation.

The fairy-tale that Jews were being transported to a "Kenyérmező Labor Camp" in Western Hungary made the rounds among the residents of the northern Transylvanian city of Kolozsvár (today Cluj-Napoca, Romania).[6] Masses of defenseless Jews accepted that they would be sent to a camp *simply to perform agricultural labor* until the end of the war. The only exceptions were those Jewish leaders who chose to flee instead at the end of May. (Among the first to leave Romania were the well-informed Neologue rabbi, Dr. Mózes Weinberger, and his wife.) However, after the war had ended, they were unable to satisfactorily explain how, if they had really believed in the Kenyérmező rubbish, why they had escaped, leaving the defenseless masses to themselves.[7]

---

[6] Approximately 165,000 of the 2.6 million inhabitants of the Northern part of Transylvania, which was re-annexed by Hungary on August 30, 1940, were Jewish. As in most of the reannexed territories, the majority of these Jews were committed Hungarians both in their language and culture. This made no difference to the new Hungarian state administration. In the fall of 1940, most Jewish civil servants lost their jobs. They were gradually followed by lawyers, journalists and others skilled professionals. By the end of the year, Jews had been almost completely excluded from the industrial and trade sectors.

[7] Randolph L. Braham, *Román nacionalisták és a holocauszt* [Romanian Nationalists and the Holocaust], (Múlt és Jövő Könyvek, 1998), p. 103.

The occupier used similar ruses in the western region of the country. They forced the Jewish Council in Szombathely to comply rigorously with their demands. A register of daily commands was kept.

Separate slips of paper came from the Gestapo, the camp gendarmes, the SS and others, all specifying precisely what they needed, and in what quantity or size. Then the so-called 'acquisition unit' that the Council had established just for this purpose would either collect the required things from among the members of the local Jewish community or went out and purchased them at the Council's expense ...

The Germans got paper, pencils, typewriters, radios, binoculars, cameras, civilian clothing, underclothing, linen, curtains, gramophone records, toys and eau de cologne in this way. There hardly exists a common or luxury item that did not appear on the lists.

They often requested that these things be packed in wooden crates, so they could send them home to their families in Germany. They weren't ashamed to admit that they favored suitcase-shaped wooden containers because these could be sent back by their families empty, and then loaded again.[8]

German agents went around the country dressed in clothing and leather jackets arbitrarily confiscated from Jewish shops. Homes of affluent Jews were simply seized without much ado, and they removed any furniture that they wanted for themselves. They took great pleasure in publicly humiliating the former owners of these homes. For this reason they were forced by the Germans wash their service vehicles and clean camp toilets with their bare hands. At other times their German guards would force them to do "physical exercises" under the most humiliating circumstances at any time of the day or night.

The German embassy in Budapest sent reports to Berlin specifying the number of Jews who had been individually detained and the number of those transferred to ghettos after April 16. The following data have been taken from these reports:

---

[8] Personal recollection of Iván Hacker, contained in the following book: Edit Balázs and Attila Katona, eds., *Baljós a menny felettem. Vallomások a szombathelyi zsidóságról és a soáról* [Sinister Are the Heavens over Me. Testimonies Regarding the Jews of Szombathely and the Shoah], (Szombathely: 2001), p. 45.

| Date | Number of Jews Arrested | Number of Jews Transferred to Ghettos |
|------|------------------------|----------------------------------------|
| 1    | 3,441                  | —                                      |
| 15   | 6,461                  | —                                      |
| 18   | 7,289                  | unknown                                |
| 20   | 7,493                  | 38,000                                 |
| 21   | 7,580                  | 100,038                                |
| 24   | 7,802                  | 135,000                                |
| 26   | 8,046                  | 140,000                                |
| 27   | 8,142                  | 194,000                                |
| 28   | 8,225                  | 194,000                                |

The number of Jews placed under arrest individually decreased at the end of April when these prisoners were transferred to camps. SS *Obergruppen-führer* Winkelmann played a part in these transfers, ensuring that there was a sufficient number of railway carriages to accommodate them.[9]

Eichmann's staff itself started to directly prepare the deportation schedule beginning on April 20. This work was especially urgent, because the German foreign ministry had been treating it as a *fait accompli*: "There are 500,000 Jews in Hungary who are ready for immediate placement in Germany."[10]

The German security services chose the most efficient means possible. On April 22, Veesenmayer reported to Berlin that the Security Service had sent a „consultant specialist" to work alongside Undersecretary of State for Internal Affairs László Endre, who had been handling matters related to the implementation of anti-Jewish provisions. An SD liaison officer was also assigned to the office of the Reich plenipotentiary envoy to Hungary.[11] The day after his arrival he confirmed that the Jews' "final destination is Auschwitz."

Veesenmayer's report indicated that two trains each began their travel northwards on April 29, carrying selected prisoners[12] from the following locations: the Kistarcsa internment camp; the auxiliary vagrants' detention center in the southern town of Topolya; the Csáktornya ghetto in the *Muravidék* (the

---

[9] According to a telegram that Veesenmayer sent on April 19, "The transfers can commence, since we have the necessary railway carriages at our disposal. This is, however, presently running into the greatest possible amount of difficulty." *Wilhelmstrasse,* p. 823.

[10] Ibid., p. 832.

[11] Ibid., p. 835

[12] *The Destruction*, vol. I, p. 363. László Németh and Zoltán Paksy, *Együttélés és kirekesztés. Zsidók Zala megye társadalmában 1919–1945* [Cohabitation and Ostracism. Jews in Zala County Society 1919-1945], (Zala County Archives, Zalaegerszeg: 2004), p. 49. The figure of 800 deportees contained in this work is incorrect.

Mura River region in present-day Slovenia); the Barcs ghetto; the Nagykanizsa internment camp in western Hungary; and the local coffee warehouse and ghetto.

*The departure of these two freight trains meant the commencement* of the deportation of hundreds of thousands of Hungarian citizens. The first victims of the *Ungarnaktion* went through the "selection" process at Auschwitz–Birkenau on May 2. From among the new arrivals, 486 able-bodied men and 616 women were registered at the camp. They had their prisoner number tattooed on their arm. Some of these prisoners were assigned the task of laying new railway tracks at Birkenau; others were transferred to Gross–Rosen to join that camp's forced labor detachment and others still to Wüstegiersdorf and Mauthausen near Linz.

The 2,698 detainees considered "useless" among the first shipment of Hungarian Jews were gassed to death.[13] In SS jargon it was called *Sonderbehandlung*, or "special treatment."

## b. The Organizations of Terror Settle In

German security organs, which often competed as rivals, initially established their Budapest headquarters in the Astoria Hotel. At the end of March, they evacuated some of the modern resort hotels that had been built on the picturesque slopes of *Svábhegy* [Swabian Hill] located in the arc of the Buda Hills. Dr. Geschke and his staff (*Befehlshaber der Sicherheitspolizei und des SD*) took up residence in the Majestic and Kis [Little] Majestic guest houses; the latter five-floor building housed SS *Obersturmbannführer* Eichmann's office as well.[14]

SS *Obersturmbannführer* Alfred Trenker and the thirty-two members of his staff established their headquarters at the Melinda Resort Hotel. During the first wave of arrests it was they who interrogated, tortured and maimed Poles who had fallen into their hands. The Gestapo occupied the Éden and Széplak

---

[13] Danuta Czech: *Kalendarium der Ereignisse im Konzentrationslager Auschwitz–Birkenau 1939–1945* (Hamburg, 1989), p. 764. The Hungarians promised that each of the two shipments would include 2,000 able-bodied Jews between the ages of sixteen and fifty.

[14] The twenty-four-room building was completed in 1937. Adjacent to it were a well-tended park, a hanging garden and athletic fields. András Juhász Gyula-Szántó: *A svábhegyi üdülő-szállók története* [History of the Svábhegy Resort Hotels], (Városháza kiadása, 1999), p. 48–50.

villas on *Svábhegy* and the Hotel Bellevue in the elite Buda neighborhood of Rózsadomb (Rose Hill).

SS *Hauptsturmführer* and Police Inspector (*Polizeikomissar*) Otto Klages (according to some sources the original spelling of his surname was *Clages*) had his headquarters in the Mirabel Condominium, also on *Svábhegy*. He was the head of Special Rapid-Deployment Team "F," which coordinated various operations for the SD. His task was to monitor Zionist organizations and to see that the effort to liquidate Hungarian Jewry went smoothly. It was also his job, when the deportations had begun, to take good care that the true implications of the *Endlösung*, which qualified as a state secret, should remain concealed.

General Winkelmann occupied the luxurious Perényi villa and its environs on Gellért Hill; SS *Obersturmbannführer* Kurt Becher moved into a villa which was the property of the immensely rich Chorin family, while his colleagues appropriated another mansion in the neighborhood, owned by the Weiss family. Eichmann settled in the hillside villa of the industrialist Lipót Aschner, from which he commanded a panoramic view of the city.[15] *Hauptsturmführer* Franz Novak, the SS "railway specialist," took up quarters on *Svábhegy*, in the villa of the president of the Hungarian Commercial Bank.

Apprehending and deporting to concentration camps the former occupants of the commandeered buildings and residencies was a routine job for the Gestapo. Those who were given two hours to vacate their homes could count themselves "lucky."[16]

The Supreme Command of the SS and the *Waffen SS* established their headquarters in a quaint building on Castle Hill that belonged to the beleaguered Hatvany family.

The twenty-nine-year-old SS *Sturmbannführer*, Dr. Wilhelm Höttl, had been head of the Hungarian desk and one of Himmler's most-respected officers at Department VI (foreign intelligence) of the RSHA in Berlin. He found office space to his liking in another building on Castle Hill, on Dísz Square, in a mansion that had previously been under Jewish ownership.[17]

---

[15] In his mémoirs, László Zolnai states that Eichmann threw raucous parties with Undersecretary of State for Internal Affairs László Endre and his wife, Countess Katalin Crouy Chanel. See *Hírünk és hamvunk* [Our Hide and Our Hair], (Magvető Könyvkiadó, 1986), p. 329.

[16] This is how much time the Germans gave to the Mauthner family, for example, when they were ordered to leave their home on Lendvay Street in Budapest. Four days later all four members of the family were taken into custody.

[17] Gyula Vargyai and János Almási, eds., *Magyarország 1944. Német megszállás* [The 1944 German Occupation of Hungary], (Budapest, 1994), pp. 135–136.

Höttl settled in comfortably at his charming new residence on Castle Hill. His voluntary Hungarian advisers were happy to visit him there. Two former prime ministers, László Bárdossy and Béla Imrédy, gladly passed the time in any one of his twelve dining rooms.[18] Höttl's immediate Hungarian "partners" numbered close to eighty.

The Commander-in-Chief of the German military forces in Hungary was Field Marshal Maximilian von Weichs. Instead of the Buda heights, von Weichs and his staff chose to set up their headquarters along the banks of the Danube, at the *Nagyszálló* (Grand Hotel) on Margaret Island. The Commander-in-Chief had expected a general uprising among Hungarians, "in which Jews and those under communist influence would play a large role."[19] Von Weichs had miscalculated on this account. His mission was completed by April 24, when he moved on to Belgrade.

The Budapest section of the *Abwehr* was being led by Dr. Schmidt. (He was presumably identical with the person of the same name who was a member of the National Socialist German Worker's Party and served as Secret Agent *V-30* of the SD, though this could have been another Johann Schmidt). Dr. Johann Schmidt, whose mother lived in Hungary, first moved to Budapest from Prague in 1940. After working for a time at the Danube Steam Shipping Company, he left the country. In September 1943, he returned to Budapest, this time from Berlin, working to establish a local network of German and pro-German sympathizers.[20]

Following the occupation, the Budapest section of the *Abwehr* had much less influence and operational duties than the aforementioned organizations.

Gendarme Lieutenant-Colonel *Vitéz* László Ferenczy, who in his capacity as a liaison officer between the Germans and the gendarmerie of the Kingdom of Hungary was among the most active sponsors of the deportations, established his office at the Lomnic Guest House on *Svábhegy*. Péter Hain and the duo Ödön Martinides and László Koltay, whom the Germans had appointed to lead autonomous security and police organizations, established their offices in the same *Svábhegy* building as Ferenczy and at number 2 Karthauzi Street, respectively (the official job of Martinides and Koltay was to oversee the "implementation of legal measures pertaining to individuals to be classified as

---

[18] Both of these politicians were found guilty of war crimes and executed in 1946.

[19] Péter Gosztonyi, *Légiveszély Budapest!* [Danger Over the Skies of Budapest!], (Népszava, 1989), p. 110.

[20] *TH* O-11541/1, p. 30.

Jewish." Many people referred to the State Security Police, of which Hain was the leader until June 21, as *the "Hungarian Gestapo."*

The Trenker-led Gestapo detail and the State Security Police headed by Hain soon worked in concert. The larger-scale tasks were assigned to the Germans. Among these was the blackmailing of Budapest Jews and the location and procurement of their property and valuables. During these operations the Hungarians were left to "study living conditions" and provide intelligence.

The "security people" were free to cast suspicion upon anybody for alleged antipathy toward the Reich or for having somehow acted in opposition to the Germans. People were sometimes incriminated for being anti-German or pro-British, for listening to foreign radio broadcasts, for maintaining contacts (formerly or allegedly currently) with individuals in enemy countries, or for being hostile to the Reich in one way or another. Undersecretary of State for Internal Affairs László Baky assisted these security officials in their "investigative" duties when he sent them a list of wealthy Jewish lawyers to be taken into custody.

Those on the suspect lists of the Germans, detained right after the occupation—Christians, Jews, those belonging to no specific denomination, Hungarian citizens, registered refugees, citizens of foreign countries, political dissenters and resistance members—awaited their fate in the grip of the German security apparatus. Others, however, did not even suspect that sooner or later they would end up being targeted for some reason or another, and if they did, there would be no avenue of escape left open for them by the security forces of the invaders and those serving them.

The detainees became more helpless by the day. The authorities occasionally permitted relief organizations to provide food for their co-religionists. Then they would limit deliveries at their own whim, sometimes presenting the food donors with a new set of guidelines every other day. The emphasis was on striking fear in their hearts. It was part of the same policy that Gestapo prisoners and internment camp inmates were not allowed to have visitors during the weeks following the occupation. Only after extensive investigation and a great deal of bribery was it possible to locate detained relatives and family members. People from the provinces who had been arrested in Budapest awaited their fate in complete isolation.

## c. March 26—Deportation of the First Captives

Contrary to their practice in other countries, the Germans did not conduct large-scale or partial local roundups in Hungary. The process of individual arrests, however, continued unabated. Every real or imagined enemy of the Reich was destroyed one by one, with merciless efficiency. The number of detainees reached 3,441 on March 31, increased to 3,459 by April 4 and nearly doubled to 6,461 ten days later.[21]

For two months, beginning on March 26, the Gestapo sent Hungarians in its "protective custody" to Vienna in groups of various sizes. The first to be leave were some of the hostages taken at the time of the occupation, prominent public personalities of known anti-German sentiment, Jewish industrialists and bankers, as well as citizens, including women, seized in the wake of denunciations by informers. (In the middle of April, Interior Minister Andor Jaross received a list of Hungarian politicians held in German captivity. Most of them were not even on Hungarian soil by then.)

Along with these bigger and smaller groups of Hungarians, the Germans deported captured Polish patriots, members of the Italian colony and even French and Turkish prisoners.

The first groups of Hungarian prisoners were transported to Vienna by train or, more often, by trucks. Subsequently the SS personnel stationed at the Budapest Gestapo prison (referred to officially as the *Deutsches Polizeigefängnis*), which, as the Kistarcsa internment camp, functioned under the command of Sipo, sent the Hungarian detainees to the Vienna *Polizei Gefangenenhaus* (police prison). "Newcomers" spent one or two days at the latter location, after which they were taken by bus to the Oberlanzdorf work camp on the outskirts of the city.

Oberlanzdorf was a filthy and overcrowded camp. The ragged prisoners were treated brutally. Following their days of forced labor, the prisoners were frequently subjected to beatings and torture in the evening. Local residents reported hearing dreadful noises and cries of pain emanating from the prison at night. One of the favorite "pranks" of the sadistic guards, for example, was to push prisoners from the flat-topped roof of the camp's main building. SS *Untersturmführer* Schmidt was in command of the SS veterans and freshly recruited *volksdeutsch* (Ethnic German) volunteers who served as guards at

---

[21] Hungarian National Archives microfilm collection, box number 13 970. Based on Auswärtiges Amt. Inl. ii. Akten E-421954. The commiqués from the Budapest embassy are contained in Randolph L. Braham, *The Destruction*, vol. II, pp. 539–546.

Oberlanzdorf when the Gestapo sent its Hungarian captives to this camp in 1944. (Presumably, the next destination of most of these prisoners—a concentration camp—had already been decided by the Germans.)

The first consignment of Hungarian prisoners left the railway station Budapest East late in the evening of March 28 in a passenger car that attached to a train carrying German soldiers returning home on leave. Among the train's nearly fifty captives were Ferenc Chorin; Baron Pál Kornfeld; Leó Budai Goldberger; the tycoon Lipót Aschner; General Rudolf Andorka; the retired president of the Hungarian National Bank, Lipót Baranyai; Dezső Laky, a university professor and former cabinet minister; the parliamentary deputy Lajos Szentiványi; the Pécs professor Dr. Iván Lajos; and the journalist György Parragi. These prisoners arrived to the Oberlanzdorf work camp by two buses from Vienna's South Station at noon on the following day. They did not even know where they were for an entire week.

The next group of Hungarians, which consisted of aristocrats, parliamentary deputies, social-democratic leaders and people classified as Jews, arrived to Oberlanzdorf by truck on April 3. There were also Italians, Poles and provincial Hungarians among them, who had been placed under arrest in Budapest. The leaders of the Jewish communities of Pécs, Szekszárd and Barcs were deported to this camp in several transports. Among this group of deportees were thirty women from Pécs, including Mrs. József Sombor-Schweinitzer, and Countess Andrássy, the daughter of the former Prime Minister of Hungary, Count Gyula Károlyi (the latter was taken away from her four children in place of her wanted husband).

Families and married couples were immediately separated from one another. Some spouses saw each other for the last time upon being disunited at Oberlanzdorf. The final destination for most of the women at this camp was the Auschwitz–Birkenau death factory.

A few of the Hungarian inmates were perfunctorily interrogated following their arrival to the Oberlanzdorf by agents of the Vienna Gestapo, though, for the most part, they did not take a great interest in these new arrivals.

## d. The *Ungarnaktion* in Full Swing

Jean de Bavier, the Budapest representative of the International Red Cross, made these notes in a confidential internal communiqué:[22]

On May 13, a day before my departure from Budapest, leaders of the Jewish community informed me that railway officials would be holding meetings on the 15th and 16th. The subject of the talks was to be the transportation of 300,000 Jews to Kassa and, if possible, to Poland.

Both the public as well as many authorities are being told that the plan is to employ the Jews as a fresh source of labor. However, the deportees include both old people and children, which indicates that the real purpose is something very different. I was actually told, and not even by Jews but by high-ranking government officials, that the final destination of the trains is Poland, where there are up-to-date installations for the gassing of people. The Jewish community here says it has credible evidence that their religious kin in Poland perished in this way.

This shocking text is another piece of evidence that in the summer of 1944 *there were people who were aware of what was going to happen.* Still they chose to remain silent. Others simply sat at their desks and "did only what was their job." Most of them performed their daily chores, implementing orders, decrees and commands with efficiency. They did not ask why, they did not raise objections. They did not make the slightest effort to make life just a little bit difficult for the Germans and their zealous Hungarian supporters who were organizing this "massive relocation."

The Hungarians simply acknowledged the pillaging and ghettoization of the country's Jewish population. They enveloped themselves in a shroud of docility. Most local communities bore passive witness to the increasingly widespread German terror, to the ready collaboration of Hungarian authorities, to a whole chain of inhumane, anti-Semitic measures and actions that were in profound contradiction to Hungary's tradition of hospitality and accommodation. The invaders' scheme worked. Hungarian society acquiesced in the unprecedented crime, the all-out persecution that was taking place in front of their eyes. Many Hungarians compromised themselves to one degree or another during this process.

---

[22] Ben Tov, p. 81. The signatories of this document testified that several leaders of the International Red Cross had read it.

The mass deportation of provincial Jewry began in the Kassa (today Košice, Slovakia) gendarme district. The executives of the "Jewish operations" were sent to Munkács. (The 13,000 Jews living in the city were herded into a ghetto between April 16 and 18.) On May 11, the forty-eight-man German task force arrived by car to the Munkács police headquarters. *Hauptmanführer* Novak and Wisliceny presided over the established German deportation committees. On the Hungarian side, the Police Chief and the Subdivision Gendarme Commander (or Gendarme Flank Commander) led the urban "operations." In locales without a police station, the Chief District Administrator (*főszolgabíró*) and the Flank Commander of the local gendarmes were put in charge.

Undersecretary of State for Internal Affairs László Endre ruled that members of the German committees must always be treated with "courtesy, attentiveness and discretion." He also instructed local authorities to provide for the Germans' comfort in every way possible.

On May 14, two forty-five-wagon trains carrying 3,200 and 3,169 "transport Jews" departed from Munkács and the eastern Hungarian city of Nyíregyháza under the close supervision of Eichmann's staff officers. Hungarian armed forces dispatched to these locations in order to assist in the deportation operations "completed their mission" in every case. On May 16, these deportees arrived to Auschwitz–Birkenau packed in freight cars, after which they immediately went through a rapid selection process. Guards marched the rejects directly to the gas chambers in groups of five. Smoke poured from all chimneys of the crematoria throughout the night.

Twins were being picked out from among the new arrivals for SS *Hauptsturmführer* Dr. Josef Mengele, nicknamed "The Angel of Death," for the purposes of medical experiments. Their camp identification numbers ranged from A 1,419 to A 1,437.

From the beginning of May, the loading and dispatching of four daily trains became "routine business." According to the so-called Vienna Plan adopted in early May, by the end of June most deportation trains were to take a northerly route, in the direction of Kassa-Hernádtihany. A dispatch report was prepared for every departing train. The text of the notification of the "shipment" bearing Eichmann's signature was usually the same as that of these dispatch reports. In Nazi bureaucratic jargon it was phrased in this way: "The consignment intended for special handling (*Sonderbehandlung*) is proceeding along its designated route."

Meanwhile veteran SS officers lined their own pockets whenever possible, before the Hungarian authorities got the chance to take notice. In Debrecen, the largest town in the Great Hungarian Plain, SS *Hauptsturmführer* Seidl assumed a lifestyle of oriental opulence. Threatening Gestapo action, he extorted furniture, carpets and leather furnishings from the local Jewish Council. The local SD commander (*Sondereinsatzkommando 5*) pocketed nearly 600,000 pengő in cash installments in exchange for a guarantee to Jews that "he would do them no harm and would shield them from any form of brutality."

Often it was only a lack of available freight cars that limited the number of "labor consignments" which Eichmann's staff (those operating on the ground were primarily Wisliceny and Novak) dispatched, unhindered, with full Hungarian cooperation. The death factory sent proper verification of the arrival of the trains. It contained the precise number of Jewish men, women and children arriving. It also included information on how many had been selected for labor and how many for "special handling."

By then there was hardly any more possibility for escape. Before the establishment of the ghettos there had been a better chance to flee: crossing the border into either Romania or Slovakia (usually with the help of a Zionist organization); going into hiding within the country; or blending in with the urban masses. Intrepid Zionist youths engaged in self-defense action managed to liberate several dozen young Jews from provincial ghettos, sheltering them in Budapest.

It was another element of the German tactic to covertly regroup the occupation forces that had arrived to the Kingdom of Hungary on March 19, and to redeploy them to another country. The Gestapo and the SD, on the other hand, were kept in place. These troops were provided with reinforcements whenever needed to help perform duties pertaining to "public law and order."

In June the deportation trains carried an average of more than ten thousand people, devastated from the degradations and confinement in the ghettos and relocation camps, from Hungary to Auschwitz–Birkenau via Kassa. The Hungarian gendarmerie provided armed escort for the train cars full of expelled Hungarian citizens—the so-called "transport Jews"—until they reached the city of Kassa, where their guarding was taken over by German police detachments.

Records kept by Reich Emissary Edmund Veesenmayer and gendarme Lieutenant-Colonel László Ferenczy have provided much of the evidence regarding the program of "worker relocation." The latter drafted daily reports of the number of deportees transported out of Hungary's six deportation zones (corresponding to ten Hungarian Gendarme Districts) during the process of "de-Jewification" lasting from May 3 to July 9.[23]

Veesenmayer was also reporting continually to Berlin. On July 11, he added up the data received from Eichmann's forces: up to the previous day 147 trains left the country, carrying 437,402 Jews.[24] This signified that the elimination of Jews from the provinces had been completed. By then, the Germans were already making preparations for the next phase, the "operation" against the Jews of Budapest.

Battalion Commander Giebe took control of the deportation trains once they reached Kassa. Units of the *Schutzpolizei* opened the locked and chained doors of the freight cars, and took a rough head count. From this point on, the trains were being escorted by a unit of specially trained armed guards taking place in a passenger car in the middle of the train, along with an unknown number of railway personnel.

It took a single day for the police commando to deliver a full "consignment" to the ramp at Birkenau, the scene of the selection preliminary to the mass murder, still to be seen today, which had to be specially extended to accommodate the *Ungarnaktion*.

## e. The Hungarian Prisoners of the Vienna Gestapo

Deportation both to and via Vienna continued in May. A continual stream of people—the majority were Jewish women and men from Budapest— "summoned" to the Gestapo (often on the ground of denunciations), and detained and interrogated by them, suspected of espionage, rumor-mongering, transmitting or listening to illegal radio broadcasts, conspiring with the Allied powers, maintaining contacts with the resistance and other suspected anti-German activities, were being transported to Vienna.

The next station was Oberlanzdorf, from where they were taken to Auschwitz–Birkenau or Bergen-Belsen. Fragmentary evidence indicates the number of these unknown victims to have been at least 300.

Captives held at Oberlanzdorf, still in one of the antechambers of the SS camps, witnessed numerous atrocities. Most of them were compelled to think

---

[23] These so-called "event reports" are contained in: László Karsai and Judit Molnár, *Az Endre–Baky–Jaross per* [The Endre–Baky–Jaross Trials], (Cserépfalvi: 1994), pp. 497–522. According to Ferenczy, the total number of deported Jews was 434,351.

[24] *Wilhelmstrasse*, p. 881.

over and reject one or another period of their past, to draw conclusions from the events of the previous years, and to part with illusions. Their discussions with other inmates led them to recognize the limitations of Hungary's foreign-policy options, the consequences of the country's pro-German servility, and the horrible reality of life in Hitler's Third Reich.

At dawn on May 5, thirty-six Hungarians who had been detained for *suspicious political activities* were sent from Oberlanzdorf to the Mauthausen concentration camp, known by its official abbreviation of KLM. (They include Rudolf Andorka, Manó Buchinger, Gusztáv Gratz, Iván Lajos, György Parragi, Károly Peyer, Károly Rassay, Count Antal Sigray and Lajos Szentiványi). There were no women in the group. The Jews were separated during the trip in precisely the same way as they would be at the concentration camp.

The next group of "politicals" (Imre Bálint, Dr. József Domonkos, Frigyes Párkányi, Dr. Elemér Pollatschek, Editor-in-Chief Károly Rátkai and others) arrived to Mauthausen on May 20. In the months following the occupation, 356 Hungarian detainees were transported to Mauthausen via Oberlanzdorf.[25]

An estimated 120 of these political prisoners were victims of informers serving the interests of greater Germany in southern Hungary.

The *Zentralstelle der Geheimen Staatspolizei Wien* (the Vienna Gestapo headquarters) also played prominent role in the campaign against Hungarian political and military figures suspected of preparing and supporting the initiative launched in secret for the withdrawal of Hungary from the war. Individuals deemed particularly dangerous to Germany's war efforts were also taken to the Vienna Gestapo headquarters, which functioned as an important element in the Nazi terror apparatus. Its affiliate branches, agents and security men continually collected information, which they sent on to the center. The information was sifted through and analyzed by Gestapo and SS specialists, who collectively decided whether the individuals concerned would live or die.

The Vienna Gestapo headquarters located at 4 Morzinplatz exercised exclusive authority over matters pertaining to the scanty remnants of Austrian Jewry, constantly persecuted ever since the *Anschluss* in 1938. Dr. Karl Ebner, the deputy chief of the Vienna Gestapo, was in command of those who dealt with Jewish matters. (During the German occupation of Hungary he also spent some time in Budapest). From July 1944 on, SS *Obersturmbannführer* Hermann Krumey's special SS commando, responsible for Hungarian deportees, which had been ordered from Budapest to Vienna, was also authorized to take

---

[25] *Magyarok az SS ausztriai lágerbirodalmában* [Hungarians in the Austrian SS Camps], pp. 55–56.

action with regard to Jews in cooperation with the Gestapo but independent of it.

From the beginning of 1944 until the collapse of the Reich, Ebner and his narrow group of subordinates, Dörrhage, Rixinger and Dr. Weinz, sent 800 Jews, among them Hungarians, from the Vienna Gestapo headquarters to concentration camps, primarily to Auschwitz–Birkenau and Theresienstadt. Some died in the gas chambers.

The notorious Gestapo building in Vienna was reduced to rubble in the Allied air raids. A memorial to the martyrs was raised at the site, which had been depicted as "hell itself."

The following notable Hungarians were held captive at the Gestapo's Vienna headquarters that fall: the commander of the Budapest corps of the Hungarian army, Lieutenant-General Szilárd Bakay; the former foreign minister of Hungary, Lieutenant-General Gusztáv Hennyey; the son of former Prime Minister Miklós Kállay and former commander of the Hungarian Royal Bodyguard, First Lieutenant András Kállay; and Lieutenant-General Károly Lázár. Kállay had taken part in a gun battle on Castle Hill, which broke out between the Germans and the regent's bodyguards on the day of the occupation. Following his capture the Germans took him by airplane to Vienna, from where he was sent to Mauthausen, just as his father had been.

## f. In the Buda Prison of the Gestapo

Most prisoners of the German secret police awaited their fate at the Buda Prison. From the last week of March this building was like a piece of Germany within the heart of the Hungarian capital. The Waffen SS and SD guards at the prison performed their duties with a discipline typical of military and state functionaries of the Third Reich, strictly enforcing National Socialist regulations and shouting German commands.

The German guards were quartered on the third floor of the prison. Some inmates were kept on the second floor, while most were crowded behind heavy iron bars on the fourth floor. The unit of SS guards (Wachmannstaff) at the prison was not permanent; they were being rotated every ten to fourteen days. From the time of the German invasion until the end of April, most of the guards at the prison were ethnic Germans from the vicinity of Budapest who had joined the ranks of the Waffen SS. Many of them chose not to reveal the fact that they spoke, or at least understood, Hungarian.

The ability of individual inmates to endure the humiliating conditions of the prison often determined the nature of their relations with the guards. Their chances would be much better if someone interceded on their behalf, or a prisoner received underclothing, food, cigarettes and other daily necessities from outside. It was all in the hands of the prison's highest internal authority, SS *Hauptscharführer* Werner Lemke. It was up to him whether or not prisoners were permitted to take exercise outside, use the showers, and receive medication and medical treatment. In some instances there were two inmates to a bed; in others there were five to two beds. Some prisoners slept on straw mattresses laid out on the floor or on the single table located in each cell.

Daily deliveries to the prison were frequent until July, then their rate decreased somewhat. The guards, who were relieved every two hours at night, devised many ingenious ways of tormenting their captives through deprivation from sleep and rest. They did their best to strain their nerves, to drive them mad, and to keep them exhausted and tired, so they would be easier for German security personnel to "handle." Naked prisoners were forced to perform swimming motions on the corridor floors, some of them the breast stroke, others the backstroke. Then they were ordered to do various types of calisthenics. Some were forced to do frog jumps, others were hosed down with cold water. The guards subjected the inmates to an incessant flow of mockery and verbal abuse.

The number of prison blackouts increased with the onset of Allied air raids. The Gestapo did not allow the prisoners into the bombing shelters, which were reserved exclusively for the prison guards. The bombings terrified the inmates, many of who took refuge in silent prayer.

The prisoners felt similar distress upon hearing the rumors of their impending transportation from the prison: they listened to foreign inmates, many of whom had survived more than one stint in German captivity, escapees caught over and over again, some of whom had already seen the inside of concentration camps, whispering stories of Nazi terror, who told about the circumstances and operation of the SS concentration camps, the ongoing genocide.

These accounts of mass murder first seemed unbelievable even within the confines of a Gestapo prison, though the ongoing regimen of cruelty and brutality gradually lent them credibility. With the passing of many blood- and tear-soaked days of captivity the prisoners began to feel that a heinous death lay just around the corner.

# 4. The Deportation of Hungarian Jews in the Eyes of the World

## a. Indifference

The question is being raised over and over and again: how much did the world know? Were the democratic powers of the world really aware of what was happening to Hungarian Jews: to the lethal danger they faced, their rapid isolation following the German occupation of Hungary, to their having been caught in a trap? There is no simple, black-and-white answer. There is little doubt that the Allied Powers' war effort, their will to secure Germany's unconditional surrender, defeating Germany's satellite states and separating them from the Axis, as well as developing their postwar spheres of interest and increasing their own geopolitical power, took precedence over humanitarian issues.

One may come up with a very real list of statements made in support of the Hungarian Jews, protests of varying degrees of loudness and other gestures. However, as had been previously pointed out, the Germans were able to deport practically all Jews from the Hungarian countryside unhindered, without the slightest complication or obstacle.

It took hardly fifty days to "de-Jewify" Hungary's historic counties. What was still hanging in the balance at that time was the fate of Budapest's Jews (or Jews who had taken refuge in the city), and of the Jewish men serving in the forced-labor battalions, both inside Hungary and abroad. The SS was quite clearly intent on getting hold of these Jews too, *thereby fully completing the Endlösung on the territory of Hungary.*

The deportations were not hindered by major bombing attacks or other planned military operations. Nor was there a single partisan raid or an act of sabotage which would have hampered the systematical implementation of the *Ungarnaktion*. The deportation plan devised in Vienna proceeded with the precision of a Swiss watch. The question "how it was possible," the issue of share in the responsibility for the genocide, will linger on for a long time to come; the answers will be increasingly subtle and ever more accurate.

The facts of the tragedy point to the conclusion that there was essentially nobody willing to stop the mass-murder of Jews. Even in 1944, those willing to actively help or shelter persecuted Jews formed a distinct minority.

In the United States, the accelerated production of armaments and other war-related goods led to a vigorous economic upswing and increasing profits from exports. However, the American administration feared that the sudden return of the multitude of mobilized men might have dire economic consequences.

Anti-Jewish feelings were not unknown either, even among those at the very pinnacle of the American political hierarchy. The Department of Defense and the leaders of the general staff suggested that Jews would be liberated from the concentration camps with the eventual military defeat of Germany and an Allied victory in the war. Thus the armed forces were to be utilized to vanquish the *Wehrmacht, not to assist or rescue the Jews.*

Air strikes on the concentration camps were ruled out as too risky (threatening disproportionate losses). They speculated that bombing even within close range of the extermination installations might result in killing hundreds of prisoners. At that time, this option was rejected by *even Jewish organizations* for fear of the casualties it would cause among the camp inmates.

This was another reason why neither the installations of mass death at Auschwitz–Birkenau, most of which had already been pinpointed, nor the railroad tracks that carried the victims to the camp were bombed in order to render them useless.

Neither was it unfavorable for the strategic interests of the Red Army that in addition to transporting supplies and war materiel much needed by the *Wehrmacht,* the German railroad network, overextended anyway, was being forced to bear the extra burden of transporting tens of thousands of Jews back and forth. (Besides the Hungarian "consignments," the continuous shifting of inmates from one camp to another also encumbered the German railroads).

## b. Protests

News emerging from Hungary of the ghettos and deportations produced an international backlash that was very embarrassing for the Sztójay government. In April and May, the press in several neutral countries published reports condemning the persecution of Hungarian Jews. By the summer, anti-Hungarian sentiments were running high all over Europe.

The increasingly negative international reputation of the Hungarian government manifested itself in a March address by President Franklin Delano Roosevelt of the United States, in the ever more frequent BBC reports on Hungary, and in an early April appeal to the Hungarian people by William Temple, the Archbishop of Canterbury. At the end of April several foreign radio stations broadcast reports on the mass persecution and ghettoization of Hungarian Jews.

The circulation throughout Budapest of the so-called "Auschwitz Reports," based on the testimony of two young escapees from Auschwitz–Birkenau, Walter Rosenberg and Josef Lanik, increased the shock.[1] The detailed account contained in the reports, detailing what was taking place at the death factory, reached both Horthy and several leading clerics of various Christian denominations.

Angelo Rotta, the papal nuncio to Budapest, repeatedly informed Vatican officials of the intelligence he had received regarding the deportation of Hungarian Jews. Consequently Pope Pius XII sent a personal message to Regent Horthy on June 25 entreating him to intervene on behalf of Hungarian Jews.

In Switzerland, several public personalities, university professors and leaders of the Catholic political party waged a resolute campaign to have news of the persecution of Hungarian Jews publicized in Swiss newspapers. Leaders of the Lutheran Church also wanted to publish what they considered to be credible information regarding the butchering of Jews in the Auschwitz gas chambers, but government censors prevented them from doing so. The necessity of maintaining Switzerland's neutral status was cited as the cause for the silence of officialdom, nevertheless, an increasing number of Swiss citizens adopted the view that it was no longer possible to remain quiet about the horrible atrocities, now verified and widely regarded as credible.

Lutheran Minister Paul Vogt delivered momentous sermons in Basel on June 27 and in Zurich on July 1 in which he castigated the murderous National Socialist régime. He spoke openly of the tragedy of the 450,000 deported Hungarian Jews, of the mass killings by gas taking place in the camp in Upper Silesia, and the cremation of the corpses. The Swiss Federation of Jewish Religious Communities also made a concerted effort to publicize news of the genocide, distributing leaflets throughout the country.

Swiss newspapers, kept on a tight leash by censorship on account of the continual threat of German intervention, published an unprecedented series of

[1] For more detail see Rudolf Vrba and Alan Bestic, *The Conspiracy of the Twentieth Century* (Star & Cross Publishing House Inc: 1989).

articles containing the facts (almost daily) of the persecution of Jews in Hungary. One paper wrote that the scale of the deportation operation was so large that *"if it does not stop soon, the entire unfortunate population will be exterminated."*[2] An article appearing in the July 7 issue of the *Neue Zürcher Zeitung* provoked a storm of indignity throughout Switzerland.

Questions of morality also came to the surface: *"One cannot be both Swiss and anti-Semitic. As Christians and Swiss we must join the courageous protests that have been raised against the criminal persecutions."*[3]

These newspaper reports, published in three languages had a part in persuading officials and the government to reexamine their response to the persecution of Jews as well as in the Swiss cabinet's decision to grant asylum in Switzerland to people subject to persecution, without any other recourse to refuge. Several newspapers voiced the opinion that the majority of Hungarian society *must be regarded guilty of complicity* in what was taking place.[4]

King Gustav V of Sweden turned to Miklós Horthy in order to ask clemency for Hungarian Jews. The King's telegraphed letter was delivered to the regent of Hungary by Carl Ivan Danielsson, the Swedish ambassador to Budapest, at Buda Castle on July 1. The Swedish monarch, citing traditional Hungarian chivalry, implored Horthy to use his political influence to save Jews from further suffering and persecution.[5]

Regent Horthy himself had been in an advantageous position up to then vis-à-vis the issue of his country's beleaguered Jews: following the German occupation of Hungary, he had given his government a "free hand" to implement measures involving the Jews, "refraining from exerting his influence." Horthy had acted like Pontius Pilate, allowing the deportation of hundreds of thousands of Jews from the Hungarian provinces, then washing his hands of the affair.

This time, however, Horthy could not evade his responsibility for putting an end to what he referred to as the *"excesses."* He had already received a great deal of information on what had happened to the Jews. Both he and his family

---

[2] *Gazette de Lausanne,* June 29, 1944.

[3] Ibid., July 8.

[4] Among these publications were the *Berner Tagwacht, Basler Nachrichten, Der Freisinnige* and *Die Nation.* Jenő Lévai, *Zsidósors Európában* [The Jewish Destiny in Europe] (from now on simply *Jewish Destiny*), (Magyar Téka: 1948), p. 118.

[5] The Swedish press subsequently published several inaccurate articles, whose optimistic tone was based on misinformation emanating from Budapest regarding positive changes in the status of Jews.

were also aware that the persecution and deportation of Hungarian Jews had pushed the country into a moral abyss in the eyes of world public opinion. He also had to consider not only the upsurge in international protest and the deterioration of Hungary's military situation, but the counsel of several of his confidants as well.

In his written response to the King of Sweden, Horthy promised *to ensure that the principles of justice and humanity are honored*, and to do his best "under the present conditions." (The text of the letter originally read "in Hungary's situation at the present time," but was moderated at the behest of Prime Minister Sztójay.)

The news bulletins that formed part of the international press campaign spread the word of the horrors associated with the persecution of the Jews. The Hungarian government was again forced to defend itself. It turned to its reduced number of diplomats abroad, to those who remained at their posts following the disgraceful German occupation, issuing an official denial of the facts surrounding the persecution of Jews in Cipher Telegram No. 6264-74, which stated that news regarding the deportations were false and that "Hungarian Jews are being sent to Germany to work."

The same cipher telegram, dispatched on June 26, also contained a shameful lie regarding the deportation of families: "Evidence has shown that the readiness of Jews to work is reduced when they are separated from their families, therefore we are sending their family members along as well."[6] Where Sztójay got that "evidence" has never been discovered.

With this telegram the press deluge became unmanageable. It also galvanized several international Jewish organizations into action, which bombarded high-ranking Hungarian governmental officials with appeals. Ben Tzvi, head of the Palestine-based Jewish National Council, began to organize, as did the Roosevelt-supported War Refugee Board (WRB) in the United States.[7]

A June 26 memorandum from the President of the United States reached the Sztójay cabinet via the Swiss government. In a repeat of his March 23 speech, President Roosevelt used a *harsh tone* in calling for a halt of the deportations and the anti-Jewish actions and regulations. He made it unambiguous that, while he spoke the language of humanitarianism, he was relying on the power of arms.

---

[6] The complete text of this telegram can be found in: Jenő Lévai, *Fehér Könyv. Külföldi akciók magyar zsidók megmentésére* [White Book. Foreign Efforts to Save Hungarian Jews], (Officina: 1946), pp. 54–55. Several former diplomats refer to this telegram in their mémoirs.

[7] President Roosevelt ordered the establishment of this organization in January 1944.

Roosevelt deemed the Hungarian government responsible for what was happening. He threatened heavy reprisals; and since his words remained ineffectual, he acted, too: reprisals did follow.

The Sztójay government continued to maintain that it was doing *all within its power* to stop the deportations. However, the *approval of the Germans was also needed, and the government would make efforts to secure that approval.* This response hardly satisfied those who had taken up the cause of the Hungarian Jews.

On July 2, Budapest and other parts of the country were the target of heavy bombing. (This was the largest air raid conducted over Hungary during the entire war.)[8] The resulting damage and casualties did not have a sobering effect on the Hungarian government, quite the contrary, what followed was a loud exaggeration of the circumstances and consequences of the Allied "terror attack."

Anti-Semitic propaganda gained fresh momentum. Jews, it was claimed, had used radio transmitters and light signals to direct Allied pilots, thus conspiring to inflict the greatest possible amount of destruction on the country. Such rumors were spread blaringly by national radio, and the newspapers published concocted stories. In several locations, dreadfully misleading posters were hung up in order to foment the anger of the population.

US Secretary of State Cordell Hull also protested in the name of the American people the mass deportation and slaughter of Hungarian Jews. He threatened the Sztójay government with retaliations. One of the American wire services summed up the situation succinctly: "Hungary is committing *national suicide.*"[9]

In London, Foreign Secretary Anthony Eden declared in the House of Commons that "the actions and behavior of the Hungarian government fills Great Britain with disgust."[10] The House of Commons—for the first time in its history—paid a one-minute standing tribute of silence to the victims. The BBC harshly condemned the Hungarian government in its broadcasts, calling for those guilty of war crimes to be held accountable.

The World Jewish Council revealed detailed evidence of the persecution of Hungarian Jews at a press conference held for British journalists.

On July 7, after all the delay, Horthy put a long-overdue halt to the deportations. The Germans and their Hungarian accomplices still dispatched several trainfuls of deportees even after these orders had come into force. Interna-

---

[8] For more detail see Iván Pataky–László Rozsos–Gyula Sárhidai, *Légi háború Magyarország felett* [Air War over Hungary], (Zrínyi Kiadó: 1989), pp. 88–109.

[9] Exchange Telegraph, June 30, 1944.

[10] Quoted in *Jewish Destiny*, p. 143.

tional protest had come too late to save Jews living in the provinces, but, for the time being, it saved the lives of the approximately 200,000-strong Jewish population of Budapest as well as the men serving in forced-labor battalions.

There were some who remained adamant about continuing the "resettlements." Among these was Minister of the Interior Andor Jaross, who was still willing to "prove" Hungarian loyalty to Germany. He informed the Reich's envoy to Budapest, Edmund Veesenmayer, that he was prepared to continue the deportations in spite of the regent's order to stop them.[11]

The Germans were nonetheless surprised that after so many years of silence, this time the Western powers and the occasionally collaborative neutral countries raised their voices in favor of the Jews. Until that time the Germans had managed to keep the lid on their death machinery. Even though some information did filter out about the Polish ghettos and the horrors of the concentration camps, the German news services did a first-rate job in neutralizing this. Most often the reports were successfully denied as sheer Jewish propaganda. News of mass murder in some distant place or other soon faded away in a sea of indifference, passing practically unnoticed.

The press campaign prompted a new development: it alarmed American Jews, who had been rather passive and skeptical until then. They seemed to realize with a shock that there were solid and finished facts behind the news coming from Hungary. A terrible drama involving millions of people was playing itself out all over Europe, the drama of the liquidation of Jews in many countries, especially the Polish Jews, with whom the American Jewish community maintained the closest ties.

That community had simply discarded the many appalling reports about places like Treblinka, Majdanek and Lublin as impossible to believe or absorb. It thought they were mere figments of the imagination. However, the Swiss campaign, which had been launched by distinguished Christian leaders and was based on diplomatic sources, was impossible to disregard. The large population of Jews living on the other side of the Atlantic was now stunned and filled with bitter remorse.[12] (Another reason for the resounding success and surprising effectiveness of this campaign was that, contrary to the Jewish rescue appeals of the previous years, it did not include "the usual" solicitations of financial support of any kind.)

Another peculiar aspect of this sympathetic response was that it had been the demise of Hungarian Jews, whose quick assimilation had made them un-

---

11 *Wilhelmstrasse,* p. 880.
12 This includes Australia.

popular in Jewish circles abroad. The wave it created reached all the way to the White House. This is true even if one is aware that it was directed only partially at the rescue of Hungarian Jews.


## c. Another German Cover-up Game

To counter the wave of international protest, German officials staged a new bit of theater. On July 19, a press conference was held in Berlin for foreign correspondents. Deputy Press Secretary Helmut Sündermann adroitly denied all allegations, citing "*grave misunderstandings*" with regard to the alleged mistreatment of European Jews and its "isolation." Sündermann claimed that it was not only the right, but the duty of Germany and its allies to "take defensive measures." It was for this reason that Jews were segregated and incorporated into the work force. This was done with utmost humanity. At this juncture the German official emphasized the significance of Theresienstadt, where, he claimed, there functioned a Jewish self-government, and nobody was forced to work. It was the place for all elderly Jews and for all those with special merits and capabilities. These people worked only to provide for their daily needs.

Sündermann claimed that Theresienstadt's inmates were permitted to maintain correspondence with anybody and to send and receive packages freely. He followed this with a blatant lie: over the past month more than 20,000 parcels had arrived from Portugal alone, he said. He also asserted that representatives of the International Red Cross (IRC) had been allowed to inspect the "Jewish City."

He did acknowledge that *other Jews sent to work had been concentrated in a large camp* for inspection before being detailed to specific tasks. Efficient work missions after had to be specifically organized and took planning. Those deemed unfit for work were sent to so-called family ghettos. All Jews are assigned tasks in accordance with their professional skills; married couples are permitted to stay together. Their housing and daily rations would correspond to those of other workers.

Sündermann concluded with the assessment that the Jewish question had been a thorn in the side of the enemy as well, and that there would be peace in the world only once this restive element was quarantined in order to prevent it from setting nations against one another in order to advance its own interests. The German way of solving the Jewish question, with its 'humaneness' *will once be seen as a model for the whole world.*[13]

---

[13] Sündermann's declaration appeared in the July 21, 1944 issue of the *Pester Lloyd*.

In order to provide a complete view, it will be fitting to quote from *Note Verbale* A No. 405, presented to the Hungarian Foreign Ministry, by the Germans. This diplomatic communiqué indicated, on August 12 (!), that Hungarian Jews would need better nourishment for their long journey to the "work" camp. *They requested the Hungarians to furnish sufficient provisions.* And in order that they might be able to *live comfortably* at their initial work place on the territory of the Reich, German officials recommend that Jews bring with them sufficient clothing, household goods, blankets and straw mattresses.

The German embassy would appreciate if the Hungarians ensured that Jews designated for labor in Germany be permitted to keep the supplies and provisions they took along or were supplied. Poorly trained border guards would thus be prevented from confiscating such items from the Jewish deportees.[14] The hypocrisy of this German communiqué hardly deserves commentary.

Meanwhile, on August 12, Regent Miklós Horthy sent his response to Max Huber, the director of the International Red Cross in Geneva. In it the increasingly isolated Hungarian head of state briefly addressed the concerns that Huber had expressed in his letter of July 5, explaining that IRC officials[15] had been apprised of the true situation with regard to Jews in Hungary, and affirming that he was "*completely aware* of the vital importance of this problem (that is, of what was happening to the Jews—*author's note).*"

Unfortunately, he wrote, he was not in a position to prevent inhumane acts. He instructed the Hungarian government to resolve the Jewish question on its own. His fear and servility toward Germany and the Gestapo is clearly revealed from the concluding sentence of the communiqué, in which Horthy says he hopes that "this statement by him will not lead to serious complications."[16]

There is no evidence to indicate that German occupational authorities took particular interest in the regent's correspondence. They were too busy preparing for a new round of deportations, that of the Jews of Budapest, which was scheduled to commence on August 25. Only a sudden shift in the military situation and a concomitant lack of Hungarian support prevented them from carrying through with these plans.

[14] *Jewish Destiny,* pp. 141–142.

[15] They outlined a series of proposals, mostly with regard to facilitation of Jewish emigration. With Horthy's permission, these were sent on to Washington and London. Their intention was to rescue all Jewish children under the age of eleven from Hungary.

[16] Geneva archives of the International Red Cross, G 9/1-5.

# 5. The SS Trading in Human Lives

## a. The First Meetings of the Rescue Committee

Zionist leaders learned of the impending German invasion days before it took place, primarily through Joel Brand, yet the occupation still caught them off guard, because they were also under the illusion that this would never happen.

During the first weeks of the occupation, they waited in hiding to see how events would develop. This was when a forty-year-old chemical engineer by the name of Endre (Andreas) Biss began to participate actively in the rescue operations, first by allowing use of his apartment for this purpose.[1] Biss, who had supported the Zionist cause up to then passively, through financial contributions, was a well-traveled, self-assured businessman. His connections in Budapest, his financial background (he owned a factory in Beszterce—now Banska-Bistrica in Slovakia), and foreign language skills became very helpful.

On March 19, Kasztner and Ernő Szilágyi hid with their families at Biss' apartment. Ottó Komoly and his wife soon joined them. Joel Brand, with help from Josef Winninger and his connections within the *Abwehr*, found shelter in the home of a female dancer. Ironically enough, Brand's wife Hansi had planned to weather the first weeks of the occupation with their two children at the Hotel Majestic. Fortunately they left the Svábhegy resort before the German terror organizations commandeered it. Eventually the Brand family also ended up at the Semsey Street hideout.

Following the initial shock of the occupation, several members of the Zionist committee contemplated taking refuge in the Hungarian countryside. However, they soon abandoned these plans once they found out about the continuous identity checks going on at the train stations, and the hostage-takings and

---

[1] Biss' mother was Jewish but after the divorce of his parents he grew up as a Catholic. His apartment and business meeting rooms located at No 15 Semsey Andor Street had first been used as a shelter for Polish refugees. He had the premises officially registered with the police as the office of the Transylvanian German Lutheran Confession.

other German measures implemented in the provinces. After making an assessment of the situation, the fugitives started making cautious attempts to establish contacts on the outside. At the same time they concluded that they would thereafter concentrate their efforts on *rescuing Hungarian Jews*. They then divided up the immediate tasks.

Ottó Komoly endeavored to make contact with Hungarian politicians and seek the support of Christian Churches and their organizations. In the meantime they learned of the establishment of a Jewish Council, the main objective of which was to gain time. The Council gradually realized that the connections of the Zionists, some of which were already known by the Germans, could prove to be very beneficial, perhaps even help to save Hungarian Jews.

The life-saving role of money had turned into a well-established practice over the previous years, at which the Zionists had increasing experience. Kasztner and his associates pondered the potentially enormous cost of saving Hungarian Jews. They calculated the amount of wealth that certain Jewish organizations in Poland, Holland, France and Belgium had yielded to Eichmann's deportation squadrons. They were also aware of the fact that on several occasions the SS had politely accepted the ransom money, then sent the Jews thus "liberated" to their deaths in the Majdanek gas chambers.

In contrast, there was the experience of Slovak Jews who had been able to redeem tens of thousands of lives through payment of ransom money to the SS.[2] The Hungarian Zionists also entertained hopes of establishing some kind of anti-German front by allying up with certain Hungarian political officials when they decided to continue rescue operations.

It was the result of secret negotiations between the Rescue Committee and Eichmann's officers—with SS *Obersturmbannführer* Kurt Alexander Becher, who had been overseeing the exploitation of Hungary's economy, looming large in the background[3]—that a fragment of Hungary's Jews ultimately escaped the Auschwitz death factory in the summer of 1944. SS Reich Commander Heinrich Himmler knew, and likely approved, of the deal. Compared to its unbending will to implement the "final solution," this readiness to negotiate showed *a different face* of that SS than the one known so far.

These intense negotiations were based on the intention of several high-ranking SS officers in Himmler's inner circle to seek profit from Jewish lives,

---

[2] The following work addresses this question in detail: *Freikauf von Juden? Verhandlung zwischen dem nationalsozialistischen Deutschland und jüdischen Representänten von 1933 bis 1945* (Jüdischer Verlag: Frankfurt am Main, 1996), pp. 103–193.

[3] His original name was Kurt Andreas Ernst Becher.

which they saw as a nearly worthless "trade commodity." Consequently they drew up an exchange plan (*Austauschplan*), of which only those at the apex of the SS hierarchy were aware, already in 1943. Initially they were thinking only of exchanging Jews with either British or American dual citizenship[4] for citizens of the *Reich* or ethnic Germans deported as enemy aliens by the Allies. The number of Jewish prisoners considered suitable for exchange grew steadily, for both political and economic reasons.

This scheme, known in Nazi jargon as the Europe Plan (*Europaplan*), was also designed to highlight the strength of the SS and the "flexibility" of its leadership at a time when German positions were deteriorating and their room for maneuver was narrowing down. This would establish the preconditions for negotiation with the Allied powers and appear as an appeasing gesture to "Jewish world power." Such human trade efforts, their architects thought, might alter the image of SS leaders and also provide a significant source of income.

In order to expedite this scheme, on April 30, 1943, at Himmler's orders, the SS took over a segment of the prisoner of war camp (Stalag XI C/311) operating inside Bergen-Belsen, located forty kilometers (twenty-five miles) to the north of Hannover, near the town of Celle. Here the SS established a holding camp (Aufenthaltslager),[5] in which it would gather 10,000 potential „exchange Jews with important connections." Among the eight large subdivisions at this camp, the *Sternlager*, the *Neutralenlager*, the *Sonderlager* and the *Ungarnlager* were reserved for "prominent hostages" and "exchange Jews."[6]

At the beginning of 1944, Dutch Jews (along with their families) were forming the largest nationality group at the holding camp. They were obliged to work. Several hundred Spanish, Portuguese, Argentinian, Turkish and North African Jews were held in another subdivision of the camp where they were not subject to forced labor. An increasing number of "exempt" Jews awaited release owing to the SS exchange program.

---

[4] The first groups of dual citizens, consisting of 2,500 Poles and 441 Greeks, arrived during the summer of 1943. At the beginning of 1944, the largest number of "exchange Jews"—3,670—arrived from Holland. At that time they also transferred 205 North African Jews and 200 French women to the camp; in June, they were joined by several hundred Yugoslav and Albanian Jews who held foreign passports.

[5] It essentially functioned as an internment camp, though it was not technically defined as such so as to circumvent Geneva Convention guidelines that permitted international inspectors access to civilian internment camps. The new sector of Bergen-Belsen, partitioned into eight distinct subdivisions according to function and treatment of prisoners, was classified as a concentration camp by the start.

[6] Bergen-Belsen Hameln, 1990, p. 53.

The prisoners of the *Sonderlager* were Polish Jews exempted from work. Most of them held temporary exit permits or entry documents of some kind to various South American countries.[7] Due to a lack of documentation, the precise "yield" of the exchange plan devised by the SS is unknown. In fact, up to the summer of 1944, the number of Jews who had gained release from the camp in this way was only a couple of hundred.[8]

Thus part of the reason for the meager results of the "exchange plan" is to be found in the exorbitant demands, based on pressure and blackmail, of the SS. However, it is equally important to note the procrastination, negligence and indifference on the part of the Allied powers as well as the governments of South American countries with regard to the Jewish crisis.[9]

The Hungarian state laid hands on all property and assets owned by provincial Jews. Only the rest was left to the Germans. The occupiers had to wrest as much as possible of what was left of Jewish wealth in the country—that of the Budapest Jews and the still existing Jewish organizations—in order to support their lavish lifestyle in Budapest and to secure their postwar financial prosperity. They were completely unabashed at that. They were not content with their bills and continuously increasing demands being met. The German overlords had their eyes on bigger "business": a lucrative trade of human lives in Hungary.

Officers on Eichmann's staff first negotiated the conditions (the exorbitant ransom) for allowing 600 "Palestinian emigrants" to leave the country. Kasztner played a decisive role in these negotiations. The head count grew in proportion with the net worth of the property and assets that the Zionists offered to the

[7] During the summer of 1944, the majority of these inmates were transferred to Auschwitz-Birkenau, where they were killed. Approximately 350 of them were retained at the holding camp. The number of "exchange Jews"—including Hungarian citizens sent to the *Ungarnlager* following negotiations in Budapest—reached 7,300 by July. Located right next to the section of the camp designated for the Hungarians was a so-called *Häftlinglager* with 500 wretched and utterly exhausted Jews in striped camp uniforms.

[8] In June 1944, 222 people arrived in Palestine one month after their release. A total of 136 Jews regained their freedom at the end of January 1945, traveling to Switzerland pursuant to a German–American exchange agreement involving civilians. We can add to this number the 1,683 Hungarian Jews and several hundred Jews of other nationalities who also wound up in Switzerland by the end of 1944. See *Studien zur Geschichte der Konzentrationslager* (Deutsche Verlagsanstalt: Stuttgart, 1970), pp. 138, 141; and also *Bergen-Belsen*, p. 57.

[9] G. E. Schaft and Gerhard Zeidler, *Die KZ-Mahn-und Gedenkstätten in Deutschland*, (Dietz Verlag GmbH: Berlin, 1996), p. 38. This theme is also addressed in the following works: Barnard Wasserstein, *Britain and the Jews of Europe 1939-1945*, (London, Oxford, 1979) and David S. Wyman, *Das unerwünschte Volk. Amerika und die Vernichtung der europäischen Juden* (München, 1986).

Germans. It soon reached a thousand. Krumey, Wisliceny, occasionally Hunsche as well as SS *Obersturmbannführer* Becher and his associates geared the length of the list of potential travelers to the amount of hard currency, diamonds, gold, and internationally recognized bonds that they would be receiving. There is evidence indicating that "slots" were being sold also by some high-ranking Gestapo officers.

The completion of the final version of the list took more than three months of bargaining. Zionist leaders entertained no illusions regarding the objectives of the SS officials involved in the scheme; recalling their past devious tactics, they carefully followed their movements within Hungary. They struggled with doubts as they ran a race with time to save as many Jews as possible from the deadly ring drawing ever tighter around them.

The Jews were at an enormous disadvantage vis-à-vis the Germans, who had so many means of intimidation at their disposal and such extensive experience in dealing with the behavior and reactions of their victims. On the other hand, Germany's military prospects were becoming increasingly dim with the imminent Allied invasion of continental Europe and the Red Army's anticipated spring offensive against the incessantly retreating *Wehrmacht.*

Brand and Kasztner first established contact with SS *Hauptsturmführer* Dieter Wisliceny on April 5 via *Abwehr* agents, who had been looked down upon and pushed into the background with the arrival of German personnel following the occupation.[10] SS *Hauptsturmführer* Erich Klausnitzer represented the Gestapo at the talks, which were held at his elegant, requisitioned apartment overlooking Szent István Park in Budapest.

Brand and his associates wanted to put out feelers to the *Sonderkommando* to find out if "economically based" negotiations were conceivable. If so, how might it be possible to avoid, or at least delay, what Jews dreaded the most—ghettoization and deportation? Dr. Schmidt and Agent Winninger were also present at the first meeting at which Wisliceny presented a letter from Rabbi Michael Dov Weissmandel on behalf of Jews living in Bratislava, Slovakia.[11]

In response to the Zionists' questions, Wisliceny declared that *the mission of the German authorities which brought them to Hungary was not to ghetto-*

---

[10] Several personal mémoirs indicate that the first nominee to represent the Zionists in their negotiations with the Germans was Dr. Nison Kahane, but that he declined to accept this task.

[11] Three letters arrived written in Hebrew. These were addressed to Baroness Edit Weiss, Fülöp Freudiger and Dr. Nison Kahane. Edit Weiss, who had previously done much to help refugees and thwart German deportation plans, had gone into hiding. The other two addressees met separately with the SS captain before Brand did.

*ize or deport Jews.* The German officer claimed that this would only happen if Hungarian authorities requested permission for it straight from Berlin "over the head of the SS." They were having *a different task*, so he and his associates were suitable for negotiating about "the preservation of the Jewish average."

The objective, he explained, was to eradicate Jewish influence at all levels of Hungarian society, and they saw it conceivable to achieve that objective by Jewish emigration. While their superiors retained the authority to make the ultimate decisions on this matter, the SS officials deemed drawing up a preliminary plan involving 10,000 Jewish emigrants to be a realistic proposition. The German officers informed the Zionists that they would be willing to act as "spokesmen" for the plan in Berlin for a fee of two million dollars "for their pains." Brand and his associates would be required to make a down payment of ten percent of this sum—or 6.5 million pengős at the black-market exchange rate—within a week as proof of their *good faith and financial solvency.* The Germans soon let it be known that the two million dollars "should only be considered an advance."

It is worth taking note of the chronology of these negotiations: meetings between the Zionists and the SS started on the very day in which it was announced that Hungarian Jews would be required to wear the yellow star in public. On the day before, the Sztójay government brought a secret decree, issued April 7, calling for the ghettoization and eventual deportation to Germany—referred to euphemistically as "labor resettlement"—of Jews living in the provinces. *Sonderkommando* officials were doubtlessly behind this measure, which affected the lives of hundreds of thousands of people. They were doing their diabolical job in a masterly way.

The confidential interior ministry decree "pertaining to the matter of designating Jewish residences," was issued by Dr. László Endre,[12] the notoriously Jew-hating undersecretary of state for internal affairs of the Sztójay government, which was totally subservient to the Germans. Naturally, Wisliceny had prior knowledge of the contents and objectives of the decree.

SS officers served as advisors during the preparation for the deportation of Hungarian Jews, dubbed "worker resettlement." They retained strict secrecy regarding these proceedings, which was all the more easy as Hungarian Jews had essentially been handed over to them fully. *Their fate had become sealed.*

Brand and his associates evaluated their negotiations with Wisliceny at a meeting including Ernő Szilágyi, Károly Wilhelm and Samu Stern that took

---

[12] The text of this decree is contained in *Jewish Fate*, pp. 97–99.

place at the home of the latter. They deemed the outcome of the talks to have been paltry, but they thought they must not miss even the slightest opportunity for their people getting out of their plight; therefore these Zionist officials elected to pay the 6.5 million-pengő advance. Stern, the President of the Jewish Council, began to make efforts to raise this immense sum of money by beginning to summon the richest Jews of Budapest one by one to his office. In just a few weeks, he collected 5 million pengős; the Rescue Committee then came up with the rest.

The money was handed over to the SS in installments. Eichmann's deputy, SS *Obersturmbannführer* Krumey, and SS *Hauptsturmführer* Hunsche arrived to collect the first 3 million. They announced that the negotiations had assumed a formal character, which suited the Rescue Committee well. The Zionists repeated the statements Wisliceny had made regarding ghettoization and deportation.

The SS officers were unwilling to discuss these matters in the absence of Wisliceny, who they claimed had gone to Berlin. This was another lie; it subsequently turned out that he had traveled to Munkács to oversee the ghettoization of Sub-Carpathian Jews.

Krumey declined to take up the previously discussed issue of emigration, because he had "not yet received any orders." He promised that the SS would prevent the Hungarian authorities from taking the measures they had introduced against the Zionist organizations. The Hungarian political police led by Péter Hain nevertheless arrested several Zionist leaders, three of whom were released as a result of German intervention. In this way Krumey was able to show that he fulfilled his pledge to help the Zionists, and to demonstrate his "cooperative" attitude.

The third round of negotiations took place on April 21. This time the subject of the discussions were the prospects and procedures related to emigration; it turned out that Hungarian officials would not be allowed to take part in this transaction. Krumey declared that the emigration scheme they were devising with the Zionists was a "purely Reich matter."[13] What the SS Lieutenant-Colonel was hinting at was that the human-trade venture, the trafficking in Jewish lives, was being handled on the highest level. But he also implied that any breach of confidentiality on this issue would entail the heaviest of consequences. At the meeting, Krumey and Hunsche received another installment on the payment: a total of 2.5 million pengős.

---

[13] Knowledge of confidential Reich affairs (*Geheme Riechssache*) such as this was almost always limited to a very limited circle of officials.

In the meantime, the Zionists had learned from their *Abwehr* contacts that, in spite of all official statements to the contrary, the German plan for the ghettoization and deportation of Hungarian Jews undoubtedly reached the point of being actually carried out. Undersecretary Endre pressed for the deportation of all the Jews. Only money, and vast amounts of it, might forestall this. (Negotiations "along the Hungarian lead" came to a dead end; several Zionist initiatives along this avenue ended in a fiasco. One member of the Jewish Council, Ernő Pető, managed to establish contact with Finance Minister Reményi-Schneller, who had long enjoyed the complete confidence of the Germans; but this did not produce any concrete results either.)

Critical intelligence involving the fate of Hungarian Jews got through even the strictest German wall of secrecy: the crematoria at the Auschwitz–Birkenau death factory had been expanded and renovated. This prompted the Zionists to turn to their Istanbul contacts in order to expedite the emigration plan, but they were not able reach them by telephone, even with German assistance. Every passing day was crucial: at the end of April deportation trains departed from Kistarcsa and Southern Hungary. The facts again contradicted the claims and promises of the SS officers.

A call was received from Eichmann's deputy, Krumey, who laughingly said that they should concentrate on real business, since Berlin had granted permission for 600 Jews to emigrate from Hungary. According to the agreement, half of this number would be made up of provincial Jews in possession of a *Zertifikat* entitling them entry to Palestine. The SS would escort them to Budapest, where they would be held at a "privileged camp" until their departure.

The SS officer went on to state that he had been permitted to negotiate the exit of a further 300 emigrants; for this the gallant Germans would ask for a total of $100,000. Krumey called the collection of such an enormous sum of money "child's play." He nonchalantly mentioned that he had once been offered three million pengős to arrange for the emigration of a Jewish family of three.[14] Cognizant of his superiority, Krumey commented that the SS did not want to deal directly with such issues, and that it was up to the Zionists to raise the money.

In response to questions regarding the "resettlement" trains that had left at the end of April, Krumey said (*lying again*) that the deported specialists would soon be writing home from Waldsee. According to the SS officer, this

---

[14] There may have been a grain of truth to his claim; desperate people were willing to pay any price to save their lives.

place[15] "was not far away, West of Hungary," though he had never been there himself.

On May 3, Brand and his associates discovered that Wisliceny was staying in Kolozsvár. With Krumey's assistance, and after payment of another million pengős, Kasztner was given permission to travel by car to Kolozsvár with Sedlaczek.[16] They reported seeing several forlorn caravans along the way. Gendarmes with bayonets escorted columns of tired and famished provincial Jews and their horse- and ox-drawn wagons. Village Jews were being gathered in local ghettos.

During a meeting with Wisliceny at a Hungarian police station, Kasztner, using a personal tone, attempted to find out precisely what had taken place in the country over the past few days. The SS captain, a skillful liar, claimed that he himself had been *powerless* at that particular period of time: due to his "good reputation" with the Jews, Eichmann had decided to exclude him from the negotiations, assigning him instead to do the dirty work of forcing Jews into the ghettos. He contended that Eichmann was attempting to ridicule him by obstructing his effort to save Jews, but that his uniform obliged him to comply with his orders. The true culprit for the ghettoization of these provincial Jews was László Endre, who "wanted to eat all Jews alive—and Eichmann sure isn't the one to appease him."[17]

Kasztner continued to ask questions: were the impending deportations to include all Jews, or would they involve only those deemed fit for labor, as they had been in the case of Kistarcsa?[18] Dieter Wisliceny made no response; he made more promises instead, telling Kasztner that he would soon be traveling to Budapest, where he would obtain further information from Eichmann, and pass it along to the Zionists.

Though it was, perhaps, possible to confront a question of life and death, there was no such thing as good response to it. Ottó Komoly and Ernő Szilágyi were forced to deal with the bitter issue of precisely whom to choose for the

[15] Waldsee was a fictitious name. Letters that the SS had the deportees write in fact arrived from Auschwitz–Birkenau.

[16] His brother, Ernő Kasztner, later became a member of the local Jewish Council, the *Judenrat*. The following work represents another study of the Kolozsvár ghetto and deportation: Dániel Löwy, *A téglagyártól a tehervonatig* [From the Brick Factory to the Freight Train], (Erdélyi Szépmíves Céh: Kolozsvár, 1998). Following the war the leaders of the Kolozsvár ghetto were criticized harshly.

[17] *Haladás*, April 3, 1947, p. 6

[18] It is not true that the Germans deported skilled labor from Kistarcsa; sixty-one percent of the deportees were murdered by gas soon after arriving at the concentration camp.

emigration list, because the *Palamt*, the Palestine Office, would have made the selection based on personal and political criteria. The emigration list was, nonetheless, the subject of much wrangling and debate. Zionists or non-Zionists, beginners or experienced members of the movement, provincial or Budapest Jews, Polish and Slovak refugees, young or old—which of these, and others, should appear on the roster and in what proportions?

The list of names changed constantly. The mortal danger to which the Jews were now exposed naturally gave rise to heated disagreements regarding the final version, which took weeks to produce. Its implementation, the actual, much-coveted departure from the country, however, remained entirely in the hands of the Germans. Instead of the one or two weeks promised, authorization was finally given after two months. In the meantime, Swiss vice-consul Carl Lutz granted diplomatic protection to Krausz, who had been drafted into a forced-labor battalion. With the granting of political asylum to him and living quarters at the embassy, the Swiss had made their first attempts to place *Palamt*, which began its Budapest operations with a staff of thirty, under their protection.[19]

The SS was busy with many things; for example, on May 4, it sponsored the two-day Rennwegen Transportation Conference in Vienna. At this gathering, railway officials, including representatives from MÁV (the Hungarian National Railways), coordinated international schedules for lines involved in the German "worker resettlement" program, establishing various duties to be performed at various locations on certain dates. SS *Hauptsturmführer* Franz Novak, a transportation specialist known as "death's stationmaster," arrived from Budapest to represent the German deportation unit operating there.

The preconditions necessary for implementation of the previously discussed *Ungarnaktion* had been established; all that was needed to start it was a wave of the conductor's baton from the maestro of the *Endlösung*, Lieutenant-Colonel Adolf Eichmann.

The event that the supreme leadership of National Socialist Germany had been demanding and anticipating for two years took place on May 14. It was the turn of the Europe's largest remaining Jewish community, nearly intact until then, to fall prey to Nazi extermination plans. Eichmann had made some further moves before the big day. After reviewing the negotiations conducted

---

[19] Theo Tschuy: *Becsület és bátorság. Carl Lutz és a budapesti zsidók* [Honor and Courage: Carl Lutz and Budapest Jews], (Well-Press Kiadó Kft.: Miskolc, no year specified), pp. 136–137. The title of the English-language edition of this work is *Dangerous Diplomacy* (William B. Erdmans Publishing Co.: Grand Rapids, Michigan/Cambridge, United Kingdom, 2000).

with the Zionists thus far, he concluded logically that first of all the circle of participants, eager to have their cut, must be narrowed down. With one swift and powerful stroke, Eichmann pushed the Budapest agents of the *Abwehr*— who he believed had broken National Socialist regulations by collaborating with the Zionists and demanding a middleman's share of the ransom—from the human-trade business.

The details are little-known and largely irrelevant. The role of Judas in betraying the agents of the *Abwehr* was played by Bandi Grosz, whose financial enrichment made him susceptible to blackmail in the eyes of the Gestapo. Joel Brand himself had intended the Zionists to play some role with the Gestapo as well. (Kasztner later made a very subtle reference to this.) The *Abwehr* was thus eliminated from the scene and in the seventh week of the occupation the omnipotent overlord of the Jews (the *Judenkomissar*) took center stage. He summoned Brand to his headquarters on Svábhegy.

Eichmann referred to Krumey's negotiations as a trifling affair. He spoke of a new chapter in the negotiations in a strident, domineering voice and short sentences, one in which he, personally, would represent the Jews' best chance for survival. Eichmann had heard about Roosevelt's radio address in which the US president had voiced concern for the fate of Hungarian Jews. Now, he said, the President would get a chance to turn his words into action.

> I don't need money. What would I need it for? I need war matériel and equipment—trucks if possible. I have therefore decided to send you to Istanbul in order to present your friends there with my generous proposition.
>
> I will have each and every Hungarian Jew transported to the Reich, where they will be collected. I will wait two weeks for a response from Istanbul. You will return to Budapest immediately with the response of your friends. If it is positive, they can take all one million Jews as far as I'm concerned; if it is negative, the Jews will suffer the consequences.[20]

According to Kasztner, Eichmann deemed the Joint organization to be financially solvent during his May 8 "briefing" of Brand. (In Eichmann's mind, everything connected with Jews and money was inseparably associated

---

[20] *Haladás*, April 10, 1947, p. 6. During Eichmann's trial in Jerusalem, Brand emphasized that the SS officer was obsessed with the idea of genocide. He quoted a statement that Eichmann had made before his departure for Istanbul: "One million Jews for ten-thousand trucks— they're getting by pretty cheap!"

with the Joint.) He awaited response to his blackmailing offer from this quarter, simultaneously rejecting Brand's suggestion that the deportations be delayed.

Kasztner met with Wisliceny on the same day. At the talks, which took place on Svábhegy, the SS captain confidentially informed Kasztner that *collective* and *total* deportation of the Jews from Hungary was irrevocable.

Contacts with the occupying forces thus underwent a fundamental change. That change led to newer and newer turns, producing a series of increasingly thriller-like situations and events.

## b. The Columbus Street Camp

As a direct consequence of the negotiations, Eichmann placed individuals referred to as "sample goods" in camps. At the request of the Zionists, the Jewish Council had began constructing living quarters inside the Aréna Street Synagogue, near the Városliget (the biggest Budapest town park). However, work on these accommodations dragged on too long. In early July, however, a rapid housing solution was needed, so the Rescue Committee had a camp built at 46 Columbus Street, in the Zugló (14th) District of Budapest.

On July 7, Jewish School Commissioner Dr. Zoltán Kohn and a Kolozsvár resident named Zsigmond Léb[21] informed Dr. Dezső Kanizsai, Director of the Israelite School for the Deaf, Dumb and Blind, that nearly 400 Jews would soon be transferred to Budapest from the Kolozsvár brick factory, where they were being held. They said that they had been selected from among 18,000 Jews designated for deportation and that *Eretz*[22] *was their final destination.*[23]

The institute had a courtyard with gardens and was situated on grounds whose surface area measured 135,000 square feet. (Most of the main building had already been converted into police barracks earlier; the Jewish quarters were thus placed in the empty gymnasium and several unclaimed spaces in the basement, and walled off.) In a matter of days and at his own cost, László De-

---

[21] As a highly decorated officer from World War I and a disabled veteran, Léb was not required to wear the Star of David in public. Up to the German occupation, he had served as President of the Kolozsvár Jewish Religious Community.

[22] The new Jewish homeland.

[23] For more detail see Szabolcs Szita, " 'A' Columbus," ("The" Columbus) *Remény* no. 4, September-October 1999, pp. 61-68. A memorial plaque was placed on the site in October 1994.

vecseri,[24] a structural engineer from Kolozsvár, built wooden barracks with bunk beds to accommodate 210 people. Around July 10, 388 Jews—filthy, ragged and in some cases beaten half to death—arrived at the newly constructed camp from the Kolozsvár ghetto.[25]

Jews residing at the Columbus Street camp were housed with their families; suitable hygienic conditions were established for them following construction of three more barracks. Twenty residents were later moved to the machine shed and forty to a villa located in the gardens. The population of the camp quickly increased.

This camp represented a unique phenomenon in Hungary: it was guarded by a detachment of five SS troopers, who were ordered to accord *humane treatment* to the Jews held there. According to Kasztner, the SS carried out this order with the same strict discipline as it did when, as "normally," commanded to do the opposite.[26]

A twenty-five-bed infirmary was also established on the grounds of the camp. Under the direction of Dr. Vilmos Stern, who had been a chief physician at the Kolozsvár hospital, several medical doctors treated the sick and frail. Orthodox women prepared kosher food. Workshops, warehouses and a laundry room were also established. Voluntary contributions from the residents of the camp, whose number had swelled to more than 600, covered common expenses.

With a few exceptions, the Kolozsvár Jews arrived to the camp with only the clothes on their backs. In order to compensate for this deficiency, residents with the necessary skills in garment making spent weeks in the newly built workshops stitching together clothing, backpacks, work pants and spare underwear.

---

[24] With the help of the SS and Kasztner, Devecseri, a prosperous, thirty-seven-year-old engineer, had his only living relative, Mrs. Izsó Steiner, brought from Kolozsvár to Budapest. (He also wanted to save his sister-in-law and her husband, but, out of a false sense of security, they stayed on. Both fell victim to the deportation.) The fulfillment of the first "shipment," however, allowed the conclusion that others might be rescued from Kolozsvár in the same way. A list of the first twenty people to leave the town was drawn up in mid-May. Joel Brand dealt with this matter until his departure, after which Zsigmond Léb took over. (The list of those who had paid the required $12,000 for this privilege changed constantly. This list would eventually wind up in Kasztner's hands.) Based on author's interviews with László Devecseri on December 12, 2003 and May 21, 2004.

[25] *Der Bericht des jüdischen Rettungskomitees aus Budapest 1942–1945 Vorgelegt von Dr. Rezső Kasztner*, (n. p., s. a.) p. 45.

[26] Ibid.

A welfare and assistance committee was established under the direction of Mrs. József Vészi and Jenő Ungár, while the OMZSA also contributed to this effort. The spiritual needs of the camp residents also had to be met: many of them had been torn suddenly from their habitual environment, and had lost their homes and all their possessions. Some struggled with severe depression. They knew nothing about what happened to their relatives, and their future was uncertain. In the meantime, since the Germans promised *aliyah* for them, they had to prepare for a new life in Palestine.

For many camp residents, the lack of privacy (110 people slept together in the gymnasium, for example) and the extended period of waiting became increasingly disconcerting. A disciplinary committee was established under District Community Chief Dr. Miklós Szegő in order to handle personal complaints and punitive issues. The mere fact of its existence had a restraining effect on camp life. The rabbis arriving to the camp—Dr. Izsák Pfeifer, Dr. József Horovitz and Dr. József Berend—held religious services. Hebrew-language courses were launched, and teachers, led by Sándor Szilágyi, engaged the abundant energy of the school-aged children with educational exercises.

Dr. Izsó Diamant of Kolozsvár organized a series of lectures at the camp. The volunteer speakers discussed the achievements of many branches of science. Emphasis was also laid on getting ready for life in Palestine. Ottó Komoly, Dr. Diamant and Dr. Miklós Szegő and his wife provided important information on Zionism and the new homeland.

Most participants of the first *aliyah* departed from this camp on the last day of July. The emigrants left on foot, in rows of five, many of them lost in thoughts. Each were allowed to take two changes of clothing, six sets of underwear and enough food to last them for ten to fourteen days. The old and the sick were transported by wagon to the Rákos railway station, where all would board their trains.

They still thought they were bound for Palestine.

## c. The SS Buyout Proposal Mediated by Joel Brand

At the beginning of May, the Zionists were already talking to other SS officers as well. During the Budapest negotiations, in which Fülöp Freudiger, the head of the Budapest orthodox Jewish community also took part, the SS revealed its proposition in full: the Germans would be willing to "release" one million Jews in exchange for 10,000 fully equipped trucks and other "militarily significant" goods. The trucks, the Germans declared, were to be used exclusively on the Eastern Front.

Eichmann, who had been the first to mention the trucks, later claimed that this proposition had official backing from Berlin. The Nazi jargon used to describe these negotiations as *Blut gegen Waren,*[27] or "blood for goods."

The negotiations essentially consisted of mutual bluffing. (Even if the SS undeniably had the upper hand.) What was truly tragic was that even as they spoke of mass rescue, the *Endlösung* was going on at full speed. Freight cars packed with Jews rolled unimpeded and according to plan from the Hungarian countryside toward the railway platforms at Auschwitz–Birkenau. *Both sides were aware of this, just as they were of the ultimate purpose of the deliveries.*[28]

Adolf Eichmann arranged for the representatives of the Hungarian Jewish community to travel to Turkey on May 8. The purpose of the visit was to establish contacts with representatives of the Allied powers and to obtain the financial resources necessary to carry out the *Europaplan.* The fact that one of the principal representatives of the Palestinian Jews, the previously mentioned Chaim Barlas, was working in Turkey, further raised the stakes.

Present at one of the meetings that Eichmann held with Brand prior to his departure for Istanbul was an *Obersturmbannführer* whom the Zionist leader had not yet encountered. He was Kurt Becher, the chief of the Budapest economic staff of the *Waffen SS.*[29]

A particularly dangerous agent of the Germans took part in preparations for the Brand mission: the forty-four-year-old Fritz Laufer, whose extensive experience, knowledge, special skills and secret-service background made him a valuable asset to the SS in its planning of the undertaking.[30]

[27] The expression *Waren gegen Blut* was also used on occasion.

[28] In order to dispel the "Jewish horror stories," SS *Hauptsturmführer* Hunsche informed Kasztner that, at most, fifty or sixty Jews died in each of the deportation trains.

[29] Ibid., p. 37. How he got into that situation is a mystery. Becher claimed several times that Winkelmann and Eichmann had told him about the negotiations with the Zionists. At other times he said that the Zionists had asked for his presence to provide special protection for them at the negotiations.

[30] Fritz, or Frantisek, Laufer, was born in Prague in 1900. His first profession was as a waiter. Like Grosz, he was a petty criminal, appearing before a Prague court in 1940. After being recruited by *Abwehr* captain Erich Klausnitzer, Laufer worked for the Germans in Zagreb, Belgrade and Istanbul. Returning to Prague, he worked as an SD operative under several code names (Direktor Schröder, Ludwig Mayer and Karl Heinz). In 1944, he was sent to Budapest, where he exposed two valuable members of the anti-Nazi resistance, Heinrich Maier, the Dean of the St. Stephen Church in Vienna, and Franz Josef Messner, the director of the Semperit Works. Both were executed at Dachau—Maier in November 1944 and Messner on April 23,

Joel Brand considered the trip to Istanbul and conveying the SS proposal the chance of a lifetime. On May 17, he made the first leg of his trip, traveling to Vienna. He carried letters of recommendation from the Budapest Jewish Council and the Rescue Committee, which designated him as a legitimate representative of the Hungarian Jewish community. While he was in Vienna, the SS supplied him with a fake German passport, without a Turkish visa, under the name of Eugen Brand. Brand sent telegrams to the Jewish organizations operating in Istanbul informing them of his impending arrival. He got the reply that "Chaim was ready to meet him."[31]

His travel companion, who did have a Turkish visa, was Andor Gross (aka Bandi Grosz, Andreas Grosz, András György and András Grainer). He made notes before the trip, which, as an experienced courier, first he learned by heart, and then destroyed. Grosz, to use his former alias, was a paid member of the SD network. His main mission was to keep an eye on Brand, though he was also given his own, separate, tasks as well. In addition, he was sent to ensure that the Germans received prompt information regarding the general reception and feasibility of the *Europaplan*.

Brand and Grosz flew by a German courier plane from Vienna to Sofia, where they were inspected again by the local Gestapo. The two arrived in Istanbul on May 19.

Grosz was well aware that he landed in an affair of which the order of magnitude was far bigger than any of his previous missions. He quickly realized that he hardly even qualified as small fry in such a large context. At any rate, there was definitely something suspicious about entrusting a small-time crook with the mission of laying the foundations for nothing less than a separate peace. Perhaps somebody made it clear to him that the bigger fish thought it better to keep clear of the mission, lest they would be blamed for its failure.

Brand said afterwards that he had gone to Istanbul of his free will, though he was well aware of the character of the Teutonic order wearing the black uniforms of German National Socialism, and the objectives, temperament and actions of the perpetually superior and cynical SD officers. He knew that they were plotting to exterminate the Jewish people and were determined to achieve the *Endlösung*. Still, Brand was willing to collaborate with any individual or

---

1945. After the war Laufer returned to Prague. Because he knew too much about his secret-service supervisor, Klausnitzer had him arrested and executed, along with his third wife.

[31] Brand actually thought that this referred to Chaim Weizmann, the President of the Zionist World Organization and the Jewish Agency.

organization in order to advance his almost crazy, all-consuming effort to rescue as many Jews as possible.

Brand found most of the Nazis whom he dealt with, particularly Eichmann, repugnant. He was aware that the *Judenkommissar* had been responsible for the hideous deaths of hundreds of thousands of Jews. He also knew that none of the claims and promises of either Eichmann or his officers could be trusted an inch. But there simply was no alternative. The life and death nature of the challenge he was struggling with practically destined him to cooperate with the persecutors and tormentors of his people.

Any clemency toward Jews was the exclusive prerogative of Himmler and his direct subordinates in Budapest, Becher, Eichmann and his staff. Brand had no choice but to fight these people, because they held all the strings that needed to be pulled if his rescue work was to have any chance of success.

As far as Kasztner was concerned, he was quite possibly aware that the exaggerated German demands for military supplies would never serve as a viable ground for negotiations. Perhaps he hoped that the Germans might prove willing to accept other goods or that some other sort of deal might be worked out.[32]

Many sources indicate that Kasztner's secretiveness was damaging to the Jewish leadership, because he had been the only one whom Brand had permitted to participate in many of his earlier talks with the Germans. He did not allow anyone any closer. He likely did not want others to have access to "exclusive information" that he and his inner circle had gained during their negotiations with the Germans. They were vague about what was said during their meetings, which undoubtedly benefited Eichmann.

Yet the most significant message to emerge from the negotiations was intended for the leaders of the Budapest Jewish community: its fate could still be avoided. There must still be a way out if they were able to talk to Eichmann, if they followed his orders, if they did not resist.

In the meantime, Eichmann's staff continued to operate efficiently, deporting an estimated 310,000 expelled Hungarians from the country. A further 500,000 Jews remained in Hungary as a bargaining chip.

---

[32] For example, on May 22 Rabbi Wiessmandel of Bratislava contacted Jewish organizations in Switzerland, urging them to begin immediate negotiations with the Germans in order to save Hungarian Jews. He also insisted that Auschwitz and the railroads leading to it be bombed. The Vatican was informed of these developments. František Kuruc, "A Vatikán, a szlovák állam és a zsidók" [The Vatican, the Slovak State and the Jews], *Új Forrás*, 1991, no. 8–9, pp. 58–62.

Some intelligence about the ongoing secret bargaining somehow reached the detectives of Hungarian Secret Police Chief Péter Hain. On May 27, three agents of "the Hungarian Gestapo" raided the Rescue Committee headquarters at Semsey Street, confiscating a large amount of hard currency that had been sent from Switzerland and Istanbul during their search of the premises. They arrested Hansi Brand, who they thought was well informed, as well as Kasztner and Sándor Offenbach, along with their wives.

Fortunately for the Zionists, they did not find a well-hidden suitcase that was full of thousands of blank Baptism certificates and fake military identification cards.[33] On the same day they also raided the apartment of the leader of the Zionist youth organization, Menahem Klein. This time they made a more impressive catch: identity photos, travel documents and other fake papers needed for escape were found.

Kasztner and his associates entered a new period of uncertainty while in Péter Hain's custody. They were interrogated for five consecutive days, during which they refused to answer the continually repeated questions. *Not a single one of them disclosed the subject of their negotiations with the Germans.*

Hansi Brand did nearly everything she could have in order to save her colleagues. Mrs. Brand confessed that the hideously beaten printer with whom she had been interrogated for hours on end had told the truth: she had been responsible for arranging and paying for the forged documents. She stated repeatedly that she had no idea why the Germans had sent her husband to Istanbul.

Hansi Brand showed great courage. She refused to talk, no matter how brutally she was treated by Hain's men. She was so severely beaten that for a long time afterwards she was unable to stand on her feet, and walked with difficulty even later.

Kasztner's turn came at 9 a.m. on the sixth day. Fortunately for him, the telephone rang just as he was receiving the first punches and kicks from the interrogators. Then an SS officer appeared, who took them to a nearby German Gestapo station. Two hours later they were free.[34]

In the meantime, another telegram had arrived from Brand. He inquired about the Hungarian deportations, warning that their continuation was hampering the "promising" negotiations that were under way. (This was not true: there was no serious negotiation going on in reality). The freed Kasztner

---

[33] These were the products of the young Zionists' mobile document workshop.

[34] Péter Hain was in favor of releasing them. However, the money that the Hungarian Gestapo had confiscated from the Zionists was never returned to them. *Der Bericht*, p. 40.

showed Brand's telegrams to Eichmann, but this did not produce the slightest result: the deportations proceeded at full speed.

Joel Brand repeatedly asserted that "*steady progress is being made.*" He promised a speedy return, though rumors circulated throughout Budapest about him having been sighted now Palestine, now in Lisbon; others claimed to have received irrefutable information that he was already on his way back to Budapest. The name Ottó Hatz, that of a Hungarian military attaché based in Istanbul, emerged in connection with Brand's mission.[35] Though information regarding Hatz's activities at this time is incomplete, it is certain that he served, on occasion, as an intermediary and courier between the Hungarian Zionists and the Jewish Agency.

During the protracted period of waiting, Kasztner also began to have doubts. He and Mrs. Brand kept coming up with newer and newer explanations to German and Jewish officials as to why the emissary had still not returned, and what the chances were. He requested that Eichmann halt the deportations, at least temporarily, as a goodwill gesture and in order to enhance Brand's chances for success.

The "maestro's" interests, however, ran contrary to his. Genuinely obsessed with genocide, he was not really interested in the success of the deal. He had made the realization of the German deportation plans his top priority. He was not prepared to yield an inch where the pace or scale of theses deportations was concerned. Postwar testimony from Hansi Brand and Wisliceny makes it unambiguously clear that the failure of Brand's mission actually pleased Eichmann. "He wanted to complete the deportations rapidly in order to present a *fait accompli* so that the negotiations ordered by Himmler would inevitably run aground."

Eichmann's conduct was partly the reason why Becher's influence began to grow beginning in June. Over the following months Becher basically took control over the negotiations, which caused Eichmann to begin viewing him as a rival. The relationship between the two became strained, eventually leading to

---

[35] Ottó Hatz (1902–1977), who went by the surname Hátszegi beginning in January 1945, had served as Hungarian military attaché beginning in 1941, first in Sofia, then in Istanbul. It is certain that he maintained contacts with American secret-service operatives from the beginning of September 1943. The Gestapo arrested him on May 3, 1944, for feeding misinformation to the German espionage service. Hatz was released three weeks later for lack of evidence. Until October 15, he served as the Hungarian defense minister's aide-de-camp with the rank of Colonel. On November 7, then as Chief of Staff, he flew to Soviet-occupied Szeged carrying valuable documents with him. His family was sent to a concentration camp in retribution. *A Gestapo Magyarországon* [The Gestapo in Hungary], pp. 283, 287.

open conflict. During this time Becher's position within the SS power structure strengthened steadily: soon his authority exceeded that of Eichmann, though the two were of identical rank.

According to Jenő Lévai, one of the first researchers to study the Hungarian Holocaust, Kasztner's attitude underwent a change during these weeks. He attempted to affiliate himself more closely with the Jewish leadership. He no longer stood as firmly by Brand as before, and virtually stopped covering up for him. He acknowledged that this mission had been, at least, *"an unfortunate move."*[36]

Then he reconsidered the events and came up with a new idea. If the "truck" deal could not be pushed through, then there might be another solution: the Rescue Committee could purchase five million francs worth of *tractors* in Switzerland for the Germans. And if negotiations with the American emissary of the Joint were not possible, they would have to deal with the Swiss representative of this organization.

To sum up the human trade negotiations, the first period lasted for five weeks following the German occupation. The second stage coincided with Joel Brand's trip to Istanbul, and Kasztner's role was growing all the time. Now it was the turn of the third phase to begin.

## d. Zionist Youths

The underground *Halutz* movement engaged in active resistance against the Germans in Budapest. The leaders of this 500-member youth organization were Tzvi Goldfarb, who was Polish, a Hungarian from Slovakia, Rafi Friedl (Rafael Benshalom)[37] and Peretz Révész. The following people also fought for Jewish self-rescue and resistance: Endre Grósz (David Gur), Sándor Grossmann (Ben Eretz), Yitzhak (Mimish) Horváth, József Mayer, Moshe (Alpan) Pil, Moshe Rosenberg and Ernő Teichmann (Imre Benkő, aka Agmon Efra).

Their ingrained communal spirit and the lethal danger they were facing forged a firm sense of unity among the members of the *Halutz* movement. Following the occupation, some of the *Halutzim* advocated a guerilla war on the Polish model in response to the actions of the SS, though they soon realized that in Hungary, where they could not count on serious support either

---

[36] *Jewish Fate,* p. 155.
[37] Members of this illegal movement often changed their names.

from Jewish or Christian quarters, this was not really viable. They saw that through organization the greatest number of Jews could be saved with the help of authentic or fake documents, escape routes and organized flight to Romania. They achieved significant results in these endeavors, often at great human cost.[38]

Following the occupation, the young *Halutzim* had several conflicts with the older, "moderate" Zionists, who thought the bold actions of the youthful Zionists were jeopardizing their own political position and connections. They were at loggerheads with Kasztner, who—along with the conservative-minded Krausz—opposed their anti-German activities, even thought they needed their support. Nor were they on good terms with Arthur Weiss, a committed advocate of Swiss protection and organized Jewish emigration, whose concept of Zionism differed from that of the *Halutzim*.

The Jewish Agency initiated efforts to provide assistance to East and Central European Jews via the British already at the beginning of 1944. They recruited volunteers from among young Jewish émigrés living in Palestine. Out of 170 candidates, only thirty-two successfully made it through the long and arduous selection process. Following a period of intensive training, they were sent on parachute missions to Yugoslavia, Italy, Romania, Slovakia and Hungary. Though it was not their fault, *they arrived in all these places too late.* (With the exception of Romania, where Jews were no longer in danger of being deported by then.) Due to lack of preparation and proper cover, most were captured immediately or shortly after they had landed.

The young Palestinians had taken part in a mission whose feasibility, given the difficult circumstances of the time, was questionable. They undertook to carry out organizational and intelligence activities. With official approval, they wanted to "revive the fighting spirit of oppressed, persecuted and displaced Jews."[39]

After much delay, the first agent, Anikó Szenes (Hanna Senesh), a twenty-three-year-old native of Budapest arrived in Hungary on June 9 across the country's southern border; she was soon followed by the nineteen-year-old

---

[38] For more detail on their activities see the following works: Avihu Ronén, *Harc az életért. Cionista ellenállás Budapesten, 1944* [Struggle for Life: Zionist Resistance in Budapest, 1944], (Belvárosi Könyvkiadó: Budapest, 1998); David Gur, "Iratcsata az életért" [Document Battle for Life] in *Holocaust Füzetek* [Holocaust Notebooks], no. 9, 1998; and Alexander Grossman, *Nur das Gewissen. Carl Lutz und seine Budapester Aktion*, (Verlag im Waldgut Ag, 1986).

[39] Hájim Hermes, *Amszterdam-hadművelet* [Operation Amsterdam], (Aura, 1994), p. 34. This volume presents a short history of the Jewish parachutists who served with the British army in central Europe.

Kolozsvár native Peretz (Ferenc) Goldstein and the twenty-six-year-old Joel (Emil) Nussbecher.[40] Szenes was quickly captured. The romantic, sensitive twenty-three-year-old girl, who wrote poems, endured a long and excruciating period of captivity until she was executed on November 7. Her courageous conduct in the military prison became the subject of legends.

The two male parachutists traveled to Budapest around June 20 equipped with forged documents. They first met with Kasztner, with whom they were already acquainted and had secret talks with him. They gradually realized, however, that German and Hungarian counterintelligence were on their tracks. Lacking armed support, nobody in Hungary was willing to back their mission. Nussbecher was captured.

Peretz Goldstein continued to evade his pursuers. He hid, and tried to find contacts, but all in vain. In the end his hopeless situation prompted him to surrender himself.

The "espionage case" was investigated by both the Gestapo and the SS. The Germans again arrested Kasztner and Hansi Brand, whom they suspected of knowing where Goldstein was hiding. This incident could well have derailed the rescue negotiations. Presumably the Germans concluded that Kasztner had no direct involvement in the planning or execution of the parachute mission, because talks regarding collective emigration continued unabated.[41]

At the end of November, Joel Nussbecher managed to escape from a deportation train headed from Budapest to Komárom.[42] Goldstein disappeared into the hell of the concentration camps. The parachutists dropped in Hungary were not able to achieve their original mission. Their courage and dedication were, nonetheless, exemplary. According to Randolph L. Braham, their action "undoubtedly had a positive influence on many of the Zionist pioneers and unaffiliated younger Jewish intellectuals, who had become disillusioned with the leadership and policies of both the *Vaada* and the Jewish Council."[43]

[40] Following the war Nussbecher changed his name to Palgira. An embellished account of his mission was published in Israel under the title *Jött a fergeteg* [The Storm Was Coming], (Alexander: Tel Aviv, no year).

[41] Some have held Kasztner responsible for the death of Hanna Szenes and the failure of the mission. The true reasons for its miscarriage were lack of preparation, poor planning and incorrect analysis of the conditions in Hungary. A similar Soviet attempt to parachute Hungarian partisans into the country fared no better.

[42] He returned to Budapest, where he survived until the end of the war living among the *Halutzim*.

[43] Randolph L. Braham, *The Politics of Genocide*, vol. II, (The Rosenthal Institute for Holocaust Studies: New York, 1994), p. 1132.

Young Zionists established contacts with several underground resistance groups in Budapest in the course of their perilous, life-and-death rescue operations. They were helped by these groups mostly with documents. Beginning in the summer of 1944, they waged a veritable document war with Hungarian authorities. One of the forgers, Miklós Langer, was beaten to death following the discovery of the document lab.[44]

## e. The Ordeals of the "Emissary of the Dead"

At that time Rezső Kasztner did not yet know that Brand, who had arrived in Istanbul on May 19 via Vienna and Sofia, had only had enough time for a brief interlude. Brand, who was imbued with an inflated sense of the importance of his mission, thought of himself as the "Emissary of the Dead."[45]

Following his arrival, Brand quickly realized what a strange and risky situation he was facing. It soon became apparent that his travel companion, Grosz, had arrived in Istanbul with a separate agenda—that, in fact, the SD had sent him there on a secret assignment. (A Turkish employee of a Hungarian front company providing cover for secret-service operations took "Bandi" away immediately after their arrival; Brand, on the other hand, was facing the direct threat of arrest and deportation.) Eventually the Jewish legation from Palestine sent representatives to pick Brand up at the airport and managed, with great difficulty, to obtain a temporary visa for him.[46]

This episode represented yet another surprise for Brand. He never understood how it was possible that the organization lacked the necessary resources and influence he had so much hoped to rely on. Brand met with a group of Zionist representatives at the Pera Palas Hotel. They sat in stunned silence as Brand movingly described the dire fate of Hungarian Jews and informed them

[44] David Gur, ibid., pp. 86–87. On February 24, 1998, the Hungarian minister of the interior presented the following people with honors for their courageous acts in the resistance and rescue operations of 1944: Efra Agmon, Moshe Alpan, Neshka Goldfarb, David Gur, Peretz Révész and Rafael Benshalom (posthumously). See *Holocaust Füzetek* [Holocaust Notebooks], no. 9, 1998, p. 90. A further forty-two members of the Zionist youth movement accepted these honors from Hungarian Ambassador János Hóvári in a ceremony that took place in Tel Aviv in June 2002. See *Új Kelet* [New East], June 7, 2002, p. 14.

[45] During a family gathering before their departure, Brand and Grosz talked as if "they were the gods who would save the Hungarian Jews." This information is based on the author's interview with László Devecseri, a Holocaust survivor from Leányfalu, which took place on October 12, 2003.

[46] Jehuda Bauer, ibid., p. 272.

of Eichmann's proposal. They were shocked because they were faced with new facts. Following Brand's talk, several of the representatives declared that immediate action was necessary and that the information which he had conveyed to them should be transmitted immediately to their superiors and other top Jewish officials.

On May 24, Moshe Shertok, the head of the political division of the Jewish Agency, received word of what Brand had told the Zionists from Wenya Pomeranz, a leader of the *kibbutz* movement. Together they contacted David Ben Gurion, who convened an immediate meeting of the Jewish Executive.[47] (In April, the Executive had refused to discuss the *Europaplan* without the consent of the Allied powers.) The meeting adjourned with a decision to first contact the British in regard to this matter.

The information was passed on to a British secret-service agent named Arthur Whittalt and his superior, Colonel Harold Gibson; shortly thereafter an American envoy, Laurence A. Steinhard, was also notified. The only member of the Executive to oppose disclosure of this information to the Allies was Yitzhak Grünbaum, the man responsible for rescue operations, who feared that the British would immediately torpedo the plan. On May 26 Ben Gurion and Shertok took a further step: they paid a visit to Sir Harold MacMichael, the British High Commissioner for Palestine, who passed on the information he had received to London.

The High Commissioner was suspicious. He posed an essential question: *what is the purpose of this all?* Is this "Jewish rescue" operation actually an attempt to undermine Allied unity? Ben Gurion's reply was based on the view of the Jewish Agency: the Germans must not be supplied with war materiel, but the negotiations must continue if any Jewish lives might be saved that way. Since Eichmann had given Brand only two weeks to accomplish his mission, Shertok flew back to Istanbul immediately in order to discuss the response to the proposal. In the meantime, MacMichael contacted R. G. Maunsell, the head of British Intelligence in the Middle East, in order to obtain as much information as possible on Grosz and the background of Joel Brand's mission.

The Turkish authorities were totally indifferent. They were certain that both men were Gestapo agents. They wanted to expel Brand from the country, whereas he was headed for Ankara in order to speak personally with Steinhard.

---

[47] Ben Gurion was one of the principal leaders of the Zionist movement and one of the founders of the Jewish state.

On May 26, the Turks ran out of patience; Brand found himself in the custody of the Istanbul police. He was released only after repeated and emphatic intervention on his behalf. He was allowed back to his hotel but had to promise to leave the city on the 29th. (It is possible that Germany's envoy to Turkey, Franz von Papen, had played a role in putting pressure on the Turks).

Meanwhile Brand was contemplating his personal fate. He realized that returning to Budapest would put both him and his family in mortal danger. Moreover, he did not want to travel without Grosz. His fear of the consequences of failure prompted him to write his will on the 27th. The British were also making plans, persuading the Turks to expel Brand and Grosz to a territory under their control.

The Turkish authorities had been absolutely convinced throughout that Grosz was a Gestapo agent. On the 31st of May they permitted him to cross the border into Syria. There he was immediately arrested by the British, and taken to Cairo.

Brand's case generated a flurry of documents and memoranda. By early June the Americans had produced two summary reports on his mission. They correctly identified the SS officers' motives for sponsoring the Jewish rescue proposal: they wanted to improve their standing with the Allies and, at the same time, put the burden of determining the fate of European Jewry upon the shoulders of the Allies. The reports, however, also included that, according to Brand, *every day, 12,000 Jews were being deported from Hungary to Poland, where they were being murdered.*

The British repeatedly deliberated upon the Brand mission and its possible ramifications. On June 5, they informed the United States administration of their rejection of the Brand proposal, contending that neither the Jewish Agency nor any Jewish organization should be permitted to conduct negotiations with the Germans. The British also asserted that the Jewish Agency should transmit their rejection to Hungary.

On the 9th, the United States envoy to Moscow put the State Department's information and analysis regarding this matter at the disposal of America's Soviet ally. On the 19th, Soviet Deputy Foreign Minister Vishinsky conveyed Moscow's assessment of the situation: his government deemed any negotiation with the German authorities aimless. With this Soviet rejection, any continuation of Brand's mission had become useless.

Most Jewish organizations, however, wanted to help desperately. They conceded that furnishing trucks to the Germans was out of the question; however, they continued to insist upon the validity of money-based negotiations. They also agreed that the Germans should be persuaded to allow the International Red Cross to provide Hungarian Jews with food.

Brand was allowed to leave Istanbul on June 5, crossing the border into Syria next day with Avriel Ehud. The British detained him in Aleppo. It took four days of continual badgering before the British finally allowed Moshe Shertok to talk to Brand.[48] Shertok interviewed him for an entire day, after which he decided that Brand was solid in character, clear in thought and one hundred percent reliable. Shertok took these factors into account when he considered Brand's recommendations.

The British took Brand to Cairo on June 14. He was questioned by Lieutenant W. B. Savigny, a secret-service officer, for two consecutive weeks. On July 2, Savigny submitted a thirty-seven-page report,[49] in which he asserted that the Rescue Committee member had provided him with detailed information regarding the purpose of his trip, his proposal and, to a lesser extent, his contacts.[50]

By contrast, Brand had proven extremely reluctant to divulge any information regarding the *Haganah*[51] and those who, according to British information and assumptions, maintained links with the Jewish Agency. (The British had already collected data on the matter. They intercepted letters that couriers forwarded to Palestine, tapped telephones etc. The British were particularly interested in the organization of the underground Jewish army, its purchase and distribution of arms, and the *Irgun Zvai Leumi*.)[52]

The report provides ample evidence that the general rivalry between the *Abwehr* and the SD characterized their Budapest operations as well.[53] It is also

[48] Using the name Moshe Sharett, Shertok became the first foreign minister of Israel; he was appointed Prime Minister following Ben Gurion's resignation in 1954.

[49] László Devecseri has an English-language version of this report in his possession. Documentation pertaining to the interrogation of Brand and Grosz can be found at the London Archives under the call numbers PRO/FO 371/42811/WR 422/9/G.

[50] The predominant opinion within official British circles was that large-scale rescue of the persecuted could not take place before the Allies had gained victory in the war. A series of rhetorical questions posed during Brand's interrogation bears witness to British insensitivity in regard to this issue: "Save one million Jews? Then what would we do with them? Where would we put them?" See Alex Weissberg, *Advocate for the Dead, the Story of Joel Brand* (A. Deutsch: London, 1958), p. 167.

[51] The British viewed any armed Zionist organization as a potential threat to their authority in Palestine.

[52] A radical, anti-British, armed Jewish organization. The *Irgun Zvai Leumi* was hostile toward the Jewish Agency, whose leaders it considered to be collaborators.

[53] For example, the Budapest *Abwehr* opposed Brand's mission, because it did not want to lose control over negotiations with the Zionists and the potential financial profit that these en-

apparent from the report that during the summer of 1944 a considerable number of German officers were already trying to change their image, making widely various attempts to collect proof to show that their involvement in the persecutions was minimal, and that they had somehow been "nice to the Jews."

It is worth noting in this regard that the previously mentioned leader of the Budapest *Abwehr*, Dr. Schmidt, had called upon Brand, even before the German occupation, to write letters to the British and American ambassadors to Turkey indicating that a certain group of Germans had contributed significant assistance to his rescue efforts.[54]

Nor would Eichmann's deputy, SS *Obersturmbannführer* Krumey, be left out of the "race for an alibi." Before Brand's departure for Istanbul from Schwechat Airport, Krumey asked him to make sure that the Allied response he would bring along when he returns includes a reference to their appreciation of his (Krumey's) cooperation.

Following repeated, lengthy and highly detailed interrogations, the British concluded that the Rescue Committee member was not a Gestapo agent. They saw no reason to prevent him from returning to Hungary either. However, the British Foreign Office convinced local authorities that to permit Brand to go home would only increase Soviet suspicions; therefore Brand was *barred* from traveling back to Hungary or having contact with anybody involved in the affair, even in order to buy time for Hungarian Jews.[55]

Three months following these interrogations, during which Brand suffered a nervous collapse from which he never fully recovered, he was permitted to leave Cairo for Palestine. The "Emissary of the Dead" protested continuously, but in vain. Again he was to suffer disappointment: allegedly after being taken to Jerusalem, he was interned until after the end of the war.

According to the distinguished Israeli researcher, Yehuda Bauer, Brand was eventually given the option of going back to Hungary or remaining in Palestine. Newly discovered sources indicate that he did not want to return. Brand was aware that if the Germans were to hold him responsible for the failure of the mission, then he would soon be eliminated from the scene.[56]

---

tailed. The *Abwehr* attempted to send its own agents to Istanbul with Brand, but the Gestapo took them into custody before they could leave the country.

[54] In accordance with secret-service practice, Brand would not be permitted to mention specific names, though the letter was to be written so that the identity of those said to be offering assistance was absolutely clear.

[55] Gideon Hausner, *Ítélet Jeruzsálemben. Az Eichmann-per története* [Verdict in Jerusalem. The History of the Eichmann Trial], (Európa Könyvkiadó: Budapest, 1984), p. 358.

[56] Yehuda Bauer, ibid., pp. 306–307.

Brand's nervous condition prompted him to go on hunger strike twice. He also threatened to commit suicide if his were forced to return to Hungary. For the remainder of his life in Jerusalem, Brand was an active member of the small, extreme radical group known as the Stern Gang.[57]

As for Grosz,[58] British Counterintelligence quickly concluded that he was a paid agent and spy of the Gestapo. Following his thorough interrogation, the British interned Grosz on the island of Samos. (According to another version of the events, Grosz practically begged the British to arrest him. Ultimately the British Secret service decided that it could put the information to be gained from Brand and Grosz to good use.[59] This is why they received entry permits for Syria.)

The Brand mission was merely a short intermezzo in the larger games of the SS. The chance of escape would be dangled before the remaining Jews in Hungary in order to becalm them and keep them obedient, as well as to lessen the influence of the "panic mongers." Several publications, however, indicate that the SS was also interested in gaining the greatest possible financial profit from its commerce in human beings.

However, casting a great deal of doubt upon the seriousness of the entire scheme—even though Brand took it for granted—is the question of just how much compensation the Germans expected from the transaction, a question hardly even raised during the preparation of the human trade message. Brand tried to lay proper emphasis on it, but the Germans virtually avoided the question, practically treating it as a small and harmless detail. The "emissary" received only vague allusions suggesting that the Jews abroad would know exactly what goods to send to the Germans. Finally the Germans sent him a single-page, typewritten wish list that contained only fifteen to twenty items.

Brand was surprised to notice that the German demands that he was to mediate contained no specific conditions as to either quality or quantity. They did not even bother to put the proposal into an envelope. All of this evidence suggests that Brand's proposed "deal" rested on flimsy foundations indeed.

---

[57] Beginning in 1944, the Stern Gang waged a merciless campaign of terrorism aimed at weakening British influence over Palestine. Dr. Yeshurun Eliyahu, *Szabadságharcosok* [Freedom Fighters], (Netanya, 1985), pp. 122–124.

[58] Grosz had left Hungary under the name Endre György.

[59] Little is known about what became of Grosz following this episode. When the war was over, and the State of Israel was founded, he demanded to be financially rewarded for his efforts. Among others, Teddy Kollek, the Mayor of Jerusalem, supported his petition, but there is no evidence of his receiving anything.

The SS appears to have devised the *Europaplan* with its "greater" objectives in mind. The architects of the plan hoped that by various manipulations they would create faultlines and drive a wedge in the anti-Hitler coalition, which the Germans might exploit to establish a new, anti-Soviet alliance.

Meanwhile, the number of Jews who would be "redeemable" was rapidly decreasing. The Allied powers that had united against Hitler proved unwilling to engage in negotiations regarding this matter (either). The position of the British war cabinet, above all, that of the Prime Minister, Sir Winston Churchill, was critical to the chances for success of the proposed deal. Churchill wrote the following after the war:

> There is no doubt that this [persecution of Jews in Hungary and their expulsion from enemy territory] is probably the greatest and most horrible crime in the whole history of the world ... There should, therefore, in my opinion, be no negotiations of any kind on this subject. Declarations should be made in public, so that everyone connected with it will be hunted down and put to death.[60]

A few days following Churchill's decision, news of the secret negotiations became public. On July 19, the *New York Herald Tribune* published an article on Brand's mission that presented it as part of a Gestapo conspiracy to subvert Allied unity, noting that the Germans had declared their intention not to deploy the aforementioned trucks *on the western front*. On the following day, the *London Times* described the proposal as "one of the most shameful," particularly in light of the fact that the Germans were then clearly losing the war. The *Times* also reaffirmed that *only Germany's defeat* could bring security to Jews and all Europeans.[61] On July 21, the BBC provided more information on the affair during one of its broadcasts.

The reaction of the Jewish Agency Executive to the surfacing of the news was characteristic. It deemed the proposal's becoming public a *breach of confidence* and *equal to the death sentence for Hungarian Jews.*

---

[60] Winston S. Churchill, *The Second World War,* vol. 6, *Triumph and Tragedy,* (Houghton Mifflin: Boston, 1953), p. 597.

[61] This article appeared in the *London Times* under the title "Shameful Proposal—German Blackmail—Barter: War Matériel for Jews." This article claimed that 400,000 Hungarian Jews had been liquidated and provided details of the German attempt to blackmail the Allies. The article concluded that the proposal was nothing more than a brazen attempt to sow mistrust among the Allies.

Himmler's rival, the Reich's foreign minister, Joachim von Ribbentrop, had not been apprised of the negotiations that had been taking place in Budapest. On the 20th—the date of the assassination attempt on Hitler—he sent a telegram to Veesenmayer demanding an explanation for this omission. The Budapest plenipotentiary replied two days later, making not the slightest reference to his own involvement in the affair while implicating Winkelmann. Veesenmayer went on to mention Brand, but not Grosz, and characterized the deal as an exchange of "a few Jews" for commodities that were scarce in Germany. Veesenmayer also stated that the Western powers were receptive to the proposed deal. This convinced Ribbentrop that the affair was positive from a German standpoint in spite of the gross indiscretion of his subordinates in not informing him of it.

On July 26, the Hungarian Ministry of Foreign Affairs issued a communiqué that referred to the "malicious news" that had appeared repeatedly in the British press over the past few days.[62] It cited the following excerpt as an example of the slander: "A delegation of Hungarian Jews under German authority is supposed to have arrived in Istanbul to negotiate the release of 400,000 Jews." These Hungarian Jews, the British were saying, would be delivered in exchange for military trucks and consumer goods. In reality, the Hungarian government was determined to find a *permanent, humanitarian solution* to the Jewish question, the communiqué stated. The Anglo-Saxons could take that for certain.

The Foreign Ministry communiqué speaks about ridiculous newspaper hoaxes and the naiveté by which "conditions in Hungary are unfortunately being judged in enemy circles."

The German embassy in Budapest sent a report on the affair to Berlin on the 28th of July. According to this dispatch, the Hungarian foreign ministry had defied established practice in its publication of commentary on the Jewish question without first having notified the German embassy. Mention of the "humanitarian Hungarian solution," the report concluded, served only to add credibility to the enemy, to "Anglo-Saxon propaganda."

Jenő Zilahi-Sebess[63] presented the official Hungarian response to the German grievance, commenting that "unfortunately this passage slipped through the cracks."[64]

---

[62] This was published in the *Budapest Értesítő* [Budapest Informer].

[63] Zilahi-Sebess worked as an official at the Hungarian foreign ministry beginning in 1935. From March 24, 1944 he served as the head of the ministry press division.

[64] *The Destruction*, vol. II, p. 634.

The German report indicated that the foreign ministry communiqué had been published only in the July 27 issue of the evening newspaper *Magyarország*.

# f. Some Conclusions

An examination of the history of the four months following the German occupation of Hungary suggests that *the tactics* of the occupational apparatus, of Eichmann and his staff, *actually worked out.* They made clever use of the Rescue Committee for their own ends, to demonstrate that, in spite of the grim reality of the deportations, they were prepared to compromise and cooperate with the Allies on the Jewish question.

Along with the cautiously maneuvering Jewish Council, Kasztner and his faction were being manipulated as effective means of giving the Jews "something to keep them busy." The Germans were experts at such diversionary tactics. Among the latter was their seeming willingness to permit Jewish emigration, which large groups of well-informed Jews, particularly in Budapest, believed might represent their salvation.

The maneuver also served to undermine the unity and self-saving efforts of the Hungarian Jewish community. It was crucial for the Germans to *divert attention* from what had been going on in the Hungarian countryside, where they vigorously pursued the Final Solution.

The mysterious methods and the secrecy with which the *chosen* Jewish leadership handled the emigration affair served only to facilitate the deportation operations of the SS. The Germans successfully neutralized all Jewish leaders who would have been capable of organizing resistance.

The number of activists among the Jews was reduced because they were busy making preparations for emigration, contentious meetings, drawing up the register of those who would be permitted to emigrate, and ensuring that their families, relatives and acquaintances would all be included on the final list.

The possibility of a *Hungarian repeat of the Warsaw ghetto uprising*, which the Germans had feared from the beginning of the occupation, had essentially *vanished*. The German occupational forces were thus no longer in need of so many troops, which could be withdrawn gradually from the country. Units of the German terror organizations, with the help of the Hungarian Gestapo and other authorities, were able to effectively stifle the feeble efforts of Hungarian resistance and prevent Jewish escape attempts.

The conductor of the deportations dealt with the leaders of the Hungarian Jews with skill. He eventually had all the Zionist leaders and members of the Rescue Committee under his thumb. Kasztner's dealings with Becher only appeared on the surface as being aimed at providing a separate route of escape. Adolf Eichmann in fact knew about all of it. The two SS officers worked in reality as the two arms of a pincer squeezing the Hungarian Jews. Few were aware of this, because, once again, Becher simply nourished their hopes. As a result of his actions, rational thought among Hungarian Jews was replaced with false illusions, a genuine belief in the preventability of deportation and the need to cooperate with the murderers.

In retrospect it is clear that the Germans, who were highly experienced at this game, were aiming to divide and demoralize the Jewish leadership from the start. They succeeded, too, because the debates over the tactics to be followed and over increasing collaboration also disrupted the unity of the Rescue Committee. Ernő Szilágyi, for instance, as has already been mentioned, quit the Rescue Committee, because he considered further cooperation with the Germans to be a grave disservice to the interests of Hungarian Jewry.[65]

---

[65] Szilágyi moved to Basel after the war. He was preparing to write a book provisionally called *I Did Wrong*, though there is no record of his having finished it. He later returned to Hungary, where he died in 1973.

# 6. The "Sample Train"

## a. Departure

Retrieving the "emigrants" from the ghettos was no easy task. Eichmann viewed this as another opportunity for blackmail. He employed a broad array of pretexts to prevent the Rescue Committee from taking the designated individuals. Eichmann even threatened to send Rezső Kasztner, who continually urged him to expedite the emigration plan, to Theresienstadt, or at times to Auschwitz, for some "relaxation."

The Zionist leader's instant response was bold and clever. He said that Eichmann could do to him whatever he wanted but that would mean the end of any further bargaining, since nobody was willing to take his place. (That is, that would be the end of the SS' human-trade venture.) Eichmann bellowed about the responsibility he had undertaken to "clear out" every last Jew from the Hungarian provinces and declared that, for him, *Jewish tears and arguments meant nothing.*

Kasztner countered this by saying that in this case, the arguments that the Hungarian Zionists were to put forward in Istanbul would be futile. The dispute continued until Eichmann, who was weary that word of the Jewish rescue scheme might somehow be leaked to László Endre and his associates, finally agreed to allow approximately 200 Jews to be taken from the provincial ghettos to Budapest.

The adept Captain Wisliceny found a pretext for this concession, asserting that he had informed Gendarme Lieutenant-Colonel László Ferenczy that his forces had uncovered a *dangerous Zionist plot*, which they were in the process of suppressing. Wisliceny told Eichmann that Ferenczy had "swallowed" the story and informed his superiors, Deputy Undersecretaries Baky and Endre.[1] Therefore if SS operatives were to remove certain Jews and Jewish families from the ghetto, the Hungarians would assume that they were uprooting Zionist conspirators.

---

[1] *Der Bericht*, p. 44.

The Jewish Council and the Rescue Committee selected the majority of the "emigrants" from the Columbus Street camp and from those set up in the synagogues located on Aréna Street, close to Városliget, and Bocskay Street, in the Kelenföld District.[2] Compilation of the list of travelers was a source of great friction, generating debate and conflict of various degrees. (This issue severely undermined hard-won unity and harmony brought about in the Zionist movement by the ordeal of the German occupation.) The grim reality that the various promises of massive "emigration" had all gone up in smoke would soon become apparent.

This "solution" was a source of desperation to Jews, many of whom put the blame not on their true enemy, Eichmann and his men, but on the very Jewish leaders who had done their utmost—and taken the greatest personal risks—to help them. A Zionist leader named Mihály Salamon recorded one of Kasztner's outbursts in reaction to one such attack from fellow Jews: "Do you really think we could just stand up and leave the Gestapo's table anytime we want to? So why didn't you put your heads into the lion's mouth yourselves?"[3]

The personal risks and internal debates of the Jewish leaders hardly interested those who wanted only to save their lives. The people preparing the emigration list inside the Budapest Jewish headquarters were virtually mobbed by throngs of desperate and angry Jews. Pushing and shoving, they tossed jewels, gold and other valuables into a collection sack intended as compensation for a place on the emigration list. There was never any detailed inventory taken of the wealth thus accumulated, though the subsequent appraisal of its cumulative worth required several days to complete.

Survivors recalled that the approximately 150 people coming from the three groups of Jews, combined into a single group at the train station, had already turned over all their assets, at least two million pengős, in order to confirm their spot on the emigration list.[4]

Ottó Komoly and his colleagues included on the list people who had done outstanding work for the community in the Zionist movement as well as those

---

[2] Others made the list as well, such as the daughter, son-in-law and grandchildren of Samu Stern. Space was also reserved for candidates whom the Palestine Office had designated.

[3] Mihály Salamon, *"Keresztény" voltam Európában* [In Europe I Was a "Christian"], (An "Our People" publication: Tel Aviv, no year), p. 80.

[4] Nearly $12,000 at the prevailing exchange rate.

who had prominent positions in the provincial ghettos and relocation camps.[5] Also included were forty rabbis whom the highly active Kasztner managed to rescue from the relocation camps before they would be taken to the death factories, with the help of Wisliceny, who was richly rewarded for his trouble. Kasztner also coordinated the transfer of 388 people from the Kolozsvár ghetto to Budapest for eventual emigration; though Zionists comprised the large majority of this group, it also included Jewish refugees from Poland, Yugoslavia and Slovakia as well as seventeen Polish and some forty Hungarian orphans in the charge of the teacher Elza Jungreisz, who went along with them.

The world-famous psychiatrist Lipót Szondi was also a passenger of the train, as were more than thirty doctors as well as young Zionists of all stripes.

The head count of 1684 passengers of the 35-carriage train[6] included the young people,[7] mostly forced-labor conscripts, who had managed to clamber aboard the thirty-five-car train under the cover of the descending darkness just before its departure. Several more people boarded the train at the Ferencváros station in Budapest. For reasons unknown, the SS crew on the train paid no attention to the interlopers.

More groups of people squeezed into the cars in the Kelenföld station. Among the "emigrants" were Dr. Kasztner's wife, several of Joel Brand's family members as well as Ernő Szilágyi.

What Eichmann commonly referred to alternately as "sample goods" or "the sample train" left Budapest with three German escorts at around midnight on June 30. The passengers had been told that, in eight to ten days, they would be arriving in Spain, from where they would continue on to Palestine. The truth of the matter would soon indicate otherwise.

It took days for the train to cover the distance of 200 kilometers (126 miles) to the town of Mosonmagyaróvár, on the Western border of Hungary. There the train stopped and was shunted to a sidetrack. (The cars were packed so tightly that the passengers had to sleep in shifts, lying tightly side-by-side on the floor.) They began to camp out. Soon they consumed all the food that they had brought with them. They bought some in a nearby village, but local offi-

---

[5] The following people served on the committee responsible for drawing up the list: Cvi Hermann Federit, Endre Marton, Ernő Szilágyi and József Weinberger. Kasztner did not personally take part in the work of this committee.

[6] According to Hungarian sources, there were either 1,684 or 1,685 prospective emigrants on the train. German authorities at Bergen-Belsen recorded 1,683.

[7] Seventy-two of these young people were on the list of the *Ha-shomer Ha-tzair* ("Young Guard" in Hebrew), the socialist-Zionist youth movement. Thirty-four belonged to the Gordon Circle of intellectuals and approximately thirty more were children.

cials instantly stopped them from doing so under the pretext that this constituted illegal "price-raising." Tense days of waiting passed one after another.

László Devecseri, who was exempted from the obligation to wear the Star of
David, left his family behind to travel back to Budapest with German permission, to meet with Zionist leaders. In the meantime, the rumor spread that
Hungarian authorities had prohibited the train from leaving the country. This
is contradicted by the fact that the Hungarians were, at this same time, cooper-
ating fully with the Germans in their daily dispatch of at least four deportation
trains bound for foreign concentration camps abroad. During the wait in
Mosonmagyaróvár, the dreaded name of Auschwitz also surfaced as the true
destination of the train, filling the passengers' minds with terror, as most of
them had already heard a thing or two about the gas chambers by that time.
The SS escorts denied this hearsay, claiming that it had likely emerged as a
result of a "miscomprehension" of the name Auspitz, where, according to the
Germans, they were scheduled to stop for a two- or three-day layover.[8]

Devecseri returned from Budapest with encouraging words from the Zionist
leaders: "The passage of the train is being watched. There will certainly be
more inconveniences and difficulties, but nothing really bad can happen to
you."[9] The line of railroad cars did indeed start, only to stop again at the border of the German Reich, where the passengers were served a hot meal. They
then traveled via Vienna to Linz, where they were made to take showers and
subjected to a humiliating medical examination.[10] The train then headed north;
the passengers could only guess where they might be going. On July 8, they
arrived to the Bergen-Belsen concentration camp near Hannover.

The "emigrants" were shocked at the sight and the experience of the SS
camp, a perfect embodiment of German National Socialism, operating under
the command of SS *Hauptsturmführer* Josef Kramer. They no doubt considered the camp to be a wretched destination indeed, though they were, in fact,
considered to be "privileged." The segment of Bergen-Belsen where they were
placed, the so-called *Ungarnlager*, had many advantages in comparison to

---

[8] The town of Auspitz is close to Brno. The following play-on-words made the rounds during their forced stopover: "What is the difference between Auspitz and Auschwitz? The same as
the difference between Zionite and Cyanide."

[9] The source of this optimistic quote was Rezső Kasztner, with whom Devecseri met at the
Keleti Café. Kasztner also sent some letters back to the train with Devecseri.

[10] The crowd of passengers was forced to wait, naked, for hours in order to take a shower.
According to certain sources, uncouth local guards taunted them with quips about the gas
chambers. Several women were shaved bald during the "lice inspections" that were commonplace at the concentration camps.

other parts of the camp. The "emigrants" were housed in large barracks in which 80 to 130 people slept in two-tiered wooden bunk beds.

The staple of their daily diet was a black gruel, which they ate both in the morning and the evening. At noon they were served a tasteless vegetable stew made with onion stems or turnips—and twice weekly with meat as well. Children and the sick received milk, semolina purée and oatmeal, while every three or four days healthy adults, too, got a supplementary portion of food, known in camp idiom as *Zulage*, which contained butter, cheese, a small scrap of sausage, jam and, occasionally, honey. The former cook of the Kolozsvár Jewish hospital prepared separate meals for people with special dietary needs.

They were not forced to work. However, the agonizingly long and tedious morning roll call known as the *Appell*[11] was obligatory for them too. During the day both children and adults engaged in activities that had been introduced at the Columbus Street camp (Hebrew and English language lessons, presentations on Palestine, sports and other physical activities). After several weeks in the camp the physical condition of the new inmates began to deteriorate, which was manifested in a sharp increase in the number of sick among them. The adults commonly suffered from stomach ailments, the children from measles, inflammations of the nose and throat, ear infections and the misery of confinement within the barbed wire fences.

It is worth noting that the SS and Gestapo continued to keep meticulous records. The "emigrants" were being registered by the Vienna offices of SS *Obersturmbannführer* Herman Krumey, the *Sondereinsatzkommando Aussenkommando Wien*.[12] Around July 18, authorities at the camp distributed new index cards, instructing the new inmates to describe, in detail, "the destination of emigration." The Germans then drew up new lists, compiling separate ones for the relatives of Dr. Kasztner and Brand. For many, the drafting of this and subsequent lists was a cause for great anxiety and excitement.

At first those left behind in Budapest knew nothing of the fate of the "emigrants." After much speculation, the *Shomer,*[13] who were always ready to undertake a dangerous mission, initiated action to determine where the train had gone. Milan Grigorijevič, a paid Gestapo agent who dealt primarily with

---

[11] The very old and mothers with children under the age of three did not have to stand for the roll call—the Germans counted them inside their barracks. The bed-ridden were recorded by number of bunks.

[12] The headquarters of this unit was located in a Jewish school at Castellezgasse 35 in Vienna's second district.

[13] Name designating a member of *Ha-Shomer Ha-Tzair*.

the release of Yugoslav prisoners, went to Vienna accompanied by his interpreter, a pretty girl named Támár Friedl. (Grigorijevič, whose true identity
is unknown, was generally considered to be "a somewhat mysterious character.")

A plain-clothes official of the Vienna Gestapo took them to the transit camp
(*Durchgangslager*) in the nearby town of Strasshof, where they witnessed a
shocking sight. After inquiring about the Hungarians, they were escorted to a
dim and bug-infested barracks, where Miss Friedl encountered a group of Jews
who had been deported from the Great Hungarian Plain, but found no trace
of the passengers of the "sample train."[14]

SS *Obersturmbannführer* Krumey appeared at Bergen-Belsen one day in
the middle of August. He brought a prepared list, from which he read the
names of 300 camp inmates whom, he announced, would be permitted to
leave for Switzerland. The names of an additional eighteen people were put on
the list on the basis of a letter of unknown origin. Kasztner, the Hungarian
camp superintendent, Dr. Fischer, and Joel Brand's family members were
missing from the list.

The personal notes of Mrs. Emil Devecseri reflect the drama of their departure from the camp:[15]

> The release of 317 people was an exciting and uplifting event. We all still
> believed that everybody would get out sooner or later. Many, perhaps even
> most, people who left were forced to part with members of their family. We
> all stood outside as they left the camp singing a farewell rendition of the
> *Hatikhvah*.[16]

## b. The Swiss Reception

The 318 "lucky ones" made the trip from Bergen-Belsen to the Swiss border in freight cars. At the Weil border station the SS again searched their belongings. They confiscated all their documents, ripped up photographs and
took personal mementos from many people. While this was going on an SS

---

[14] Avihu Ronen, ibid., p. 160.

[15] Quote from of Mrs. Emil Devecseri's reliable personal notes, which can be found in the
Beit Lohamei Haghetaot collection in Israel, pp. 19–20.

[16] This song became the official national anthem of Israel.

officer shouted in László Devecseri's face: *"You swine, you're being set free and now you're going to turn right around and fight against us."*[17]

On August 21, Swiss officials gave them a surprisingly warm reception. During the war years, the Swiss had repatriated or expelled Jewish refugees in the most stiffly bureaucratic manner possible. On several occasions, border patrol guards prevented groups of people, many of them pleading for their lives, from approaching the Swiss border, most of which was reinforced with barbed-wire fence.[18]

On December 29, 1942, Swiss officials informed appropriate state agencies that *"individuals who seek asylum in Switzerland on racial grounds are not to be considered political refugees."* The rigidity of that approach, the unwillingness to face reality, sent thousands to their tragic death.

On July 12, 1944, Swiss authorities issued new orders regarding "people persecuted on racial grounds." The new rule declared was that *"those foreign nationals who, for political or other reasons, face actual bodily harm or death, and have no other recourse but to seek asylum in Switzerland, must be rescued from danger."* International and Swiss reaction to the brutal mass deportation of Hungarian Jews was a major factor in facilitating this change in policy.

Beginning on June 5, the Swiss press—the *Tat*, the *National Zeitung*, *La Liberté*, the *Berner Tagewacht* and other newspapers—published numerous reports on the plight of the Hungarian Jews. A dramatic account describing in clear terms the grim reality of Auschwitz–Birkenau, the gas chambers and the crematoria, appeared in the June 5 issue of *Juna*. The article referred to the camp complex as a gigantic German *death factory*. Many people found this report deeply disturbing, though there were others who regarded it as mere fabrication and anti-German propaganda.

At the same time, the so-called *Auschwitz Report*, based on information and testimony from two former inmates who had escaped from the camp on April 7, was publicized in Switzerland. The July 7 issue of the *Neue Zürcher*

---

[17] From the personal notes of László Devecseri: "Life," p. 66. Manuscript in the possession of the author.

[18] Between April 1940 and May 1945, Swiss authorities expelled 24,398 refugees from the country. Between 1938 and 1945, they officially rejected a further 14,000 applications for entry visas. Many more cases were not registered; therefore the true numbers must have been much higher. Jürg Stadelmann, *Umgang mit Fremden in bedrängter Zeit. Schweizerische Flüchtlingspolitik, 1940–1945, und ihre Beurteilung bis heute,* (Orell Füssli Verlag, 1988), pp. 111–112. According to a detailed summary published on April 1, 1945, a total of 92,724 emigrants and refugees were staying in Switzerland. Ibid., p. 167. These sources estimate the number of Jews among these emigrants and refugees to have been between 28,500 and 30,000.

*Zeitung* treated the information contained in the report as fact. The new account once again shocked and galvanized Swiss public opinion. Prominent Swiss organizations, such as the Governing Council of Zurich Canton and the Lutheran Aid Committee, virtually laid siege to the Federal Governing Council, demanding that it employ every means at its disposal to rescue the mortally endangered Hungarian Jews.

The newly liberated inmates from Bergen-Belsen were taken by bus to the Mustermesse building in Basel. A shower and dinner of rice pudding were their first experiences in Switzerland. Doctors treated those in need of medical attention. Under the watchful eye of Swiss public opinion, the refugees were then moved to Montreux, where they spent three weeks quarantined in the vacant Bellevue Hotel on the shores of Lake Geneva. (As time passed, those with connections in Switzerland and sufficient financial resources were permitted to leave the camp.)

Little is known of the events that led to the transfer of the Hungarian Jews from captivity at Bergen-Belsen to asylum in Switzerland. On August 29, there was an exchange of messages between the German Red Cross, presumably playing an intermediary role, and the IRC regarding the Hungarians held at the Bergen camp, which was discretely referred to as a *holding camp.* The subject heading was "Jewish Transports from Hungary" (*Judentransporte aus Ungarn*), which referred to the arrival in Switzerland of the 318-person "partial transport."

In reference to Switzerland's stated "concerns," the Germans indicated that the Swiss police had encountered "entry complications." Further, "regularly arriving" transports were, nonetheless, to be expected.[19] The German Red Cross' cynical message, which was signed by the chief of the organization's foreign operations, *Generalhauptführer* Hartmann, stated that "we rightfully cannot understand the reason for the difficulties" ... which the Swiss are causing, primarily by withholding entry permissions.

On September 6, the bureaucrat responsible for running the official apparatus of the IRC wrote a memorandum from which it becomes apparent that the Hungarians who arrived on the "partial transport" were subjected to thorough questioning. According to information the Swiss gained during the interviews, 1,366 prospective Hungarian emigrants, who hoped to travel to Palestine via Spain, were being held at Bergen-Belsen. The memorandum concluded that

---

[19] This phrase might also be translated as "arriving according to regulation." Geneva archives of the IRC, G/59 (0) - 2, p. 15.

"Their care has been adequate. Their greatest need is for winter clothing (since they arrived to the camp wearing light summer clothes) and medicine."[20]

According to the official, the 318 people who had arrived to Switzerland suffered primarily from a lack of winter clothing. Their appointed leaders were Dr. Tivadar Fischer, Zsigmond Elek, Dr. Nison Kahane and camp superintendent Miklós Speter.

The Swiss authorities did not permit correspondence. For the time being, those liberated were allowed only to send a few telegrams to Palestine via the British consulate.

Indicative of the rigidity of the Swiss' conduct was their refusal to permit the Hungarians to receive boxes of donations containing food and chocolate that the Argentine Red Cross had sent from Geneva. Swiss camp wardens immediately confiscated these boxes, denying repeated requests by the Hungarian "internees" to hand them over.

According to the author of the memorandum, M. Metter, the Hungarian Jews were afraid that they would soon be separated from one another. Rumor had it that those fit for labor were to be sent to Zurich, while all the others would be taken to Les Avants. They preferred to remain together, even in an enclosed structure. First and foremost they wanted to go to Palestine.

In a memorandum sent to *Generalhauptführer* Hartmann from Geneva on September 19, Hans Bachmann again described the surprise arrival to Basel on the previous day of Jews "who are to be interned in Switzerland." Before the transfer of these people from the reception camp, the local section of the Swiss Red Cross had "provided them with soup, tea and bread."

Bachmann likewise informed the Hungarians held at the Belmont internment camp that standing regulations prohibited them from sending written correspondence during their twenty-one-day period of quarantine. His letter to Tivadar Fischer (whom he addresses as "Highly Esteemed Herr Doktor") was basically a reaction to the experiences of IRC representatives during their visit to the Belmont camp.

Bachmann maintained that he had discerned no official intention to separate or segregate the Hungarians. He thought that he expected them to soon receive several shipments of aid containing mostly clothing and medicine; however getting such aid to those members of the group who had been left

---

[20] Ibid. This memorandum also indicates that there were several hundred Polish Jews at the *Vorzugslager* who were in possession of valid travel or residence documents issued by various countries in North and South America.

behind at Bergen-Belsen would be much more difficult.[21] Shortages and nearly insurmountable transportation obstacles had hampered other relief efforts as well.

Deputy First Secretary Bachmann was somewhat evasive regarding the resolution of some more difficult issues. He recommended that the Hungarians contact Roswell D. McClelland, the Bern-based special representative of the War Refugee Board whom they could reach at the American embassy. Bachmann also commented that the Argentine Red Cross had erred when it sent them food parcels, because Swiss regulations prohibited distribution of donated provisions in the internment camps. Thus the shipment was being returned to the Argentines (and the Swiss chose to ignore the earlier suffering and starvation of the "internees"—*author's note*).[22]

On the 23rd, *Generalhauptführer* Hartmann received another, somewhat contrite, letter from the Swiss, signed this time by a chief Red Cross physician and army colonel. This letter contended that German objections to the Swiss reception of the Jews (a product of Goebbels' propaganda) were groundless: the Basel train station had not been festooned with garlands; no local authorities or organizations had arrived to welcome them; there were not a dozen army officers present; no banquet had been held in their honor. The reception of the Jews from Bergen-Belsen had taken place under purely military (*rein militärisch*) circumstances.

Based on their information, Swiss authorities had prepared for the arrival of 700 to 800 refugees, dispatching a team of twenty-five Red Cross soldiers and forty nurses to examine them for infectious diseases and other medical problems. Soldiers and police were present to secure the site, from which civilians had been strictly prohibited. The Swiss medical corps colonel requested that

---

[21] In another letter written that same day, Bachmann stated that he had managed to obtain medicine, a trial shipment of which was to be sent to Bergen-Belsen at a cost of 25,000 Swiss Francs. More such shipments would be forthcoming pending the success of this initial enterprise. Geneva archives of the IRC, G. 59/2 123. On September 8, Dr. Mihály Bányai, the secretary of the Zürich-based Swiss Aid Committee for the Jews of Hungary (*Schwiezerisches Hilfskomitee für die Juden in Ungarn*) also sent a letter in which he urged the IRC to respond to the distress of the Hungarians left at Bergen-Belsen, specifically to send them food. Ibid., G 59/2/00-8. The *Hilfskomitee* collected and disseminated data on the Nazi persecution of the Jews, making special recommendations regarding relief and rescue operations to those organizations and individuals with which it maintained contact. For more detail on the activities of this committee see Jacques Picard, *Die Schweiz und die Juden, 1933–1945*, (Chronos Verlag: Zurich, 1994).

[22] Dated from the Hotel Metropol in Geneva on September 19, 1944.

Hartmann publicize the true facts surrounding the reception "so that colorful stories of what took place in Basel do not spread to a wider audience."

At the end of the lengthy letter, the reader gains an insight into the motives of the Swiss authorities. The letter states that over the past ten years they had never once expressed approval of the persecution of Jews, a transgression that contradicted both Swiss tradition and their Christian faith. On the other hand they recognized the Jews merely as fellow human beings, distancing *themselves from any glorification of their martyrdom*. This basic attitude was unchanged.

On September 25, the united relief division (*das vereinigte Hilfswerk*) of the IRC informed the Swiss committee responsible for providing assistance to Hungarian Jews that it had sent packages of food worth sixteen Swiss francs each to "the internees at Bergen-Belsen" (that is, the former passengers on the Kasztner train whom were being held at that camp—*author's note*). In the event that the committee was preparing to send relief assistance to these internees, the following information regarding each individual incipient should be included on the packages: first and last name, date of birth and nationality.

This applied only to Bergen-Belsen; therefore further inquiry would be advisable "with regard to other camps."

# 7. Another Chapter in Human Trade; Forced Labor for the SS

## a. Provincial Jews Sheltered in Strasshof

When dealing with the self-rescue efforts of Hungarian Jews, international specialist literature devotes most space to the *Musterzug*, the "sample train" or the "Kasztner Train;" its route and the precarious experiences of its "privileged" passengers have also been preserved in numerous memoirs as well as in fictionalized accounts.

The evidence that we have unearthed, however, points to the conclusion that the operations of the Rescue Committee achieved considerable success over and above that celebrated incident, including the rescue of a part of the Jewish families deported from the Great Hungarian Plain region. At the end of July, in the shadow of mass death, passengers of the trains departing from Debrecen, Szeged and Szolnok were granted a fair chance for *survival*. They were unaware of what was happening.

All this came about as the result of the continuous negotiations that the Rescue Committee had been conducting with the Germans regarding the exemption of large groups of Jews from their planned deportation to Auschwitz. The contours of this human trade scheme that emerged during these discussions were similar to those of the "sample train" deal, although this time the "head money" was a hundred US dollars. This was, of course, to take place in such a way as to make it appear as if SS *Obersturmbannführer* Eichmann had *compromised* with the other side.

In truth, this was all just *tactical maneuvering* that had nothing to do with preferential treatment. The Grand Master of the deportation exploited his informational superiority as well, gaining crucial intelligence regarding previously unknown demands before the Zionists did. With these in possession, Eichmann appeared willing to temporarily spare a further 30,000 Jews, sending them, instead of Auschwitz–Birkenau, to a camp in Greater Vienna.

There were several factors behind this newer "gesture" of the SS. On the one hand, Eichmann calculated that if negotiations were to take place with the Western Allies regarding the release of Jews, then the 30,000 Hungarians who would be, in his words, "put on ice" in the vicinity of Vienna, might come in useful as "exchange stock." On the other hand, the mobilization of most able-bodied men in the Reich produced a significant shortage of labor in Greater Vienna and other parts of the country, which these Jewish camp inmates might help to alleviate.

Last but not least, there would also be the direct income: the payments received from the Zionists, topped by the profits produced by Jewish "hired labor," i.e. the money paid out to the SS by businesses and private persons in exchange for the slave labor.

When considering this scheme, the SS certainly factored in its potential for generating revenue, either directly from the Zionists or in return for lending this source of "wage labor" to local business enterprises.

The Zionists could hardly have known that the chief of the security police and security services, Ernst Kaltenbrunner, had acted upon the request of the Mayor of Greater Vienna, SS *Brigadeführer* Hans Blaschke, to "kindly allocate" Hungarian labor. According to his letter, dated June 30, Kaltenbrunner had received this request from "Dear Blaschke"[1] more than three weeks earlier, on the 7th. SS *Brigadeführer* Dellbruegge also contacted Kaltenbrunner on this matter. Therefore he ordered a few "evacuation transports" to Wien/Strasshof.

Rezső Kasztner might have been aware of the first, decisively important, factor. On June 14, Kasztner informed the Jewish Council of the recent negotiations.

> We agreed that 15,000 people would go from the provinces and another 15,000 from Budapest. All of those who are physically capable of working will be required to do so. The young, old and the sick will all be kept alive, and families will stay together. Eichmann said that there are no resources in the Reich's budget to pay for support of these people, care for the sick, etc. It will be incumbent upon the Budapest Rescue Committee to cover these expenses as well as to provide supplementary provisions and administrative assistance. I immediately agreed to the proposal. I offered an advance payment of 100,000 pengős.[2]

The Jewish leaders accepted Kasztner's recommendations. Negotiations with the SS continued. It is worth noting the SS pledge that this group of departing Jews would "be *kept alive.*" This indicates that the Hungarian party was

---

[1] The form of the address used in the letter. *The Destruction*, vol. I, p. 415.
[2] *Der Bericht*, p. 50.

well aware that this would not be the case, should these people arrive at Ausch-witz–Birkenau.

But the Germans were up to their usual devious tricks. In May and June, the German embassy in Budapest repeatedly corresponded about increasing labor needs in the Reich. Plenipotentiary representative Veesenmayer also wrote a series of telegrams describing the establishment in Hungary of an "efficient, civilian worker deployment apparatus" that would be continually monitored in order to provide for Germany's ever-changing labor needs.

On June 15, Veesenmayer reported that he had satisfied a request received from Berlin on May 26 to provide 3,000 laborers for construction of the Air-port Gau Wien and that an *order* had been placed for a contingent of 15,000 more workers, which he would send in the coming weeks.[3] On the 30th, Veesenmayer sent a telegram to Berlin that, in addition to providing "everyday" information on the dispatch of deportation trains, stated that *"a few smaller special consignments of Jewish political leaders, intellectuals, skilled workers and families are also en route."*[4]

As Vienna and Berlin were being notified of their departure from Hungary, these deportation trains were moving up the Nordbahn grain-transport line near the Strasshof "transit camp" that had been established to accommodate so-called "Eastern workers."[5]

At Eichmann's behest, a total of 15,011 Jews—6,641 from Debrecen, 5,239 from Szeged, 2,567 from Szolnok and 564 from Baja—arrived to the labor camp with their families.

These registered figures were further reduced by the ordeal of the trip to the camp in sweltering, overcrowded and poorly ventilated railway. The Vienna *Landeswirtschaftsamt* (regional economic office) recorded 14,700 Hungarian prisoners. Existing records from the end of August and beginning of Septem-ber indicate that 5,972 people (41%) performed forced labor in the Greater Vienna region of the Reichsgau. According to data collected by one of the record keepers, a deportee from Mezőtúr named Éva Friedmann, there were 6,889 men (41.05%) and 9,812 women (58.95%) among the Hungarians who had been sent to the Strasshof camp.[6]

---

[3] *The Destruction*, vol. I, p. 403.

[4] Ibid., p. 413.

[5] For unknown reasons, the 15,000 additional workers were never sent. Perhaps the Germans wanted to avoid the attention that this would have attracted, since the deportation plans were still officially secret.

[6] DÖW E 19 287.

After arriving at Strasshof, the new internees underwent a preliminary medical examination, after which fingerprints were taken and their basic personal information written on an index card with a five-digit identification number (some of these cards indicated whether the individual in question was fit for industrial or agricultural labor). Those sent off to work had their index card stamped, and a stamp was printed on the backs of their hands prior to being loaded into freight cars; the mark *Gd* denoted the town of Gmünd, for example, while *WN* stood for Wiener Neustadt, a hub of the Reich's ammunitions industry. Those deemed unfit for work had the letter *R* (the meaning of which cannot be resolved) stamped on their arms.

In regard to the status of the Jews, it is worth mentioning that non-Germans working in the military industry were *placed in official categories* that distinguished between so-called foreign workers, forced-laborers and prisoners-of-war. The precise "hierarchy" was as follows: free foreign employees; volunteer or conscripted workers from Wehrmacht-occupied territories abroad; forced laborers; prisoners-of-war and Italian military internees; *Jewish forced laborers from Hungary*; and concentration camp prisoners.

In the summer of 1944, there were 165,000 foreign workers (21% of the total labor force) in the Vienna Labor District and 208,000 in Gau Niederdonau, now known as Lower Austria (38.1 % of the total labor force). Foreign civilian workers and prisoners-of-war accounted for 21% of a total labor force of 2.4 million in Austria (then an integral part of the German Reich).

The number of foreign workers in the German Reich at this time was 7.6 million, or 26.5% of the total labor force. In terms of national origin, most of these workers were from the Soviet Union (2.8 million), followed by Poland (1.7 million) and France (1.3 million), with the remaining 1.8 million came from at least twenty other European countries.

According to statistics published in the Republic of Austria in 1999, the number of civilian men and women coming (mostly recruited) from Hungary and working in what was then known as the region of Ostmark decreased steadily between 1941 and 1944.

| Date | Total Number of Foreign Workers | Total Number of Hungarian Foreign Workers | Percentage |
|---|---|---|---|
| April 25, 1941 | 128,730 | 8,285 | 6.4% |
| July 10, 1942 | 302,464 | 12,335 | 4.0% |
| November 15, 1943 | 527,590 | 12,018 | 2.0% |
| September 30, 1944 | 580,640 | 10,795 | 1.8% |

The data clearly demonstrate that Germany's imported workers from Hungary could not even meet the demand for labor in the neighboring regions of the Ostmark. Therefore aggressive intervention and *military occupation* were needed in order to ensure that a sufficient labor force be provided to the Reich (through deportation) to work in the factories, on the grandiose construction projects, the fields and the service industries. Moreover, based on recent scholarly analysis, Austrian historians have concluded that the *uncompensated work and suffering of the forced laborers laid the foundations for the current thriving economy of Austria.*[7]

## b. Camp Life in Greater Vienna

A special unit of the SS, the previously mentioned *Sondereinsatzkommando Aussenkommando Wien* under the command of *Obersturmbannführer* Herman Krumey, was put in charge of the Hungarian Jews who performed forced labor in the Reich. Krumey established his unit's headquarters in Vienna with technical help from the Gestapo.

Krumey's staff consisted of his deputy commander, *Hauptsturmführer* Seidl, *Hauptsturmführer* Schmidtseifen, *Oberscharführer* Neumann, Richter and Vrtoch and *Unterscharführer* Voss. The name of *Unterscharführer* (later *Oberscharführer*) Matthias Schefzik also surfaced in the winter of 1944 as a camp commandant in the vicinity of Wiener Neustadt, though there is no evidence indicating that he was ever officially assigned to the *Sondereinsatzkommando*.

SS *Hauptsturmführer* Seidl was posted to the Vienna *Aussenkommando* in the middle of July, after which he became a frequent visitor to the labor camps and quickly assumed the role of the unit's iron fist.[8] Next to Seidl, Krumey was able to make himself look like "a good soul." This tactic worked for the SS

---

[7] For more detail on the role of forced labor in the wartime economy of the Ostmark, see the following summary of the recent research of Austrian historians on this subject: *Wieder gut machen? Enteignung, Zwangsarbeit, Entschädigung, Restitution* (Studien Verlag: Innsbruck, Wien, 1999).

[8] While serving as Commandant of the Theresienstadt camp, from November 1941 to July 1943, Seidl had a "model ghetto" constructed there. Seidl was transferred to Vienna following the completion of the deportation of Jews from the Hungarian provinces in 1944. He returned to Hungary on August 28 of that year, serving as Eichmann's liaison officer with the Hungarian gendarmerie. Following the war, the Vienna district court sentenced Seidl to death in October 1946. He was executed.

officers, who succeeded in duping the Red Cross representatives with whom they conducted negotiations in the winter of 1944.[9]

The deployment of Krumey's SS detachment to Vienna produced a shift in the handling of Jewish affairs in that geographical area. Beginning in July, Krumey and his staff received formal authority to oversee implementation of the Reich's policies vis-à-vis the Jews in cooperation with, though independent of, the Gestapo. Records pertaining to the Hungarian Jews at the Strasshof camp were stored at the unit's Castellezgasse headquarters. The files were kept under the strict supervision of eight or nine Jewish women from Hungary in a department called the SS-*Arbeitszentrale.*

All data pertaining to the Hungarian Jewish camps (*Judenlager* or *Familienlager*) was registered on index cards. Éva Friedmann maintained a deportee cash receipt book in which she kept track of the compensation paid to the SS for the work of the Jewish labor detachments.

Accounts for this labor were settled on the basis of a seventeen-point directive (*Anordnung über die Beschäftigung von Juden*) issued by the President of the Labor Affairs Office, Alfred Proksch, on June 27. It contained detailed measures relating to Jewish labor and sustenance, as well as the means of settling accounts. The document declared that German labor statutes were *not applicable* to Jews, and that they would only be allowed to work in groups with no special allowance for families or children.

The deportees from Hungary were officially referred to not as *Transportjude*, but as *Tauschjude* or *Joint-Jude*, which likely reflected a change in the German approach to the Jewish question (the latter designation emerged in connection with the Jews performing forced labor in Vienna). According to Wisliceny, that "appropriate" term was concocted by Krumey, suggesting to Eichmann that he apply it as well. The SS clearly considered the Hungarian Jews being held in Vienna as potential collateral for future negotiations, "*to be shown to Joint representatives at any time.*"[10]

Grandiloquent names, of course, did not change in the slightest the conditions under which the Jewish deportees slaved away for days and weeks on end. In practice, these Jews were qualified as *KZ-Häftlinge,* or *prisoners registered in the concentration camp system.*

The Germans obliged the "employers" to provide living quarters and a determined amount of provisions to the Jews. Compensation, based on the age of

---

[9] Geneva archives of the IRC, G. 59/2/118. Activities of the Vienna delegation in January 1945. Memorandum to the Secretariat.
[10] *The Destruction,* vol. II, p. 440.

each individual Jewish worker, was to be deposited monthly in Reichsmarks in the Vienna bank account of the Jewish Council (Länderbank, Wien, Postscheckamt Wien Nr. 16447, special account "U," Nr. 72500). The rates, based on the years of age of the Jewish workers, were as follows[11]

|  | Labor in Agricultural and Forestry Sectors | | Labor in Industrial Sector | |
|---|---|---|---|---|
|  | men | women | men | women |
| 21 and over | 23.5 | 15.0 | 30.0 | 20.0 |
| 18 to 21 | 21.0 | 12.5 | 27.0 | 17.0 |
| from 17 | 18.5 | 10.0 | 24.0 | 14.5 |
| from 16 | 15.0 | 7.5 | 20.0 | 12.0 |
| below 16 | 11.0 | 6.0 | 15.0 | 10.0 |

Each "employer" was required to pay a health-care tax of three Reichsmarks. Expenses related to the support and care of non-working deportees were also regulated. Krumey's detachment had access to the special account at the Länderbank, where they also brought the postcards that labor-camp inmates were occasionally permitted to write. Rarely did this mail, which typically consisted of a few condensed lines scrawled on a bare note card, make it to the Hungarian addressee; most often it ended up in the wastepaper basket of SS *Hauptsturmführer* Seidl, who was well aware of the fate of the Jews deported from the Hungarian provinces.

A few letters did, nonetheless, arrive to Hungary from the camps in Vienna and the Austrian countryside. Sympathetic local camp personnel, Austrian "employers" or other contacts gained during the course of forced labor occasionally posted mail on behalf of the Hungarian Jews in spite of a strict prohibition on doing so. Some deportees even managed to get small packages and money through to Hungary by mail.

During the first ten days of July, the 6,000 Jewish laborers deported from Hungary to Vienna were dispersed from the district administrative centers and railway-station relocation camps where they had been held. Their employers sent people to pick them up, and take them to their new living quarters and workplaces. The deportees were engaged in a wide variety of labor—from municipal services to clearing rubble, from light and heavy industrial work to seasonal occupations.

[11] DÖW, 18 929.

The Hungarian Jews were housed in agricultural or industrial buildings, schools, barracks, empty halls and a variety of other locations. There was no barbed wire surrounding these improvised living quarters, though their occupants were not allowed to leave the premises without permission. Families were allowed to live together. These accommodations were often severely overcrowded, sometimes the whole group lived in the same space, which gave rise to frequent conflicts between people of different ages, families and other groupings.

Children and those deemed unfit for labor also lived with their working family members. Leaving one's designated living area was forbidden, even during leisure hours.

German authorities made a concerted effort to ensure that the Hungarian Jews would be isolated. They were not allowed to have contact with prisoners of other nationalities or civilians with whom they worked. An agent of the *Judenpolizist* (Jupo)—most often a fellow prisoner—was assigned to every ten or twenty Jewish deportees in order to enforce compliance with established regulations. Some of these *Judenpolizisten* were recruited by the local Gestapo headquarters, while others were appointed by the camp commandants.

The Jupo were given the authority to impose punishment for minor disciplinary infractions. Camp officials, local authorities and, in extreme cases, the Gestapo were summoned to handle more serious transgressions. The latter decided whether the offender would be permitted to remain at the detention camp or further measures were necessary.

From time to time entire families—parents, children and relatives—were transferred from one of the camps in the vicinity of Vienna to Laxenburg, from where it was not possible to return.[12]

Officials from the various sites where the deportees performed forced labor were required to report major disciplinary violations and instances of insufficient work output to the Vienna Gestapo headquarters on Morzinplatz.

At most places, the Jewish forced laborers worked in several shifts, the length of which varied depending on the nature of the tasks to be completed. One of the primary employers of forced labor was the Floridsdorf Shell Oil refinery, where Jewish deportees worked in *ad hoc* groups of ten. The per-

---

[12] People could be taken away for other than disciplinary reasons. In some instances seriously ill captives were "relieved" of work duties and transferred, along with their families, to Auschwitz–Birkenau.

sonal diary entries of a deportee from Debrecen, Mrs. Benő Halmos, offer an insight into their fate.[13]

6-29
We arrived to Strasshof, which is 25–30 km from Vienna. Here we were disinfected.

7-3
At 8 o'clock in the morning we again boarded freight cars. The train departed at 8 o'clock in the evening.

7-4
We arrived in Vienna at 3 o'clock in the morning. Here we walked by foot to the Rotschild's old folks' home. We were all registered and some were assigned to work at different places (there are probably 2,500 of us).

7-7
We—a total of 15 people—were taken to the Russian camp in the 10th district.

7-13
At 10 o'clock in the morning we were all taken by tram along with another group of Jews that was already there to Floridsdorf in the 21st district, where we were placed in a two-floor schoolhouse at 33 Mengergasse ... They assigned us to work at the Shell oil refinery. The camp commandant was a person named Simonovits, who was pretty fairly decent to everybody. There was always black coffee for breakfast and potatoes, pasta or grits for lunch. We got a 25-gram daily ration of bread. For dinner we got 2 dkg of butter, 2 dkg of jam and 2–3 pieces of salami ...

11-18
At noon a 3-floor residential building across from the school was destroyed in a bombing raid. The front of the school was also damaged. A delayed-action bomb fell into the cellar and exploded during the night. Since I worked at Shell, I was given a dank, concrete-walled, doorless and window-

---

[13] Sándor Halmos, the son of Mrs. Benő Halmos, permitted the author to publish these passages from his mother's diary.

less room in a building opposite the plant, where I lived with my aged parents, who couldn't work ...

11-25
We moved back to the school on Kuenburggasse, into room number 4 on the first floor ...

1-1-1945
The "Todt" organization took control of the camp and the school from the Gestapo.

1-24
They took 25 single men between the ages of 14–55 to build fortifications in the village of St. Anna. This is 323 km from Vienna, close to the Hungarian border in the vicinity of Körmend ...

3
They took families incapable of work away from the camp, first to Strasshof, then to Theresienstadt ...

3-16
Air raid from 10:45 until 3:15. A heavy bomb hit the school on Kuenburggasse. Four women were killed in the building. The two Gottlieb sisters from Szeged, Mrs. Ödön Winter from Debrecen and the Weiss girl from Orosháza. We moved to a new place, to the first floor of a school on Leopold Festlgasse.

These diary entries demonstrate that the Hungarian forced laborers were often relocated and moved in and around Vienna, a circumstance which objective conditions (bombing) made necessary. Beginning in the late autumn of 1944, prisoners were relocated to more distant sites as well.

Children as young as ten or twelve were obliged to perform forced labor in Vienna. On occasion, SS *Hauptsturmführer* Seidl personally enforced compliance with this regulation. Tibor Bauer was barely ten years old when he did forced labor in Vienna. In addition to working at the Shell oil refinery in Floridsdorf, Bauer's labor group served in Döbling and repaired damaged Danube bridges and urban residential buildings. They traveled to their daily workplaces by streetcar, without escort following the first trip. Their tattered clothing, wooden-soled boots and emaciated faces inspired pity in their fellow riders.

Júlia Lackó worked with her mother and younger brother at the Kallinger Construction Company in Sitzenberg (Niederösterreich), a village located to the north of St. Pölten, for three weeks following their deportation. Her twenty-two-member group performed heavy labor, mostly with concrete. The company foreman and his wife took most of the food that had been allocated to them. Fortunately for them, they were soon sent from Sitzenberg to Vienna, where they were assigned to work on lathe machines and drill presses at the Hermann Göring Kanonenfabrik. From January 1945, they cleared rubble left in the wake of Allied air raids, primarily on Margaretenplatz (5th district) and in Belvedere (3rd district).

The random kindness shown by some unfamiliar housewives who occasionally gave Lackó bread, croissants and other things to eat in the midst of generally indifferent crowds, made a lasting impression on the sixteen-year-old girl. A benevolent shopkeeper sold them supplementary food as well, but stopped doing so after he had been warned by the Gestapo that he would be punished.[14]

Péter Józan, a native of Hajdúböszörmény, began work in a forced-labor group at the age of ten. According to Józan, the Viennese "behaved very decently"—more than one gave Józan some of their own ration stamps, a total stranger provided him and his mother with bread and cheese, though this was strictly forbidden, and nuns regularly served them meals at a local hospital.[15]

Hungarian forced-laborers prepared baked potatoes and improvised soups for their perpetually hungry children in a makeshift brick oven that they had built in the camp courtyard. They often got very cold at night—and even during the day—in their unheated living quarters.

The near daily air raids were the most frightening aspect of their lives. (The Americans bombed during the day, while the British bombed at night). The following is an account of the carpet-bombing of Floridsdorf that took place on December 27:

> We waited in a state of suffocating anxiety for the birds-of-death that circled over our heads to disappear. We lay face down on the floor, our hearts pounding, as we beseeched the skies for redemption. Some of my companions were sobbing loudly, others were screaming.

---

[14] Based on interview with Júlia Lackó conducted on September 4, 2003. Documentation regarding the *Ostmarkwerke* can be found in the HDKE collection.

[15] *Fejezetek a hajdúböszörményi zsidóság történetéből* [Chapters from the History of the Hajdúböszörmény Jewish Community], Júlia Toth, ed., (Hajdúböszörmény, 2002).

My mother hugged her children as we lay silently, our bodies trembling in unison. We somehow survived that day as well. Afterwards we were like ghosts—pale, gloomy and famished.[16]

On April 6, 1945, the SS evacuated the camp, whose residents were forced to make a long and agonizing march westward along the Danube to a new camp.

Existing records indicate that most babies and young children survived the ordeal of deportation. Several births even occurred among the female deportees in places such as the bug-infested barracks at Anhaltelager and the open grounds of Strasshof. (Unfortunately, their precise number cannot be determined due to research restrictions imposed in the name of "data protection.")

We found no documentation regarding the type of "military related" work that the Vienna-based Gauleiter and his staff had in mind for the Hungarian deportees in the shadow of the SS's human-trade negotiations. That in most instances they were not provided with the necessary clothing and equipment, that no preparations were made whatsoever, would seem to contradict this intention. Were they supposed to bring all these things along with them? A memorandum sent from the Reich's Ministry of the Economy to the Foreign Ministry suggesting that German officials might appropriate personal belongings confiscated from the Hungarian Jews at the time of their "congregation" indicates that this might have been the case.

The following memorandum was sent to German Foreign Minister Ribbentrop:

As the Vienna economic attaché has reported, the 14,700 Hungarian Jews currently being held in that city and in the Region of Niederdonau arrived without any belongings whatsoever. According to information from the regional economic bureau, the deportees left their homes with sufficient household goods, clothing, blankets, etc.; however, the Hungarian gendarmerie confiscated most of these items before they left the country.

The Gau Niederdonau labor affairs secretary and president of the region's employment bureau wrote a letter that contained the following passage:

---

[16] From memoirs contained in the HDKE collection. Some Jewish forced-laborers were bombed out of their lodgings twice.

We are attempting to ensure that the Jews bring work clothing, footwear and, if possible, straw mattresses and blankets along with them from Hungary. We have heard that you are currently conducting negotiations with the appropriate authorities in Hungary regarding the Hungarian gendarmerie's confiscation of the Jews' personal belongings. We would be grateful if you would keep us informed of the status of these negotiations."[17]

There is no available documentation pertaining to the outcome of this matter or, more specifically, to the response of the Hungarian authorities to the German request. However, the documents cited prove that, in August of 1944, *the Germans were reckoning with a new round of deportations from Hungary; that is, the impending "delivery" of Budapest Jews.*

Forced labor took place in seventeen districts of Vienna, primarily the 21st (Floridsdorf), the 22nd (Grossenzersdorf) and the 23rd (Schwechat). The number of work camps at which deportees from Hungary were held ranged between fifty-four and sixty-seven, according to demand. Official records from September 1944, indicate that there were 1,722 men (29%), 3,253 women (54%) and 997 children (17%) among the Jewish deportees from Hungary.[18]

Of the 5,972 Hungarian captives, 4,055 (68%) were deemed fit for work. The number of those engaged in daily forced-labor decreased steadily due to the large proportion of the deportees who were above sixty years old. The general emotional and physical condition of the deportees had deteriorated greatly by the beginning of winter, when at least half of the total population of the camps was considered „unfit for being detailed" to work.

New labor arrived from Hungary only at the end of 1944. Beginning on November 6, large numbers of Jews left Budapest on foot in the direction of the Western border of Hungary. In the words of the Germans' newest puppet, Prime Minister and "Nation Leader" (*nemzetvezető*) Ferenc Szálasi, these Jews were being sent to the Reich "on loan." (According to the "supreme resolution" of the Szálasi régime, all Jewish men between the ages of sixteen and sixty and Jewish women between the ages of sixteen and forty were "obliged to work for Germany in exchange for war materiel and thus to the benefit of Hungary.")

---

[17] *The Destruction,* vol. II, pp. 465–466.
[18] DÖW 9543 (Vg 1/b Vr 770/46).

The Jews constituting this third wave of deportation were handed over to SS officers at Hegyeshalom and the Austrian village of Zurndorf for the purpose of performing forced labor.[19]

These new slaves were not put at the disposal of Eichmann's Vienna headquarters; instead most of them were sent to build fortifications on the Eastern borders of the Reich, in the region lying between the city of Bratislava and the Dráva River. "Long-distance" deportation continued as well during this period. Thousands of Jewish men serving in forced-labor battalions, Jewish women and adolescent children, as well as hundreds of Gypsy families, were sent by train to distant concentration camps. The German arms industry, just as the SS, was in dire need of this "rentable" labor force.

Evidence indicates that the new Swiss IRC representative in Budapest, Friedrich Born,[20] made repeated requests to inspect the camps in which Jews taken to Germany for "military work" were being held. (Working in the background to help these deportees was the War Refugee Board, which appealed to the Germans to provide it with information regarding their total number and location.) Both the Hungarian and German governments rejected these and other such requests for "technical reasons."

Among the prominent or well-known Hungarians deported to Vienna were the book publisher and distinguished typographer, Andor Tevan. Pianist-singer Rezső Seress, the composer of the internationally acclaimed song "Gloomy Sunday" and many other hits, was treated at the deportee's hospital in Vienna at the beginning of 1945.

The January 31, 1945 report of Péter Hain, the head of the "Hungarian Gestapo," included a reference to a group of Jews who had been deported from Hungary. Hain had dispatched detectives to Vienna to monitor the massive westward movement of Hungarians that was already going on at that time. The following is an excerpt from one of their reports:

> We have have intelligence from Jews from Debrecen and Battonya doing forced labor in Vienna, indicating that the local population has been show-

---

[19] Tamás Stark, *Zsidóság a vészkorszakban és a felszabadulás után, 1933-1955* [Jews during the Holocaust and Following Liberation, 1933-1955], (Budapest, 1995), pp. 27-28; Szabolcs Szita, *Halálerőd. A munkaszolgálat és a hadimunka történetéhez, 1944-1945* [Death Fortress. On the History of Forced-Labor Conscription and Military Work], (Kossuth Könyvkiadó: Budapest, 1989), pp. 62-89.

[20] For a detailed treatment of Born's activities in Hungary, see Arich Ben Tov's previously cited work.

ing sympathy toward them, providing them with money, food and 'encouraging words.' They have expressed the hope that their suffering will soon end.[21]

The mood at certain factories in Vienna was similar:

> Anton Lachmann was our foreman, our supervisor. He turned out to be a decent and helpful person. At night he was replaced by two foremen, Johann Winkler and Josef Lukawsky. They were also well-intentioned. I also remember the camp commandant, Mr. Mükk, who always had a Swastika pinned in one of his buttonholes. On the other hand, the camp's fire chief, Mr. Geyer, never passed up a chance to make mocking comments about the Nazis, which was often of some consolation to us.[22]

The medical care provided to Hungarian Jews at the Vienna camps was adequate compared to other camps in Germany. In July, Dr. Emil Tuchmann assumed authority over health services at the work camps in and around Vienna. One of his first moves in his new position was to pull ten Jewish doctors from a local factory, where they had been doing manual labor, in order to perform medical work. Like all Jews over the age of two, they were required to display a canary-yellow, six-pointed star on their outer clothing and they were not permitted to use the mass-transit system. They examined patients and performed treatments in the camps or surgeries.

However, transport of sick camp inmates to the hospital was subject to restrictions and required direct permission from the SS. Serious illness and accidents had to be reported to the labor office.

The district treatment centers affiliated with the Jewish hospital handled 1,000 to 1,300 patients per month. Once sick people made it to one of these centers (not everybody received permission), the doctors working there gave them the best treatment possible. As was the case in German camps of every category, inmates with any significant health problem ran a great risk of receiving insufficient treatment. The prohibition on leaving the camps made early detection and treatment of illness much more difficult.

---

[21] Szabolcs Szita, *Holocaust az Alpok előtt* [Holocaust before the Alps], (Győr, 1983), p. 113.

[22] DÖW, personal recollection of Budapest resident, Béla Varga, December 15, 1985. Béla Varga, "Nehéz napok—egy fiú naplója" [Trying Days—a Boy's Diary] in *Jászkunság*, no. 2, 1984, pp. 36–41.

SS *Hauptsturmführer* Seidl knew no mercy. Ailing inmates were rapidly transferred to the Laxenburg "sick camp." In reality here was no such camp. Laxenburg was just a collection point for transfer to a concentration camp, often the end of the line. Such was the case with diabetics and deportees with lung conditions. The former got no access to insulin. It was not unusual for Seidl to slap up Jewish doctors during his periodic camp inspections.

Daily life for the Hungarian captives in Vienna remained essentially unchanged till the end of March and early April 1945. Minor regroupings did take place in February, but their purpose and extent are unknown due to lack of documentation. During the first days of April, tension grew at the labor camps day by day. SS commandants, guards and other Nazi officials began to melt away or fled openly.

The "exchange Jews" of the SS high command were often left without official supervision in many of their various camps and holding places, but they also stopped receiving their rations.

## c. Jews from the Great Hungarian Plain in the Region of Gau Niederdonau

In July, selected Jewish families from Hungary were transferred from Strasshof to other camps. The *Durchgangslager* had the appearance of a slave market. Most of the Austrian entrepreneurs, managers and business proprietors who came to the camp in search of labor wanted strong, able-bodied prisoners, taking no interest in the large families that had arrived with children and elderly relatives.

Between 8,700 and 8,800 Hungarian Jews, most of them in small groups of ten to twenty people (three to five families) began to work in various districts of Gau Niederdonau in July and August.[23] Hardly any camp big enough to accommodate more than 100 prisoners was established, because camps of a larger size would have required fulfilling an entirely new set of complex specifications regarding provision of food, medical treatment, housing and security. Smaller forced-labor groups were quartered in vacant service buildings, sheds, stables, barns, sheep pens, lumberyards and other storage buildings. These accommodations were outfitted with wooden benches and bunks, straw floor mattresses and, occasionally, iron beds. This is what constituted the local *Judenlager*.

---

[23] For more detail see the following work: Szabolcs Szita, "Ungarische Zwangsarbeit in Waldviertel 1944/45" in *Das Waldviertel*, 42. Jahrgang Heft 4 (1993), pp. 309–334.

Many deportees lived in the barracks and makeshift structures that were so common during the war years. The duty of supervision over the camps was assigned to SS *Hauptsturmführer* Wilhelm Schmidtsiefen.

A unique aspect of the Jewish camps was the unprecedented absence of guards. Security was left instead to an extensive array of regulations and prohibitions established by the Vienna SS and the Gestapo headquarters. Under this arrangement the "employer" issued the orders and discipline was maintained by the prisoners themselves. Following their selection, the Jupo underwent thorough training, received strict instructions consisting mainly of threats of severe punishment if fellow prisoners under their watch violated camp regulations or did not meet forced-labor standards or quotas. In the event that Jewish deportees were placed in the same camp with prisoners-of-war, the two groups were separated as much as possible, and kept under guard—though often unarmed—day and night.

During the summer and fall, Hungarian Jews worked according to the established pattern in rural areas, performing various types of agricultural labor from dawn until dusk. Jewish forced laborers were generally not required to work from noon on Saturday until Monday morning, though there were certain places, such as railway shunting yards and freight depots, where they were obliged to work on Sundays as well.

Of the group of twenty-one Jews from Szeged who had been sent to Ludwig Knapp's sawmill in the town of Weitra, southwest of Gmünd, eleven performed daily labor. Jenő Ligeti, a former journalist from Szeged, wrote the following of his initial experiences at the mill:

> At first we were very amused that, low and behold, we had become pick-and-shovel men—us, of all people, who had never even laid a hand on such tools. A young lady pianist cut into the rocky soil with a pick, a lawyer's wife pushed a wheelbarrow, the merchant shoveled the earth and the insurance agent hauled the extracted rocks away. Not even a half an hour had passed before we realized that this was no easy labor ... therefore we had to work our hardest, sweating profusely.[24]

Provisions at the provincial camps were generally better than those at the camps in Vienna. This was due to the more plentiful local food supply, to more favorable workplace conditions, and to the type of labor in which Jewish

[24] HDKE DEGOB 3555. sz. pp. 21–22.

deportees in the provinces were engaged. Occasional bartering also took place between Jewish captives and French, Belgian and Italian prisoners of war. (POWs performing forced labor received double the daily "Jewish ration."). In addition, the International Red Cross sent prisoners of war a monthly "gift" consisting of five kilos of food. Canned milk, chocolate and the hard currency of camp commerce—cigarettes—often changed hands several times. French prisoners at several camps regularly provided Hungarian children with food from their packages.

During the summer of 1944, the Lénárd family regularly sent secret written correspondence from the Sager und Wohl Construction Company camp in Strasshof. Mrs. Lőrinc Lénárd, whom had been deported from Debrecen with her three children, quickly became a cook at the construction company's camp. (This camp position required a great amount of labor and a high sense of responsibility.) At the end of July, Mrs. Lénárd's mother found an Austrian man whose work required him to travel regularly (perhaps he was a railway worker), and who was willing to forward letters to the Lénárd family's relatives in Budapest. The correspondence, much of which Mrs. Lénárd wrote on toilet paper, went on for two months.

The following facts can be pieced together from Mrs. Lénárd's letters: of 240 captives at the camp, 110—both men and women—went to work at the airport. They came from eleven different communities in Hungary. There were no men between the ages of seventeen and forty-eight among the captives, though there was one seventy-two-year-old man. Over half of the camp's population was made up of children and people deemed unfit for work due to sickness, disability or age. They slept twenty to a room in the huge barrack building. They received bunk beds after spending the first three weeks sleeping on the floor. There were a total of just three toilets for all the camp's inmates, men and women.[25]

Treatment of inmates at the "family camps" was, for the most part, fairly humane. (The Lénárds testified to this as well; on one occasion they even described the treatment at the camp as *very* humane.[26]) Many civilians with whom the deportees came into contact at their workplaces expressed some degree of sympathy for them, or somehow made it clear that they had nothing against the Jewish forced-laborers. However, there were always one or two fanatic supervisors, foremen or Nazi Party or SA officials who could make life miserable for the deportees.

[25] Some inmates died of intestinal inflammation.
[26] András Lénárd (USA) provided the author with copies of all the letters.

The arrival of Jewish forced-laborers took the residents of rural communities in Austria by surprise. An increasing number of them began to feel pity for the deportees, who often arrived with only the shirts on their backs in groups that included grandparents and grandchildren.

Among the official reports on the provincial work deployment of Hungarian forced-laborers during the summer of 1944 was a memorandum composed by the head of the St. Pölten district headquarters regarding deportees who were engaged in agricultural labor in the villages of Inprugg and Tullnerbach. Using bureaucratic language, the regional official expressed the opinion of local residents that *"with few exceptions the Jews are industrious; their work is, on the whole, satisfactory. The general comportment of the Jews is not known to be improper in any way."*

On August 14, the Vienna offices of the Reichsstatthalter in Niederdonau received a report from the Zwettl district that a consignment of Hungarian families consisting of seventeen adult men, forty-three adult women and seventeen minors, which had been sent to work cutting wood in the Bärnkopf district village of Saggraben to the Firma Wenzl Hartl, Holzkonstruktions- und Baugesellschaft (a construction company) in Echsenbach. The deportees were now withdrawn from their workplaces in Saggraben and transferred to the factory in Echsenbach. Their duties there were originally to involve forest work, but since they had no experience in this field, they were instead assigned to a factory.

According to a report issued by the German Labor Front on August 12, 1944, the Jews at the Wenzl factory in Echsenbach were a true asset to the enterprise.

> They are diligent and precise. The Jewish women at the factory are a bit timid about working with the machinery, which can be explained by the fact that they have never done this type of labor before.[27]

The majority of the reports contained some derogatory remarks regarding the deportees only "for the sake of being official," which often included the standard racist drivel. The scanty documentation suggests that these pariahs, whom had been divested of everything, did their best to adapt to their new circumstances. Living in a foreign land against their will, without proper cloth-

---

[27] Niederösterreichisches Landesarchiv (NöLa) ZR 1. a-1-240.

ing and equipment, amid all the trying circumstances it was not surprising that the job performance of the Jewish forced-laborers was often inferior to that of an experienced worker.

An October 12 memorandum to the Waidhofen a.d. Thaya district commissioner provided information on 467 deported Hungarians. A total of 247 women, 148 men and seventy-two children had been sent to work to four industrial plants and nine forestry concerns (107 of the women, 56 of the men and 22 of the children had been placed in the factories). According to the memorandum, the estimation of their labor was favorable, both in terms of quality and quantity. The following comment was nevertheless appended to this praise: "*The Jews must be kept under strict police supervision, which is only natural.*"

The author of a document—dated August 17 in Amstetten—also met the Nazi requirements. It called attention to the deterioration of the Jewish prisoners' physical condition and the consequences of direct contact with human suffering. (This demonstrates the advantages, from a Nazi perspective, of isolating the Jews in closed concentration camps, where the Germans generally did not have to contend with the reaction of the local population to what was taking place inside them.) The author of the Amstetten report concluded that

> ... the experiences with deployment of Jewish labor have been very bad. These miserable figures, who pass down the street each morning and evening, generally evoke pity among the local population. This is especially due to the fact that most of them are elderly men and women, whose appearance reveals that their daily rations are far below the minimum subsistence level. The people recognize these facts ...
>
> Work deployment in large groups is not possible. Though the groups sent to work with the peasants have a maximum of ten members, this is still enough so that the Jews associate frequently with the German population and the foreign nationalities. Naturally, they establish connections and beg for food, because many people feel sympathy for them. Jewish work deployment has not even once encouraged anti-Semitic thought among our compatriots: instead the Jewish laborers have aroused pity among them.
>
> The best thing would be for the Jews to be taken away from here and taken to a concentration camp. But this must be done so that the local population sees nothing.[28]

---

[28] Ibid.

The concerns expressed in this report prove that the "compatriots" (*Volks-genosse*) witnessed the misery of the outcasts, that they noticed their suffering and attempted to help alleviate it.

A labor group consisting of thirty-five deportees from a Szeged brick factory left Amstetten every morning for work at a gravel quarry located in the woods. (Children and the elderly remained in town, at the camp). As guards escorted them to their workplaces, *they occasionally received honey, butter and chocolate* from sympathetic local residents.

To show sympathy for the "enemies of the Reich," to make supportive humanitarian gestures, was a risky proposition. Between 1938 and 1945, Nazi terror claimed tens of thousands of lives: 65,459 Austrian Jews were killed during the war years and 2,700 Austrians executed. A further 16,100 Austrians died in Gestapo captivity and 16,500 more in concentration camps.

Austria lost 372,000 people, 5.58% of its total population, during the wartime bloodletting. At least 100,000 Austrians spent between three months and seven years in concentration camps during this dreadful time of pervasive violence.[29]

Terror was part of life in the region of Reichsgau Niederdonau as well. Almost anything served as a viable pretext for the Gestapo to issue a "referral" to one of the camps. According to verified data collected by associations of concentration camp survivors, the Gestapo arrested ninety-eight Austrians for providing aid to Jews. Sixty of these people were subsequently sent to concentration camps, where two of them died in captivity.[30]

The life of the Jews deported to Strasshof was being monitored by the Rescue Committee, the International Red Cross and Swedish Red Cross representatives in Budapest. Though the precise contributions of the Swedish Red Cross to this effort have not yet been documented, records indicate that the organization attempted to obtain a list of the Strasshof captives on September 16. Nina Langlet, the wife of a Swedish language instructor teaching at Budapest University, asked the SS to provide the Hungarian Jews at Strasshof with official Swedish Red Cross postcards, which were then to be sent back to Budapest in order to establish an accurate list of deportees held at the camp.

The response of the SS to this request is unknown; however, on October 10, *Obersturmbannführer* Krumey ordered German officials at Strasshof not to release any information regarding the Jews at the camp, warning them that

---

[29] *Österreich und der Zweite Weltkrieg,* (Österreicher Bundesverlag: Vienna, 1989), p. 151.

[30] C. Gwyn Moser, Jewish *U-Boote in Austria*, 1938–1945, in Simon Wiesenthal Center Annual 2, 1985, p. 60.

violation of any commands or established regulations would be grounds for intervention on behalf of the Gestapo.[31]

The International Red Cross made repeated attempts through several different channels to provide help and support. The IRC sought to provide the deportees with clothing to replace their worn-out rags before the onset of winter (the SS did not usually furnish prisoners with additional clothing, though, under certain conditions, it distributed shoes—wooden clogs and so-called Kneipp sandals for the children—as well as caps and scarves). Krumey called upon Kasztner to have winter coats sent and gave permission to the IRC to furnish the prisoners with jackets, shoes and underwear. Several of the deportees received various items of used clothing that the local villagers provided.

With the approaching winter, this donation of clothing and blankets was a life-and-death matter for many of the deportees. The clothing of those who were engaged in field work and construction labor was in a particularly poor shape; after their own shoes had worn out, these people often improvised substitute footwear from wire and pieces of sack lined and reinforced with scraps of tattered clothing. At the same time, entire groups of Jewish captives were also transferred to other camps, from Lenzing, Mannersdorf, Neunkirchen and Pottendorf, for example, to Vienna–Floridsdorf and back to Strasshof/Nordbahn.

The several hundred Jews assembled at the "transit camps" at Laxenburg and Strasshof were transferred to Bergen-Belsen. On December 7 and 8, these deportees were placed not in the "privileged" sector of the camp, but in the *Häftlinglager* at Belsen, where they lived a bleak and precarious existence alongside Dutch Jews.[32] Dov Landau, a fourteen-year-old deportee from Szeged, wrote of his experiences at Belsen:

> My memories: terrible hunger; a perpetual sense of intense fear; the smoke and smell of the crematoria; heaps of half-dead Jewish skeletons stacked up in wagons; and corpses of Gypsies whom had been beaten to death piled up in a mound.[33]

---

[31] Based on documents from the National Jewish Museum, no. 7471.

[32] László Benjamin, "Bergen-Belsen után szabadon" [Free after Bergen-Belsen], in *Remény*, vol. 5, no. 4, 2002, pp. 91–92.

[33] Marianne Dobos, *A szívek kötelessége megmarad* [Obligations of the Heart Endure], (Kelenföld Kiadó, 1989), p. 171.

Some deportees were sent to Theresienstadt and some ended up in Auschwitz.[34]

Many previously separated family members were reunited at Theresienstadt. In the depths of the casements that served as their quarters they struggled together against the torments of lice, typhus and despair. Assistance from the Swedish Red Cross was a significant source of the sustenance that the deportees needed to survive.[35]

Fourteen-year-old Judit Weisz of Szolnok had been deported along with her family via Strasshofen to Immendorf, where they formed part of the village's twenty-one-member "Jewish camp." Every morning they reported to the Mayor's office, from where local peasants would take them to work in the fields. The five-member Weisz family worked primarily at the farm of a man named Singer—four of them at agricultural labor, while Judit's mother did his sewing. At the end of September, the Weisz family was sent to Grosskadolz, where they took up residence in the cold and damp attic of a mill.

The Weisz' were astonished to receive parcels at their new workplace. *"The Singers—to this day I don't know how—managed to find out where we were and send us parcels containing gloves and warm scarves for all five of us. We were simply astonished. Of course we all really needed these things."*[36]

On April 13, 1945, the group was taken to Hollabrunn, from where they were transported to Theresienstadt one week later in open freight cars. After returning to Hungary following their release from Theresienstadt, the Weisz family expressed its *gratitude* to the Viennese family with letters and parcels.

Mr. and Mrs. Rudolf Harrer of Meierhof (Waidhofen a.d. Thaya District) undertook great risks and showed great kindness in supporting the local Jewish forced-laborers. Mr. Harrer, a forestry superintendent, found a way to help the group of deportees from Hungary hide and stay behind after their camp had been evacuated. Those under his care survived, and the letters of gratitude sent to him amply testified to his extraordinary humaneness.[37]

An eight-member group of deportees from the town of Makó worked at the paper mill and the cement plant in Gloggniz. They included Mrs. Izidor Hirsch, deported as a labor battalion man's widow, along with her sons, 12 and 17 years old respectively, as well as her daughter Maria, 3. In the group were

[34] *Der Bericht*, p. 152

[35] Based on author's interview with Dr. György Vadász, which took place in Budapest on June 11, 1990.

[36] Author's interview with Mrs. Gábor Verő, *née* Judit Weisz, in Budapest on May 5, 1998.

[37] See copy of a letter from I.R. to Friedrich Herrer Forstdirektor in HDKE collection.

also Mrs. Hirsch's sister, another widower, Mrs. Manó Róth, and the family of Sándor Scheiber with 2 children.

Twelve-year-old Zoltán Hirsch also worked every day. Hunger forced him to beg from the locals. *"When the German's weren't watching, we kids ran into houses, and asked for bread in our rudimentary German. Once I even found myself in a house where a picture of Hitler hung on the wall. Yet when, trembling with fear, I begged and prayed for bread, to my surprise the woman of the house pressed some potatoes and piece of bread into my hand.*

*The job of us children consisted in carrying off the slag from the boilers. The grownups worked in the plant.*"[38]

In November the group was resettled in Wiener Neustadt for factory work, then sent to Strasshof again. Their way led by rail from there to the Bergen-Belsen camp, and their captivity ended in Theresienstadt.

Available evidence indicates that the deportees held in "family camps" lived under much more favorable circumstances than the Hungarian "rented-out Jews," building fortifications along the border of the Reich at the nearby fortresses, let alone the *Häftlinge* of the concentration camp system.

The *Judenkommando* made substantial financial profits from forced labor by Hungarian Jews. During a conversation with Rezső Kasztner on January 10, 1945, Krumey remarked that he had managed to "save" 115,000 Reichsmarks from the fees paid for the labor of the Hungarian deportees. (By this time the "U" account had reached a balance of 180,000 marks, which included the Rescue Committee's 65,000-Mark "deposit.") Krumey was able to do this even though "there were some enterprises whose fees did not cover the expenses spent on provisions."[39]

Beginning in February 1945, the living conditions of the Hungarian captives generally underwent a marked deterioration. By that time, it was often only the generosity of anonymous Austrians, at workplaces and in the streets, that alleviated their agonizing hunger. The Austrian researcher Karl Flanner accurately observed that *"the furtively passed scrap of bread, the few pieces of potato or an apple slid through the fence into the thin hands of starving children often signified a life saved from the clutches of Nazi barbarism."*[40]

---

[38] Reminiscences of Zoltán Hirsch in HDKE collection. Makó, 20 April, p. 3.

[39] *Der Bericht*, p. 151.

[40] HDKE DEGOB 1792. sz. jkv., Karl Flanner, *Widerstand im Gebiet von Wiener Neustadt, 1938-1945* (Vienna, 1973), pp. 266-273.

# 8. More Looting—Daylight Robbery on a Different Plain

## a. The Biggest Catch: Ferenc Chorin
## and the Families of Financiers and Industrial Magnates

International academic research has shown that the German security organizations expended a significant amount of time and energy trying to expropriate the property and assets of Jewish tycoons living in the occupied territories. The struggle of the Weiss, Chorin, Kornfeld, Mauthner and Heinrich families for survival and SS *Obersturmbannführer* Kurt Becher's Hungarian campaign of thievery and plunder represent a distinct example of this.

Ferenc Chorin was the preeminent figure associated with Hungarian finance capital. For years he had been viewed as "big game" in the eyes of fortune-hunting SS officials. Until his politically motivated ouster, Chorin had served as President of the National Association of Hungarian Industrialists (the Hungarian-language acronym was MGYOSz), Chief Executive Officer of the Rimamurány-Salgótarján Ironworks and in various important functions as a firm advocate of the interests of the Hungarian industrial sector.[1] He made every effort to protect the Hungarian economy, and rejected increasing servility to Germany.

Berlin was aware of his strong and vociferous anti-Hitler sentiment. The Germans also knew that he was to the Hungarian economy as Count István Bethlen had been to Hungarian politics.

Significantly, the Chorin family held valid Swiss visas throughout the war years.[2] Though they saw the gathering of the ominous storm clouds overhead, the Chorins' love of their homeland won over common sense. Confident that Hungary's fate would soon improve, many of the Chorins were eventually forced to take refuge in neutral foreign countries.

---

[1] For a detailed account of Chorin's economic and industrial activities, see the following work: Szabolcs Szita, *A Magyar Gyáriparosok Országos Szövetsége. A GYOSZ kiépítése és tevékenysége 1902-től 1948-ig* [The National Association of Hungarian Industrialists. The Development and Activities of the GYOSZ from 1902 until 1948], (MGYOSZ-könyvek, 1997).

[2] Mrs. Daisy Chorin Strasser and András D. Bán, *Az Andrássy úttól a Park Avenue-ig* [From Andrássy Avenue to Park Avenue], (Osiris, 1999), p. 36.

The Gestapo sought to arrest Ferenc Chorin immediately following the German occupation. They did not find him in Budapest, because he and his brother-in-law, Móric Kornfeld, had managed to flee the city with the help of the Cistercian abbot of Zirc. Several days later the Germans used telephone wiretaps to locate Chorin at the Zirc Monastery in the Bakony Hills. Hungarian detectives apprehended Chorin, taking him back to Budapest, where gendarmes confined the magnate in the cellar of the Astoria Hotel, one of the headquarters of the occupying forces.

In the first days of his captivity, Chorin underwent interrogation, during which he was accused of sabotage. These trying hours were filled with threats to his life. Chorin's interrogators pressed him for information on his industrial and mining interests, the racial origins of the Hungary's leading economic figures and their wives, as well as the nature of his connections to Interior Minister Ferenc Keresztes-Fischer and Miklós Horthy.

Chorin's interrogator wore an officer's uniform. He took great pleasure in expertly administered beatings of the short, slightly built, sixty-five-year-old Hungarian industrialist. Chorin later wrote the following description of his interrogation:

> I can't forget to this day what a humiliating feeling it was to just stand there getting slapped around and not being able to strike back. The interrogations went on at a brisk tempo all afternoon—I wasn't even allowed to sit down once. The tone of the conversation became increasingly rough, which was followed by a longer succession of blows. Eventually I got punched so hard that I fell to the ground, causing the typist to scream with alarm.
>
> Then he returned again to the theme of where my wife was. He kindly recommended that I tell him, because nothing was going to happen to her, and told me that the only reason he was interrogating me was because the financial information that I had provided them had been insufficient. I answered that she was probably hiding somewhere in the vicinity of Verőce, which he didn't want to believe, demanding that I tell him where my wife and children were, why we had fled, who had put them on the *qui vive*[3] that the Germans were coming.
>
> Since I didn't answer those questions, a big oaf jumped on my feet with all his weight and then shook me back and forth like a rag doll until I couldn't catch my own breath and started to get dizzy. Fortunately, though I

---

[3] That is, who had warned them.

am prone to dizziness, I managed to hold myself upright. He then told me that if I didn't answer he was going to kick me into the wall a few times, until I got into the mood to answer. He continued this amusement for a little while, but then quit when I didn't say anything ...

Finally, after an entire day of questioning, he put a paper in front of me, which I was supposed to sign. I wasn't in any position to read what was written on it, but I thought it would be smart to sign it, because it didn't really matter anyway. I was then led back into the cellar, where I had already witnessed so many lamentable scenes.[4]

Chorin was transferred in an open truck to the Pest Regional Courthouse, where he was again subjected to humiliating treatment. Low-ranking SS officials repeatedly insulted and abused him. Chorin was among the first Jews to be deported, leaving Hungary from Budapest's Eastern Railway Station on March 26.

When he arrived at the Oberlanzendorf camp, Ferenc Chorin was classified as a Jewish prisoner. There, one of Himmler's confidants, SS *Obersturmbannführer* Kurt Becher, established contact with Chorin.[5]

Like Reich Envoy Edmund Veesenmayer, Becher had previously been in Hungary in order to negotiate a commercial transaction for a Hamburg grain-trading company. Other sources describe him in 1942 as the head of the Horse-Purchasing Committee of the SS wearing the rank of SS-*Hauptsturmführer*.

Following the occupation, the thirty-five-year-old Lieutenant-Colonel returned to Hungary as part of the SS "economic staff" (*Wirtschaftsstab*), establishing his residence in two luxurious, Andrássy-Street villas belonging to the Weiss family, most of which had either fled or gone into hiding upon hearing news of the German invasion.[6] (Becher also requisitioned property belonging to the Kornfeld and Mauthner families as well as another villa located on neighboring Lendvay Street.)

Becher's official objectives were to obtain armaments, military equipment and 40,000 horses for breeding and military purposes. The SS officer allegedly

[4] Chorin Strasser and Ban, pp. 151–153

[5] For a more detailed account of Becher's activities in Hungary, see the following work: Karla Müller-Tupath, *Reichsführers gehorsamster Becher: Eine deutsche Karriere,* (Aufbau Verlag, 1999), pp. 123–187.

[6] For a more detailed history of the Weiss family see the following article: László Varga, "Egy finánctőkés karrier. A Weiss család és Weiss Manfréd" [The Career of a Finance Capitalist. The Weiss Family and Manfréd Weiss], *Történelmi Szemle*, 1983, no. 1, pp. 36–63.

managed to purchase 21,000 horses, an endeavor that enabled him to quickly expand his circle of acquaintances to include many influential Hungarians, such as Jenő Horthy, the brother of the Regent.

The true purpose of Becher's horse-trading venture was to provide him with reconnaissance of Hungary's economic landscape. In just a few weeks he became familiar with the personal connections and focal points that formed the foundation of the Hungarian economy. Lieutenant-Colonel Becher also strove to expropriate stocks and property from wealthy families, even after the introduction of the "Jewish laws." His diligent quest for financial profit was aimed not only at filling the coffers of the SS, but at lining his own pockets as well. Becher and his staff conducted their effort to exploit the Hungarian economy using means and methods whose effectiveness had already been established in the course of earlier "operations" of the same type.

By April 20, Becher had already made the acquaintance of Dr. Vilmos Bil-litz, one of the managers of the Danube Aircraft Factory and several of the directors of Weiss Enterprises. He also interrogated Ferenc Kelemen, the head of the brokerage firm that handled the stock interests of the Chorin family. Becher assembled data on Chorin's industrial-management activities, the commercial connections that he maintained despite having been forced into the background of the Hungarian economic scene and the assets of his extended family. Becher, a man of action, worked dutifully and decisively in the service of his superior, SS Chief Heinrich Himmler.

Becher utilized wiretaps and the services of Hungarian agents to "collect" the members of the Chorin family who had gone into hiding. On April 17, he had Ferenc Chorin apprised of the results of this effort. The SS gangsters were certain that their captive's reaction to this news would be to save his family at all costs. Blackmailed, dejected and suffering from acute furunculosis, Chorin, in an act of desperation, agreed to provide the SS with important economic intelligence. The SS intended to first extort a significant sum of pengős from Chorin, then to compel him to finance the *Wehrmacht's* purchase of heavy military trucks with money from his Swiss bank accounts.[7]

On the 26th, Becher took care of matters "in higher places." He sent his personal secretary, SS-*Hauptsturmführer* Hans Stapenhorst, to Oberlanzendorf in order to escort Chorin back to Budapest. Following his return, SS officers immediately subjected him to intense interrogation, which centered on his interests in the Commercial Bank and the Credit Bank. Chorin was then pro-

---

[7] This was part of the previously mentioned German scheme, dubbed *Blut gegen Waren*, aimed at using Jewish lives as collateral for war materiel and other goods.

vided with an office at 114 Andrássy Avenue, where the SS could find him when it wanted pertinent information. Winkelmann soon found out about this episode, for which he took Becher to task. The Lieutenant-Colonel called his attention to Himmler's approval of the plan, at the same time gaining permission to transfer Baron Jenő Weiss and his son from a Gestapo prison to the János Sanatorium, with the intention of achieving even greater results. (In the meantime he prepared a memorandum that made the bogus claim that Chorin had been brought to Budapest for interrogation and then returned immediately to Oberlanzendorf.)

The contours of another European SS campaign of plunder were gradually taking shape. The Germans recognized that by gaining control of the Chorin group's stocks—as well as the two big Hungarian banks and their complex network of industrial interests—a significant portion of Hungary's economy would come under the Reich's disposal. Negotiations to this effect had begun by early May.

The Hungarian state owned a forty-nine percent share of the Csepel Industrial Works, while the remaining fifty-one percent was owned by the Weiss, Kornfeld, Mauthner and Heinrich families. Becher sought to obtain these families' ownership rights for the SS, first through a "lease" arrangement, then by way of "confidential handling" (*Treuhand*). As compensation for himself and fifty members of his family, Ferenc Chorin requested permission for all of them to leave Hungary for a neutral country as well as 600,000 dollars and 250,000 Reichsmarks.

Becher visited Himmler twice to discuss this matter, who eventually briefed Hitler as well. Taking the Führer's expressed concerns into consideration, the SS *Reichsführer* altered the plan, insisting that one-fifth of Chorin's family members be held back on German soil to ensure that "those who go abroad would not slander Germany." Himmler also stipulated that the majority of those permitted to leave go to Portugal and only a minority to Switzerland. Himmler's lawyer, Dr. Wilhem Schneider, and Dr. Fritz Zabransky of the SD's Vienna offices were sent to Budapest to conduct this "transaction."

Establishing the "legal constructs" for this plan required three weeks of strictly confidential bargaining. On May 10, the two sides arrived at an agreement that designated precisely where those members of the Chorin family who had been "redeemed" in exchange for property and assets would be allowed to travel and who would be kept behind as hostages in Germany. (By this time Kaltenbrunner had found out about this affair. He was furious that Jews "were residing in Germany under favorable conditions.") A contract that essentially served to save the Chorin family and enhance the wealth and influence of the

SS was drawn up a few days later.[8] Winkelmann was given an opportunity to inspect the document before Becher sent it on to Himmler, who approved it without modifications.

The deal was finally consummated on May 17, when four contracts, a collateral contract and Becher's power of attorney were signed. A bastion of the Central European arms industry, the Manfréd Weiss Enterprises located on Csepel Island, had become part of the booty of the SS.

Eichmann also found out about this strictly confidential Reich affair handled by Becher. On June 3, he remarked to Kasztner that "this outrage" was preventing him from transferring prominent provincial Jews to Budapest in accordance with the agreement he had concluded with the Zionists. Eichmann feared that his most zealous partner in the implementation of the *Endlösung* in Hungary, Undersecretary of State László Endre, might inquire about any new deals that the Germans had made with Jews, a potentially awkward situation that the "maestro" of the deportations wanted to avoid at all costs.

Eichmann's worries were irrelevant when an affair of such magnitude was concerned. With the approval of the highest circles of the Order of the Skull and Bones, Becher and his staff arranged for a group of people belonging to Hungary's wealthiest families to leave the country for neutral Portugal and Switzerland. (Note that the SS did pay the part determined in Reichmarks as specified in the contract but the Chorins never got more than a third of the 600,000 dollars also specified.) The Gestapo held five members of the Chorin family hostage in the Hitzing residential district of Vienna.

Some members of the Chorin family remained in Hungary as well. Carlos Branquinho, the *chargé d'affaires* of the Portuguese embassy in Budapest, alludes to this fact in a telegram that he sent to the foreign ministry in Lisbon indicating that the Weiss family had petitioned the ambassador for asylum on July 18.[9]

Because the Germans had refused the Chorins to take refuge in "nearby" Switzerland, the list of the party of thirty-one persons leaving Hungary for Por-

---

[8] The text of this contract is contained in the following article: Elek Karsai and Miklós Szinai, "A Weiss Manfréd-vagyon német kézre kerülésének története" [The History of the German Appropriation of Manfréd Weiss' Property and Wealth], *Századok*, 1961, nos. 4–5, pp. 600–719.

[9] Éva Bán, "A Weiss Manfréd Művek német kézre kerülésének utótörténethez. Dokumentumok a lisszaboni külügyminisztérium archivumából" [Postscript to the History of the German Appropriation of Manfréd Weiss' Property and Wealth. Documents from the Archives of the Lisbon Foreign Ministry], *Kritika*, no. 10, 1992, pp. 33–36. The twenty-five people reportedly "begged" for asylum.

tugal on June 25 was as follows: Ferenc Chorin and his wife, *née* Daisy Weiss, Erzsébet Chorin, Daisy Chorin and Ferenc Chorin Jr. from the Chorin family; Baron Jenő Weiss and his wife, *née* Annie von Geitler Armingen, Alice Weiss, Baron György Weiss, Annie Weiss, Edith Weiss, Mrs. Alfonz Weiss, *née* Erzsébet Herzog, Gábor Weiss, Márta Weiss, Mária Weiss and János Weiss from the Weiss family.

Members of the Mauthner family were Mrs. Alfréd Mauthner, *née* Elsa Weiss, Anna Mauthner, two Gabriella Mauthners and Ferenc Mauthner. The Baron Kornfeld family: Baron Móric Kornfeld and his wife, *née* Marianne Weiss, Mária Kornfeld, Hanna Kornfeld and Baron Tamás Kornfeld.

Non-family members were Zoltán Fenyvesi and his wife and daughter; and a Csepel Industrial Works lawyer, György Hoff, and his parents.

Nine people flew to Switzerland by airplane: Herbert Margaretha and his wife, *née* Erzsébet Mauthner, their daughter, Elisabeth, Dr. Ferenc Borbély and his wife, *née* Mária Mauthner, Sándor Borbély, Antal Borbély and István Borbély and Dr. Antal Heinrich. Five people were held hostage in Vienna: Baron György Kornfeld and his wife and young child, János Mauthner and Baron Alfonz Weiss.

Legends soon emerged surrounding the interrelated families that had escaped from the deathtrap. Among these was the myth that they had carried suitcases full of valuables out of the country with them;[10] in fact, these people took with them into exile only the clothes on their backs and a standard civil-defense package—nothing else. They were not given a friendly welcome either by the Portuguese or the Swiss. The reason for this may have been their manner of entry (the Germans had provided those going to Portugal with forged visas; they did not even bother to do this much for those going to Switzerland) as well as the international press reaction. The thirty-one refugees were subsequently forced to endure internment, separation from family members, continuous police surveillance and inspection, and limitations on leaving their homes, lasting for a long time.[11]

---

[10] Elemér Újpétery makes this assertion, for instance, in his memoirs, *Végállomás Lisszabon* [End Station Lisbon], (Magvető Könyvkiadó, 1987), p. 451. The author's claim that the Lisbon party left the country with a ton (sic!) of gold is completely unfounded.

[11] Ferenc Chorin and his family lived at the seaside resort of Curia in northern Portugal until the middle of October, when they moved to Estoril. They left Portugal at the beginning of 1947, after American officials granted them visas to enter the United States. The Chorins arrived to New York on January 21 as part of what was essentially the first group of Hungarian postwar émigrés to arrive in the city. Ferenc Chorin later participated in the work of the Hungarian National Committee and, in the 1960s, initiated the foundation of the *Magyar Ház* (Hungarian

The head of the Chorin family, Ferenc Chorin, bore the greatest responsibility for this emigration affair. Though he seemingly acted of his own will, the SS had actually put Chorin under great physical and moral pressure in order to accept an emigration agreement on their terms. Shortly after the war, the author Miksa Fenyő provided the following critical analysis of this affair, which has remained valid to the present day:

> Is it possible to condemn someone who ... given the choice between even a remote chance of survival and the cruelest death imaginable for both himself and his extended family, elects to sacrifice his possessions? Possessions he does not even control, since Csepel, in truth was already in Nazi hands for years and would have remained in Nazi hands had the Germans won the war.
>
> It is simply impossible to understand why the Nazis placed so much emphasis on this agreement when they had long since divested the owners of the factory of their proprietary rights and anyway would have swallowed up all of Hungary—Imrédy, Csepel and Mávag[12] along with it—had they been victorious.

In November, 1945, the journalist Béla Zsolt, writing disparagingly of the Chorins' flight, commented that "the willingness to suffer martyrdom has never been a trait of the *haute bourgeoisie*."[13] Fenyő soon published a rebuttal to Zsolt's reproachful article, asserting that over recent history martyrdom "has been equally uncharacteristic of the *petite bourgeoisie*, the peasantry and the proletariat. I see no valid moral or intellectual rationale for having choosing martyrdom at the hands of the Gestapo when it was possible to survive without doing harm to any individual or to the country as a whole."

Fenyő had close knowledge of the life and circumstances of Chorin and his family. He had seen many an eminent figure on the nation's economic scene being degraded into second-class citizens and social outcasts by zealous Hungarian followers of National Socialist racial mythology. The head of the Chorin family continued to help as much as he could in spite of the ostracism to which he was subjected.

---

House) on 82nd Street. For details on Chorin's émigré life and activities see Chorin Strasser and Bán, pp. 54–55.

[12] This is an acronym for *Magyar Államvasutak Gépgyár* (Hungarian State Railway Engine Works).

[13] Béla Zsolt, "A Weiss Manfréd-ügy" [The Manfréd Weiss Affair], *Haladás*, November 4, 1945.

They had forced Chorin into a state of almost lethargic passivity. He was not allowed to concern himself with Csepel, but he, along with the rest of his family, definitely did take great concern for the fate of those conscripted laborers and persecuted Jews whom the Nazis and their Hungarian henchmen had scattered along the eastern front with the vile intention that they should be annihilated; Chorin took great concern for the fate of Jews who had fled here from Slovakia, shuttling about on their behalf between the office of Ferenc Keresztes-Fischer to that of the Regent. He eagerly took up their cause and gladly assumed the significant material sacrifices that went with it. Chorin never talked about these actions, he never flaunted his humanitarian exploits, but I am a witness to all that he and the entire Weiss family did in this domain.[14]

The contract pertaining to Chorin's vast wealth and the Csepel industrial complex was a bonanza to the SS, providing many of its officers with significant economic rewards and Becher, in particular, with a further boost to his flourishing military career. With this coup, the latter gained Himmler's unqualified confidence. Becher's meteoric rise was a *typical* phenomenon of the SS state: catapulted to the top by a single success, he gained more power and authority than many higher-ranking officers, even generals.

This blatant instance of German extortion provoked a political uproar in Hungary. The affair was kept secret so successfully that the Hungarian government never even learned about in until July 5. Cabinet minister Béla Imrédy lodged a stern protest with German occupation authorities after his government had discovered, nearly six weeks after the fact, that rights to the property and assets specified in the contract had been remitted not to the Hermann Göring Werke, but to the SS. This affair destabilized Imrédy's position, because the SS frowned upon his opposition to their business.

Meanwhile, Kurt Becher made himself at home not only in Chorin's domicile, but in the main offices of the Csepel industrial complex as well. Becher's commercial contacts branched out further: during an August 17 meeting of the Sztójay cabinet, Finance Minister Lajos Reményi-Schneller went so far as to refer to him as the "German Manager." Becher was a pragmatic and cynical National Socialist, one with whom it might be possible to conduct business even after the war. He became an important negotiating partner.

---

[14] Miksa Fenyő, "A Chorin–Weiss Manfréd ügy" [The Chorin–Manfréd Weiss Affair], *Haladás*, December 1, 1945.

In late November, with Himmler looking over his shoulder, Becher started talks with Raoul Wallenberg at the Swedish embassy regarding his mission's plan to evacuate the first 400 Hungarian Jews provided with temporary Swedish passports and its counter-value. Becher demanded 400,000 Swiss francs and financial guarantees on top. In order to obtain the money, a Zionist engineer by the name of Biss dispatched a telegram to Switzerland, with a text formulated so ingeniously that it was certain to be intercepted by the SD, which would, in turn, pass it on to Becher, thereby verifying it to him.

The ploy was successful. The Germans were thus "becalmed" by the maneuver. Kurt Becher also entered into negotiations with diplomats from the Budapest embassies of Portugal and Spain about the evacuation of Hungarian Jews whom these countries had accorded formal protection. (One of the reason why all the bargaining, and planning seemed to drag on endlessly, with ever newer lists and versions coming up, was that Becher carefully avoided taking personal risks; he always had someone higher up backing him. He never took action without the prior approval of a superior officer.)

The talks came to an end when Becher departed from Budapest before the impending Soviet encirclement of the city. It is accurate to qualify Becher's flight before the swiftly approaching Red Army as a well-planned and methodically executed "departure," in preparation for which he virtually emptied the three villas that he had occupied, removing all furniture, decor and everything else that would fit through the doorway. Leaving along with Becher was his mistress, Countess Hermine von Platen, who had taken immense pleasure in her brief experience with the Budapest high society.

According to some sources, Becher also looted the Mauthner villas in Budakeszi Street, from which he purportedly had several crates containing paintings sent to the Reich—first to Salzburg, then from there on to Rosenheim.

Over the past decades, several publications have dealt with the subject of Becher's loot. Of course, the "treasure hunter" himself denied that he had gained any spoils from his service abroad. However, there is ample evidence indicating that Becher used his mounting status within the SS hierarchy to secure a sizeable share of the German booty from Hungary and its Jewish population.[15]

---

[15] Gábor Kádár and Zoltán Vági, *Aranyvonat. Fejezetek a zsidó vagyon történetéből* [The Gold Train. Chapters from the History of Jewish Wealth], (Osiris, 2001), p. 211–218 (Published in English as *Self-financing Genocide. The Gold Train, the Becher case, and the Wealth of Hungarian Jews* [CEU Press, 2004]); and "Ki volt Kurt Becher" [Who was Kurt Becher], *Heti Világgazdaság*, June 16, 2001, pp. 69–72.

Billitz remained in contact with the SS Economic Division as well as with Becher and his aide-de-camp, SS *Hauptsturmführer* Max Grüson throughout the process of executing the stipulations contained in the far-reaching contract. He also agreed to participate in the "collaborative task" of relocating the enormous amount of industrial infrastructure located at the Csepel factory complex to Germany. (For example, seventy-six Danube barges loaded with machine tools sailed for the Reich.) Billitz died in Vienna on June 9, 1945 at the Cottage Sanatorium, of circulatory disease.

## b. Blackmail and "Buyout" Continue

Several major deals were made by SD officers who were looking for the "extraction" of ransom money that the desperate Hungarian Jews still may have had. As discussed earlier in this book, SS and Zionist officials held talks regarding the withholding of trainloads of Hungarian Jews—first one-million, then thirty thousand—from deportation to Auschwitz–Birkenau.

Some of the "small fry" still seemed too interesting to ignore. Interrogation under physical and mental duress continued in Budapest and at the Kistarcsa internment camp, regarded as "reconnaissance" to determine the financial status, including any possible foreign stock interests or other assets, of the Jews residing there.

At stake was the acquisition of as much Jewish wealth as was still possible in the city of Budapest, since the Germans, specifically Eichmann and his staff, had obtained only human assets during their expulsion of Jews from the Hungarian provinces. As previously mentioned, until the concentric deportation scheme had constricted inward around the capital city, most of the personal assets and property belonging to the outcast citizens of Hungary had fallen into the hands of Hungarian state officials and bureaucrats. Zealous Hungarian gendarme detectives brutally squeezed everything they could possibly get out of prospective deportees during their "treasure-hunting" ventures in the ghettos and concentration camps. Their humiliating, physically and emotionally agonizing, rectal examinations of Jewish girls and women were especially vile.

In the course of their forays throughout Europe, the Germans had gained much experience, which they put to good use against the Hungarian Jews. The Gestapo sometimes "assisted" rich Jews during the provincial ghettoization process. The German secret police took two daughters of the well-known art dealer, the late Károly Rosenstingl, from Szombathely to Budapest in a service vehicle that also contained a large quantity of jewelry and valuable antiques. Two SD officers had previously swindled the Rosenstingls' Budapest relatives into amply "rewarding" the officers for rescuing the two women, who were then "exposed," and subsequently divested of their suitcases full of valuable jewelry and works of art during their spurious "apprehension." Following a short period of internment, the fateful journey of Vilma and Elza Rosenstingl ended at Auschwitz–Birkenau.[16]

By way of Hungarian intermediaries, the Gestapo offered the "Sugar Baron," Albert Hirsch, and his wife Irén Hatvany, asylum in Switzerland in exchange for a large sum of money. After luring them out of hiding to negotiate this deal, the couple was robbed and placed under arrest; Hirsch later resurfaced at the Mauthausen concentration camp, while Hatvany disappeared under unknown circumstances.[17]

Authorities had concentrated all the Jews in Budapest by June 24, requiring that they display the Star of David over the doorways of their new quarters. SD officers presumed that the congregated Jews might still be holding enough assets to merit use of certain "tactics" to extract them. Such were the negotiations conducted with Zionist leaders that entailed gifts of diamonds, gold, jewels and rare coins; in a more explicit form, these tactics included continual harassment of Jewish organizations (such as the acquiescent Jewish Council) to turn over valuables, paintings, musical instruments, expensive tableware, party accessories and to pay off expensive bills.

An SS "liaison" sent actress candidates from a popular gathering place among Budapest artists, the *Fészek Klub* (Nest Club) to the given address. Unfortunately they always found a Hungarian partner to participate in their ploys, which worked to the benefit of greedy and cynical customs officers.

The Gestapo's deportation of the Glück couple from Budapest to Mauthausen in the middle of June was part of this campaign of blackmail. Mr. Hermann Glück was a bank officer who had nothing to do with politics, while Emma Glück was a language teacher. The radical right-wing Budapest press had repeatedly attacked Mrs. Glück's brother, New York City Mayor Fiorella La Guardia, for being a member of the international Jewish cabal. This kinship earned the peaceful couple a summons to Gestapo headquarters on Svábhegy, from where their destiny led them to their deaths in an SS camp.[18]

---

[16] According to the recollections of Iván Hacker, contained in *Ominous are the Skies above Me*, p. 45.

[17] *Magyarok az SS ausztriai lágerbirodalmában* [Hungarians in the Austrian SS Camps], p. 74. Gábor Németi, *A hatvani zsidóság krónikája* [The Chronicle of Hatvan Jewry], (Hatvan, 2004), pp. 134-135. Information regarding prisoners at Dachau contained in the latter work is incorrect; Baron Hirsch was interned at Mauthausen, where he died.

[18] *Magyarok az SS ausztriai lágerbirodalmában* [Hungarians in the Austrian SS Camps], pp. 39, 67, 92.

High-ranking German security officials used the vital and confidential information at their disposal in order to find the most lucrative possible means to facilitate the trade in humans. In addition to these high-echelon operations, there were mid- and lower-level ventures as well, which were founded upon the gullibility and longing to escape from their illicit partners.

This presented affluent Jews, who were clutching at straws to find a way out of their plight, with the prospect of liberation, of "certain" escape that was not lacking in danger and upheaval. (In addition to the "customary" hand-over of cash and precious metals, this scheme included transfer of insurance policies, stocks and bonds and funds from secret bank accounts). A lack of sufficient documentation precludes the possibility of a systematic investigation of these fraudulent transactions—no records were ever kept regarding pledges of passports, visas or other means of gaining egress from the country. Only a few "results" are known.

There is evidence of several mid-level, German–Hungarian "commercial exchange" schemes involving human lives, most of which ended, sadly, in concentration camps. On June 23, for example, the Vienna Gestapo headquarters had twenty-four Hungarians sent to Mauthausen. Three of these deportees—the violin-maker János Tóth, the aircraft mechanic Péter Vörös and the factory manager Rudolf Westary—were registered as "individuals under protective custody," while the rest were classified as *U Jude*, or "Hungarian Jew." Among those ranked in the latter category were the Albert brothers, noted industrialists, the factory manager Ármin Herzog, the Ribáry brothers (Frigyes, the director of the Foncière Insurance Company and Alajos, an architect) and Henrik Herz, General Manager of the First Hungarian Paper Manufacturing Company.

These people had already paid up. They had handed over to swindlers collaborating with the Gestapo 500,000 to one million pengős each in exchange for guaranteed transportation to Egypt via Palermo, and permission to carry an unlimited amount of hard currency and jewelry along with them on their trip. On the way to Mátyásföld Airport, from where they were to fly to Italy, the car in which they were being driven there ran into an "unexpected" checkpoint and a documents check, after which they were seized, robbed of their possessions and, after some further blackmail, deported.

Several of the female members of this swindled party, such as Mrs. Robert Szurday and the mother of the Ribáry brothers, were sent first to Kistarcsa, and ended up ultimately in Auschwitz–Birkenau, where they perished in the gas chambers. Other smaller groups of credulous Budapest Jews were double-crossed in a similar way by "helpful" Gestapo agents.

A horrible act committed by a three-member Hungarian criminal gang was investigated after the war. They promised the Karfunkel sisters to help them escape from the country in a Gestapo vehicle. They drove the two women instead to the home of an accomplice, a Hungarian waiter, on Svábhegy, where they murdered them, and stuffed their bodies into boxes.[19]

The looting continued unimpeded throughout the summer. The Germans targeted exclusively the wealthy Budapest Jews in a series of operations ranging from the highly conspicuous emptying of Jewish villas and homes to more "discreet" plots and machinations. By the end of August the Germans had incarcerated between 800 and a thousand Jews at Kistarcsa and the Gestapo prison in Gyorskocsi Street, relinquishing many others to the custody of the ruthless and avaricious detectives of the Hungarian political police.

The German security agencies took special care to get hold of all better known art collections. (In Budapest the owner was simply summoned to "report" to Gestapo headquarters on Svábhegy, where they were skillfully terrorized and threatened into making a "confession.") Expensive furniture, tapestries, oriental rugs, collections of minerals and rare books, porcelain and silverware were taken to Gestapo warehouses, many of them right on Svábhegy, from where they were sent to the Reich in crates. Jewish labor battalion men were often employed to handle the shipping of these objects.

The opera singer Pál Sugár, a resident of Vienna, made the following statement regarding the German plundering and covert deportations in the presence of a notary:

> At the beginning of April, I received a summons from the Budapest Jewish Council to report for labor duty at an SS-operated workshop on Svábhegy ... I did carpentry work with a man named Klein. In theory we were supposed to make fittings and furnishings for the construction of bunkers, but we were also made to do carpentry and cabinetwork needed by SS officers for their own homes.
>
> Another part of our job was to build wooden crates according to the instructions of an SS sergeant, whose name was Brunner, if I remember correctly. We were told the exact dimensions. When the crates were finished, the sergeant ordered us to fill them up with all sorts of valuables stolen from Jewish shops and homes—typewriters, radio sets, carpets, expensive paintings and other works of art; then we nailed them up for shipping. Most of

---

[19] *Kis Újság*, August 15, 1995.

these items had been brought to the workshop from SS posts on and around Svábhegy—different villas and the Majestic and Mirabell Hotels, among others.

However, it also happened quite frequently that we loaded the crates into trucks empty, then an SS driver took us to Jewish homes and shops in the city and we loaded them up there. After we had nailed them up, they were put on German military trucks and taken away.

A large amount of furniture was also taken away in German military trucks ... In addition to the crates mentioned above, there were also smaller wooden boxes that had already been packed by the time we were ordered to nail them shut. These boxes had been stored at the Majestic Hotel under strict SS supervision. After we had closed these boxes up, we had to paint various addresses on them.

I don't recall the institution in the address; but to this day I remember the destination was Berlin. When the crates were ready to be sent off, Klein and I—and sometimes other laborers when we needed them—packed them onto German army trucks. Upon lifting and loading them on the trucks, we noticed that the boxes were extraordinarily heavy in proportion to their dimensions. We were noticeably under much heavier guard than usual when we were loading those boxes ...

I should mention that my service lasted for about six months beginning in April of 1944 ...The packing and loading went on continuously all the time, which means that the number of pieces of furniture and crates that I helped to pack and ship must have run into thousands.[20]

Hungarian agents collaborating with the Gestapo took an active part in the lively trade of both authentic and forged identity papers, certificates of asylum (*Schutzbriefe* or *Schutzpässe*[21]) and other documents issued by the Budapest embassies of neutral countries and various other agencies. With the Nazi noose tightening around their necks, Jews were willing to give anything for the hope or promise of escape.

"Protection" by the German secret police also made its appearance on this peculiar market. The highly coveted *Immunitäts-Schein* came at an exorbitant price, which included a steep initial bribe to an intermediary. Naturally, there were no guarantees issued as to the duration of the "protection." It sometimes

---

[20] *A Gestapo Magyarországon* [The Gestapo in Hungary], pp. 200-205.

[21] The Swiss and Swedish embassies issued the largest number of documents intended to prevent Jews from being deported.

happened that the Gestapo itself arranged for the disappearance of its own wards.[22]

Several members of the Jewish Council were repeatedly taken into custody in connection with undocumented German blackmail rackets. Eichmann's way of doing this was confining the victims in a Svábhegy room for a longer or shorter time, while the Gestapo made use of its private prison in Buda. The latter organization detained Samu Stern on August 17; Ernő Pető and Károly Wilhelm were placed under arrest shortly thereafter along with their families.

On August 21, the Gestapo demanded a list of the names and addresses of the leaders of the Budapest Jewish community and the staff of the Executive Committee. Several people interpreted this as evidence that deportations from Budapest were imminent. The Germans were undoubtedly plotting to do just that. Fortunately for the Budapest Jews, international developments and negotiations regarding the dismissal of the Sztójay government prevented them from carrying out this plan.


## c. Hopes and Doubts—the Prospects of the Negotiations

Following Brand's departure, Rezső Kasztner emerged practically as the single leader of the Hungarian Zionist movement. His connections with the SS may even have intensified after the previous primary negotiating partner of the Germans, Fülöp Freudiger, suddenly "pulled out" of the proceedings.

On August 9, having concluded that any further wrangling with the Germans was futile, Freudiger, Jewish Council member and the leader of Orthodox Jews, who had ties mainly to Wisliceny, fled Hungary for Romania. Eichmann foamed at the mouth upon learning this news, launching an immediate investigation into how a member of the Jewish Council had managed to escape.[23]

Ottó Komoly, on the other hand, strove to expand his contacts along the "Hungarian line," primarily with major Hungarian political figures who advocated dropping out of the war and with leaders of the illegal national resistance group, the Hungarian Front. Kasztner was aware of Komoly's meetings with these people—in fact, he often took part in them, though the reverse cannot be said of Komoly. Kasztner was convinced that the "German line" was more effective.

---

[22] *Világ*, October 14, 1945.

[23] Mária Schmidt, *Kollaboráció vagy kooperáció? A Budapesti Zsidó Tanács* [Collaboration or Cooperation? The Budapest Jewish Council], (Minerva, 1990), p. 91.

With support from Friedrich Born's Red Cross delegation, Komoly established an IRC child-protection agency, the so-called "A" Section, to promote Zionist emigration from Hungary. This body planned and executed "relocation" operations involving children whom they hoped to save from the Germans.[24] Money sent from Switzerland (predominantly by the Joint) arrived through Born to Komoly, who distributed it directly to Hungarian Jews.

During the summer months of 1944, Komoly worked tirelessly to prevent the concentration and deportation of Budapest Jews. In the middle of August he undertook to broaden and revitalize his range of contacts, from senior government administrators to prominent members of the clergy. During this time Komoly spoke to political and police officials as well as diplomats from the Budapest embassies of neutral countries who were concerned about the fate of the remaining Hungarian Jews, and were prepared to act in their defense.

Among the members of the Rescue Committee, Hansi Brand, Biss and Offenbach kept one another informed of the situation. Komoly made frequent visits to the Vadász Street "Glass House,"[25] a hub of Zionist activity in which the Swiss embassy had established an office called the Emigration Division for Representatives of Foreign Interests. Komoly also maintained steady contacts with Miklós Krausz and representatives of the various, frequently rival Zionist factions active during that period. Komoly's diverse network of relations indicates that he enjoyed support across a broad spectrum of the Zionist movement. Komoly's skill at resolving or alleviating internal discord manifested itself in his successful effort to prevent Kasztner and the more deliberate Krausz from going their separate ways. On several occasions Komoly defended Kasztner against charges of financial impropriety and personal enrichment. This was not the case with many Zionist youth organization members, many of whom considered Kasztner to be impatient and condescending.[26]

Becher's influence over the negotiations continued to grow. Beginning in the middle of July, Kasztner dealt mainly with him, while in August he also met with Eichmann, Veesenmayer, Krumey and SS *Haupsturmbannführer* Max

---

[24] Saly Mayer sent money from Switzerland to finance these operations; the role of the IRC was "transmission."

[25] No. 29, Vadász Street was the former business headquarters of the glass merchant Arthur Weiss. What went on inside is discussed mainly in the above cited work by Mihály Salamon.

[26] The following observation a of former Zionist youth leader, Rafi Benshalom, illuminates this aspect of his personality: "No matter how I rejected Kasztner's negotiating style, I must admit that I took great pleasure in the amusing games that this adroit and intelligent man played with his intellectually inferior rivals." Rafi Benshalom, *Mert élni akartunk* [Because we wanted to live], (HDKE publication: Budapest, 2003), p. 64.

Grüson. On the 18th, he left Budapest with Wisliceny, continuing on to the Swiss border with German armed escorts on the 21st. There he served as a mediator in an initial round of discussions held between Becher, Grüson, Krumey and the Swiss envoy of the Joint Distribution Committee, Saly Mayer in order to "clarify the situation."[27]

In retrospect, the delegation of this crucial assignment to Mayer was an unfortunate choice. He was always a loyal citizen of Switzerland above all else, avoiding any confrontation with government authorities in his native land. Mayer served as the head of the 17,000-member Union of Swiss Jewish Communities (SIG) between 1936 and 1942, during which time he either ignored or minimized the callousness that Swiss government and immigration authorities exhibited toward Jewish refugees. Mayer became the Swiss spokesman for the Joint in 1940.

In 1942, Mayer began to receive increasing financial support for his activities.[28] His coffers began to fill even more rapidly in 1944, when American Jews finally realized that their religious brethren in Europe were in mortal danger. By then, Mayer had accrued funds amounting to 6.5 million dollars, of which 3.8 million was designated for support of Jewish refugees residing in Switzerland and fulfillment of prior obligations made toward French and Romanian Jews. The remaining 2.7 million dollars was made available for providing assistance to other European Jews as well as to Jewish refugees in Shanghai, China.[29] (These sums of money were not especially large when considering the urgency, complexity and magnitude of the crises for which they had been allocated.)

On August 21, Swiss authorities denied Becher entry into the country. The largely unproductive meeting between Mayer and SS officials was therefore held in the middle of a bridge—sitting on chairs—which spanned the border

---

[27] Information from a sworn statement that Kasztner made in London on September 13, 1945. *The Destruction,* vol. II, p. 908. Kasztner claimed that these negotiations pertained to "the cost of extermination with gas." In fact they dealt mainly with smaller concessions, such as a two-stage release of prisoners from Bergen-Belsen. Due to a lack of certain prerequisites, the Germans left the table without making any provisions with regard to the fate of Budapest Jews. Eichmann was aware that these negotiations were taking place.

[28] Mayer was born in South Africa in 1882. His outlook was strongly conservative. Though Mayer knew little of Jewish tradition, he always observed Orthodox Jewish religious prescriptions. He was strongly supportive of efforts to rescue Hungarian Jews in general and Zionist redemption plans in specific. Mayer's longstanding friendship with Nathan Schwalb, the head of the Zionist youth movement in Switzerland, likely played a large role in his support for the Hungarian Zionists.

[29] Bauer, pp. 346–347.

between Switzerland and the Reich between the towns of Höchst on the German side and St. Margarethen on the Swiss side. (Joseph J. Schwartz, the American director of the Joint's European division, was not permitted to take part in the discussions as originally planned. Negotiations were thus left solely to the Swiss citizen Mayer.) The encounter did produce one important result, though; the release of the first group of Hungarian Jews from Bergen-Belsen.

Kurt Becher, disappointed, introduced himself as the personal emissary of SS *Riechsführer* Himmler. He went on to state that he had been given full plenipotentiary powers to confer with the members of the coalition, *the representatives of world Jewry.* Becher again brought up the issue of the 10,000 trucks as a basis for exchange, which he supplemented with a request for agricultural machinery. He suggested that in return the Hungarian Jews would be released and leave by ships bound for the USA, where the specified vehicles and equipment could be loaded onto them for shipment back to the Reich.[30]

Becher also informed Mayer that he was prepared to discuss any issues pertaining to Hungarian Jews. He affirmed that Budapest's Jews were destined for deportation; only the financial and material sacrifices of international Jewry and the Allied powers could alter their fate.

Becher's threats were aimed primarily at manipulation and deception of Saly Mayer. In truth, the Eichmann team no longer had the strength necessary to carry out a systematic deportation of Budapest Jews. Romania's impending turnabout to the Allied side, which took place just a few days after the Becher–Mayer talks, further exacerbated Germany's already grave military situation. (Kasztner subsequently propagated the myth that the Germans had dropped their plans to deport the remaining 200,000 Jews in Budapest as a result of Becher's negotiations).

Mayer informed Becher that he was prepared to convey the German proposal to the appropriate authorities.[31] He also stipulated that any further negotiations would be contingent upon an immediate halt to the killing of Jews with gas. Thereafter Mayer focused his efforts not on reaching specific agreements regarding Budapest Jews, but to support for Jews throughout the territories still under Nazi occupation or control.

---

[30] Ibid., pp. 346–347.

[31] In this instance the WRB had prohibited Mayer from offering the Germans ransom money or goods. It also instructed him not to negotiate on behalf of the Joint. Thus Mayer embarked upon these discussions simply as a citizen of Switzerland and a leading member of the Swiss Jewish community.

Kasztner rapidly returned to Budapest for a meeting on the 25th with Undersecretary of State Miklós Mester. The next day, Komoly was briefly detained by two state-police detectives, but was released soon.[32] Becher notified Himmler of the outcome of the negotiations on this same day, reporting that "300 pieces" (that is, 300 Jews from Bergen-Belsen—*author's note*) had been released to Switzerland as a token of good faith.

As a result of Romania's *volte-face* on August 23, the prospect of Hungarian capitulation became the main item on the domestic agenda in Hungary. By contrast, the general staff of the Hungarian army was contemplating the particulars of a potential offensive in southern Transylvania. Politicians were primarily interested in the long-coveted idea of "bailing out" of the war with support from the United States and Great Britain, though they received nothing but rejection from the Western Allies, which repeatedly advised them to first approach Moscow with this initiative. Both Komoly and Kasztner expressed their opinions on these issues in meetings with Mester (Kasztner was familiar with Becher's viewpoints on them as well). Komoly was justifiably concerned that a Hungarian invasion of southern Transylvania would expose Jews and other nationalities living in the region to the menace of physical retaliation and other new threats to their security.

Regent Horthy's August 30 reception of Samu Stern offered a glimmer of hope to Budapest Jews who had not yet been deported. This presented previously ignored Jewish leaders with the chance to obtain the Regent's "most explicit possible expression of sympathy" toward the concept of emigration. The secret audience was a success: Horthy informed Stern that "*he was going to do everything within his power to help the Jews; with regard to emigration, he was of the opinion that the Jews should act as they see fit, that he did not want to interfere in this matter.*"[33]

Within this political vacuum, Jewish leaders and civilians waited eagerly for the occasional hint of good news, which they were typically inclined to believe and propagate. Horthy satisfied their need for optimism. (He had been presented with a preliminary request to endorse the emigration of 40,000 Hungarian Jews.) In truth, however, the isolated Regent of Hungary no longer had the authority to permit the emigration of even a small number of Jews, whose destiny lay solely in the hands of the Germans.

On August 24, Otto Winkelmann received a telegram from Himmler ordering him to put an *immediate halt* to the preliminary operations necessary

---

[32] The police agents were allegedly looking for the authors of anti-deportation leaflets.
[33] The diary of Ottó Komoly, p. 268.

for the deportation of Budapest Jews, which had initially been scheduled to begin on the 25th, but was subsequently postponed until the 28th. Himmler's directive stunned SS officials in Budapest, prompting some, like Veesenmayer, to request verification of his communiqué.[34] Himmler's order appears to indicate that in some high SS circles the fanatic effort to exterminate all Jews in Europe *fell into second place* behind the prospect of financial profit. The hypocrisy of "mercy" and "rescuing," the elements of which had been present earlier, now became more prominent. Human trade had undeniably come to form an essential part of what the SS expected to achieve through implementation of the *Endlösung.*

The status of the Rescue Committee rose perceptibly among certain Hungarian political leaders who had gained knowledge of the details surrounding the Swiss negotiations with the Germans. Their grandiose daydreams went so far as to envision Hungarian Jewish leaders being sent abroad to present the British and Americans with Hungary's peace conditions.

Also belonging to the catalogue of illusions that prevailed at this time was Komoly's frequently proclaimed conviction that there was no longer any discernible conflict between Jewish and Hungarian interests.[35]

Kasztner went to Switzerland for a second time on September 1.[36] Regarding his absence, Komoly maintained that he had left in order to conclude the ongoing negotiation process, suggesting that the *Germans would release the Jews under their control in exchange for sufficient compensation.* Kasztner returned six days later, hardly speaking about the results of his trip. On September 8 and 9, Kasztner was already discussing with SS *Hauptsturmführer* Seidl the technical issues pertaining to the transfer of control over the Columbus Street camp to Hungarian authorities and the gradual release of the Jews who resided there. They also conferred about the "payments covering the provision of necessities" to the Jewish labor camps in Austria.

On the 16th, Ottó Komoly met with Miklós Horthy Jr. in Buda Castle. Komoly's first order of business was to inquire on the prospects of the removal of anti-Jewish measures, and the possible appointment—"without any publicity for the time being"—of a cabinet commissioner to deal with Jewish matters. The

---

[34] *The Destruction*, vol. II, p. 481.

[35] From the diary of Ottó Komoly, p. 263. On September 2, for instance, Komoly agreed to take a secret nighttime flight to Switzerland in order to establish contacts and obtain "pertinent information," p. 269.

[36] Prior to Kasztner's departure for Switzerland, Ferenczy's liaison officer and interpreter, Leó Lullay, counseled him not to return to Hungary. Kasztner firmly rejected this advice.

function of this new office would first be to stop all excesses in the implementation of measures regarding Jews, then to "dismantle the entire existing
framework." These measures, in Komoly's view, would serve to avert the out-
break of the type of disorder that might pose a serious threat to the prospect of
harmonious coexistence between Hungarians and what remained of the Hungarian Jewish community. The head of the Rescue Committee also presented
arguments in favor of government sponsorship for systematic Jewish emigration
and other Zionist policies.

Horthy Jr. prefaced his response to Komoly's queries with the admission
that he was, by birth and education, an anti-Semite. This was inevitable in light
of "the way Jews were talked about in my parents' house."[37] During the discussion, Horthy went into rather confused monologues about the value of Jews,
remarking that "Hungarians need the competition that the Jews give them."

Horthy proceeded to declare that he thought that the Hungarian government was "horrible" and that if he had the power to do so, he would "have
some of them shot full of holes without thinking twice," while he would have
others "hanged." At the conclusion of the meeting he asked his guest for a
written summary of his petitions.

Komoly's assessment of Horthy the younger was that he was well inten-
tioned, though scatterbrained. He estimated that he was in need of advisers
"who could take matters into their own hands." It was as if Komoly sensed that
Miklós Horthy Jr. was about to make a reckless move that would provide the
Germans, of whom the Regent's son often spoke in mocking tones, with an
opportune windfall.

In the meantime, Kasztner was on the move again, traveling this time to
Pozsony. The suppression of the anti-German uprising in Northern Slovakia
had entailed new anti-Jewish measures and deportations there, prompting the
Slovak Rescue Committee to request immediate assistance from the Budapest
Rescue Committee. Kasztner dispatched a request for financial support to Saly
Mayer, and made inquiries on the spot into the prospect of redeeming lives for
money. Kasztner's efforts in Slovakia and his subsequent trip to Switzerland
proved unsuccessful: over the ensuing weeks, the SS deported 12,000 to 13,000
Jews from Slovakia.[38]

During this time, Shmuel ben Yaakaiv, aka Fülöp Freudiger, the former
member of the Budapest Jewish Council, wrote an account from the relative

---

[37] From the diary of Ottó Komoly, p. 288.
[38] About 8,000 of these Jews were sent to Auschwitz, while the rest wound up at either Bergen-Belsen or Theresienstadt. A further 2,000 Jews went into hiding in Pozsony (Bratislava).

comfort and security of Bucharest of the interval between the German occupation and the collective escape of which he had been a part. Freudiger's narra-
tive was highly critical of Kasztner and Brand on several fronts, particularly for
their alleged secretiveness and because they purportedly handled vital matters
pertaining to the entire Hungarian Jewish community as if they had *belonged
exclusively to Dr. Kasztner and his associates.*[39]

Freudiger's account included a detailed character profile of Kasztner:

> He is idealistic, competent, a man of vision with a great appetite for poli-
> tics; he is selfless and always willing to undertake personal risks; at the same
> time he is dictatorial in nature, jealous of the successes of others and terribly
> lax vis-à-vis deadlines and compliance with agreements.

Freudiger considered Kasztner to be a partisan politician to the core. He regarded Kasztner as an extremely ambitious man who strove to become the sole
master over the fate of Hungarian Jewry. Freudiger wrote the following assessment of Kasztner's voracious work habits:

> By nature, he was a Bohemian, an unconventional person who took not
> the slightest interest in the technical, practical and economic issues related
> to rescue work; in fact dealing with such matters was not to his taste at all...
> He nonetheless wanted to do everything himself; thus in order to maintain
> his hold over all the strings, he undertook more work than several people
> could have hoped to accomplish.

Among Freudiger's harshest criticisms was his assertion that Kasztner had
no organizational skills whatsoever.[40] This allegation is easily refuted: Lily
Ungár, the Zionist leader's secretary, later attested to just the opposite—to
Kasztner's broad perspective and keen organizational abilities.

On October 30, Kasztner traveled to Switzerland with Becher for a new
round of talks. Dr. Vilmos Billitz also went along on this trip, now as Becher's
*confidant.*[41] Kasztner was still idealistic, even though he was again forced to
recognize that the international community did not consider preservation of
what remained of Hungarian Jewry to be *nearly as important a question as he*

---

[39] Schmidt, p. 282.
[40] Ibid., pp. 280–281.
[41] From 21 September on, Billitz was continuously seeing the Swedish embassy secretary
Raoul Wallenberg, who also made contact with Becher via Billitz. In a letter to his mother,
Wallenberg described Becher as a "very pleasant man."

*had expected.* Some recent studies maintain that Zionist leaders in the Middle East deemed the establishment of a Jewish state to be more important than offering a firmer support to Hungarian Zionists, perhaps even than rescuing European Jewry.[42] The West remained indifferent as well. Many people considered the hell of Auschwitz and the tragedy of the Jews to represent only one of the many horrifying *episodes* in a ghastly war.

### d. Summer Months in Columbus Street

The Jewish camp under SS guard in Columbus Street continued to operate. Its ranks were increasing day by day with the arrival of additional persons, married couples, families hoping for an escape from the death trap. Some paid enormous amounts of money, practically everything they had, to be able to get in there. They were expecting a miracle, the departure of the "second group of emigrants."

There were Zionists among them, but their former adversaries, opposed to the movement, were also present. Their lives were at stake, and *if it were the Zionists who offered a chance for escape, then they would be happy to throw in their lot with them.*

Ottó Komoly and Kasztner made frequent visits to the camp, and often spent the night too because of the curfew. Those nights were spent in feverish discussions, of which records were being made by Lily Ungár, Kasztner's secretary. Kasztner also dictated letters, addressed mostly to Swiss organizations or persons.[43]

Waiting for the "second *aliyah*" in the Columbus Street camp in the summer months were 690 persons (229 from the capital and 461 from the countryside), 199 of whom were there along with family members, while the number of singles was 167. There were four babies in the crowd, 144 between the ages of 6 and 18. The oldest—from 75 to 86—numbered 27. By profession, 48 were craftsmen, 44 merchants, 20 clerks, 18 physicians, 13 rabbis, 12 professors or teachers, 11 lawyers, 11 factory-owners, 10 economists, 8 engineers and four pharmacists.

---

[42] Shrage Elam, *Hitler Fälscher*, (Verlag Car Ueberreuter: Vienna, 2000), pp. 33–35.

[43] TH V-129355. Note by secretary Lily Ungár to the Documentary Department of the Jewish Agency. A telegraphic code was found among her papers which were sent from Budapest to Hansi Brand at the end of the 1990s but was returned to the sender from there, stamped "Address unknown."

The provincial people came mostly from the ghettos, the brick factories and deporting railway stations. Some were summoned by the SS straight from the freight cars, or transported to Budapest in separate wagons, uncoupled from the rest of the train directly before its departure. "Lifting out" took place most of the time at the order of SS *Hauptsturmführer* Wisliceny.

That was how—as a result of negotiations between the Zionists and the SS—twenty "individuals of Jewish race" arrived on July 5th from Kaposvár, and 54 from Budakalász, 33 from Monor and 51 from Pápa[44] on the 7th. The next day another 22 came from Budakalász, then on the 9th, 40 from Sopron, and on the 14th, 14 internees arrived from Kistarcsa. Dezső Kanizsai's notes also provide information on the original place of residence of the provincial camp inmates "picked out" (or sometimes escaped) from among the deportees as well as of the contacts and protégés of the Zionists in the countryside.

According to the incomplete data, broken down by original residence, 51 of the camp inmates were from Pápa, 45 from Debrecen, followed by 44 from Szeged, 42 from Kolozsvár, 40 from Sopron, 31 from Újpest, 27 from Rákospalota, 20 from Kaposvár, 20 from Szabadka, 19 from Pestszenterzsébet, 14 from Békéscsaba, 12 from Szombathely, 11 from Berettyóújfalu, 9 from Kunszentmiklós, 8 from Sülelmed, six from Sárvár, 6 from Bácsalmás, 5 from Békés, 4 from Hódmezővásárhely, 4 from Monor, 3 from Kiskunfélegyháza, 3 from Szegvár, 3 from Törökszentmiklós, two each from Baja, Cegléd, Kecskemét, Kunszentmárton and Szentes, and one each from Bácsbodrog, Losonc and Pestszentlőrinc.[45]

With the rapid departure of Eichmann's staff,[46] the Columbus Street camp came under new threats from the Hungarian authorities. Komoly and Kasztner negotiated with SS *Hauptsturmführer* Dr. Seidl, who had been left behind, on how to avert these. Using delaying tactics, they succeeded in securing that the camp remained under the guard of the SS until September 23, after which date it was taken over by Hungarian authorities. (In the

---

[44] Zionist life in Pápa began at the end of the 19th century. Its summary is found in Gyula Jehuda Láng: *A pápai zsidóság emlékkönyve* (Memorial Book of the Jewry of Pápa), a publication of the Memorial Committee of Jews from Pápa living in Haifa, Israel. 1972, pp. 66–67.

[45] "A" Columbus ("The" Columbus), p. 65.

[46] Following the about-face of Romania and the rapid advance of the Soviet forces in Moldava, Eichmann—along with several members of his staff—were engaged in rescue operations regarding the ethnic German population in the Bánát and Bácska and the Saxons of Transylvania in September and October 1944. These people were trekking in endless wagon trains across Hungary to the Austrian territories of the Reich. See Lóránt Tilkovszky: *Ez volt a Volksbund* (This was the *Volksbund*), Kossuth Kiadó 1978, pp. 330–335.

meantime, several families lost hope and left the camp. They demanded, in an increasingly loud voice, that their money and valuables be returned. Some, however, scared by the rumors circulating in the capital, scuttled back to the camp rapidly.)

The camp door—as a residence of Jews in Budapest—ought to have been marked by the Star of David in the prescribed manner. To avoid this, Ottó Komoly secured the approval of Red Cross Delegate Friedrich Born to have a notice certifying International Red Cross protection put over the door. Still, with all this going on, the passing of time and the hoping continued.

## e. More Kidnappings and Arrests

In September, Regent Miklós Horthy and his entourage discussed strategies aimed at extracting Hungary from the war—the so-called "bail-out" plans. By this time Horthy's inner circle had lost all its capacity for maintaining confidentiality: within days, the "secret" was out and circulating throughout Budapest.

Most of the current hearsay reached Staff Colonel Gyula Kádár at his quarters in the Nándor Barracks as well.[47]

Budapest was a strange city. Gossip and personal speculation swarmed about like flies in a stable. News traveled by word of mouth: the Lakatos government was the 'bail-out government;' the Horthy boy's offices were the 'bail-out' offices; Horthy is going to capitulate, and so on and so forth.

Were the Germans the only ones not to hear this kind of talk? Looking out the windows of the Nándor Barracks, from which the main entrance of the German embassy was also visible, I often saw Szálasi[48] arrive by car in the company of the future foreign minister, Gábor Kemény, and sometimes others as well. I saw well-dressed civilians and uniformed officers sneaking into the building—traffic at the German embassy had increased noticeably. I

---

[47] The anti-Nazi Colonel Kádár had been delivered from German captivity to the safe custody of a Hungarian bodyguard regiment. The barracks today houses Institute and Museum of Military History.

[48] Ferenc Szálasi was a leading political figure of the Hungarian radical right, who became Prime Minister of Hungary on October 16, 1944.

wondered if the architects of the 'bail-out' plan had anticipated these developments?[49]

Gyula Kádár's concerns proved to be justified. The Germans gained enough preliminary intelligence to thwart Hungary's effort to withdraw from the war. (The German secret services understood the objective of *Operation Panzerfaust* to be the prevention of Hungary's conclusion of a separate peace with the Allies.)

The focus of activities in the German embassy on Castle Hill was to ensure that the policies of the Hungarian government would stay in agreement with those of the Reich. Winkelmann was, in turn, responsible for harmonizing the objectives and operations of the SS, Sipo and the Gestapo. The SS general gave priority to prevention. He concluded that the SS could force Horthy into a position of total isolation if the key members of the Regent's inner circle— principally his loyal army generals such as Szilárd Bakay, Kálmán Hardy, Béla Miklós and Lajos Veress—were detained. This would eliminate the increasingly proclaimed possibility of Hungary's "bail-out."

The Germans decided to achieve their objectives through a series of commando raids and kidnappings to be conducted in Budapest. The SS planned to first abduct the anti-German commander of the Budapest army corps, Lieutenant-General Bakay, and his aide-de-camp, Tibor Versényi, in early October. The second abduction was to be that of the Regent's son one week later. The Gestapo prepared with great vigor for these operations, bugging phones and issuing status reports. German military tacticians began planning for the possible armed occupation of Buda Castle, speculating whether it would be more easily taken by infantry or paratroopers.

The SS seizure of Bakay and his aide-de-camp, who had worked to contain the increasingly dynamic Arrow Cross movement, significantly curtailed the Regent's room to maneuver. The Germans had seized the two officers in the midst of an artificial traffic jam staged in front of the Hungária Hotel on the dark and misty night of October 8. The Lieutenant-General was a decisive and resolute commander who could have achieved a great deal in fighting German aggression.

Miklós Horthy Jr. was also well on his way toward an unexpected visit from the SS. The younger Horthy was well known for his anti-German rhetoric. He often met heedlessly with compromising groups and individuals and gave no

---

[49] Gyula Kádár, *A Ludovikától Soprokőhídáig* [From the Ludovika Academy to Sopronkőhída, (Magvető Könyvkiadó, 1978) vol. II, pp. 727–728.

apparent thought to the possibility that anything he said might be brought to the attention of the SS. According to Winkelmann, "I also complained to Lakatos[50] about Horthy Jr., who seemed to take great pleasure in his use of the term *German swine* in public and showered us with outrageous threats."[51]

Dr. Ernő Pető, a member of the Jewish Council, made several visits *incognito* to Buda Castle. According to Pető, the Regent's son was wary of German spies, but often simply could not restrain himself. On one occasion Pető was chatting in the parlor with Horthy's personal secretary, Dr. Dezső Onódy, when Miklós Horthy the younger entered the room. *"When he came in he asked Dr. Onódy if the technicians had been there. Onódy told him that they had, and that they had examined the room top to bottom and found no secret microphones anywhere. Horthy then declared, nearly shouting, that since he was now free to speak his mind openly, he would state his opinion that those stinking Germans would all be dead soon, the bastards."[52]*

The younger Horthy's October 15 departure from the Buda Castle was ill-considered and unnecessary. His supposed meeting on Eskü Square with an emissary of Tito turned out to be a German secret-service ruse that ended in a deadly shootout and his abduction.[53]

Following his apprehension, the SS special forces unit led by *Obersturmbannführer* Otto Skorzeny, operating under the pseudonym Major Wolf, took Horthy and Félix Bornemissza, the director of the National Free Port who had unwittingly provided the venue for the bogus meeting, directly to a waiting airplane, which flew the pair to Gestapo headquarters in Vienna, from where they were taken by truck to Mauthausen.

In the course of his abduction, SS agents had punched and pistol-whipped the "plotter" Horthy, leaving a gash on his head.[54] They showed the two cap-

[50] Colonel Géza Lakatos was the Prime Minister of Hungary from August 31, 1944 until October 15, 1944.

[51] Budapest Archives, "Documents Pertaining to the Budapest Imprisonment of Otto Winkelmann," no. 39, November 10, 1945, p. 344.

[52] *Tekintet*, no. 4, 1989, p. 48.

[53] This operation was primarily the work of the Gestapo, which employed the Hungarian army captain Károly Marty as an informant regarding Horthy's movements (Marty had been the confidential secretary of Major General István Ujszászy, who was already in German custody). Höttl, p. 263. The SS officer Klages was lethally wounded by the bullets of Hungarian bodyguards in the shootout.

[54] The mémoirs of Miklós Kállay dispute Bornemissza's assertion that Horthy suffered a head wound during his kidnapping, though the former prime minister concurred that he had been severely beaten, even to the point of unconsciousness. According to Kállay, SS and Gestapo agents then pulled a sack over Horthy's head and took him away. Miklós Kállay, "Magyar-

tives no mercy. Horthy was to spend seven bitter months in Gestapo captivity alongside Bornemissza.

The expectations of the SS proved to be correct: following the kidnapping of Miklós Horthy Jr., the seventy-seven-year-old Regent became largely acquiescent to German demands, though it would be an exaggeration to attribute his eventual abdication solely to this circumstance. A succession of betrayals from within the military and the indecisive leadership of Prime Minister Géza Lakatos and the vacillating comportment of Adjutant-General Antal Vattay also played into the hands of the Germans.

The occupiers acted within days—much more decisively and effectively than Regent Horthy and his circle. The contrast between the two sides was striking. The Germans demonstrated a vast degree of readiness and resolve. Political, military and police officials in the Reich coordinated their efforts down to the last detail,[55] enabling them to quickly shatter the Hungarian pipe-dream of "bailing out" of the war.

Höttl mentions in his memoirs that the SS seized Lieutenant-General Kálmán Hardy from his bed, without encountering resistance, on the 16th.[56] Hardy was subsequently held captive in Sopronkőhida, on the western border of Hungary.

On October 15, two Budapest-based armed gendarme battalions were also put on a state of high alert. However, they waited in vain for deployment orders, because the Gestapo had taken their commanding officer, Major General Endre Temesvári, into custody by the following morning. The Szálasi government, which the Germans had placed in power the previous day, then assumed direct command of the two units.

The Gestapo also arrested Gendarme Colonel Gyula Király, the head of the interior ministry's public safety department, in his office after he had transmitted a radio message to all units of the Hungarian gendarmerie stationed at borders and airports directing them to prevent the Germans from taking Miklós Horthy Jr. out of the country.

The deposed Regent left Hungary with three members of his family and a small retinue of attendants, traveling under armed guard via Vienna to the Bavarian castle of Schloss Waldbichl, built at an altitude of 700 meters, where they spent the following months under the supervision a hundred SS troopers

---

ország miniszterelnöke voltam 1942–1944" [I was the prime minister of Hungary 1942–1944], in *Európa-História,* vol. II, 1991, p. 218.

[55] *The Destruction,* vol. I, p. 331.

[56] The Danube River patrol commander was a confidant and relative of Regent Horthy.

under the command of a Commander Hueber and nine Gestapo guards.[57] (Benito Mussolini had also spent a few days at this castle after the Germans had liberated him from captivity in 1943.)

The Gestapo, with the backing of the newly appointed interior minister, Gábor Vajna, detained the former interior minister Péter Schell, the former foreign minister Colonel Árpád Hennyey, the former minister of religion and public education Iván Rakovszky, and several other former high-ranking officials from the prime minister's office, confining them in the prison located on Gyorskocsi Street. Péter Schell was then taken to a concentration camp, from where he was eventually transferred to a detention facility in South Tirol.[58]

---

[57] See the following memoirs of Count Ilona Gyulai Edelshem, the wife of Horthy's Deputy Regent: *Becsület és kötelesség, 1945-1998* [Duty and Honor, 1945-1998], (Európa Könyvkiadó, 2001), pp. 9-10.

[58] Barron Péter Schell (1908-1974) served as the Hungarian government's mobilization commissioner from 1939 until 1944, doubling as the public alimentation commissioner beginning in 1942. On September 25, 1944, Schell was named Undersecretary of State for Internal Affairs, an office from which he was promoted to the post of Interior Minister just a few weeks later, on October 12.

1. Members of Ha-shomer Ha-tzair in Garany, 1943

2. Ottó Komoly, president of the Hungarian Zionist Association

3. Rezső Kasztner, his wife and daughter

4. The Majestic house on Svábhegy, Eichmann's headquarters in Budapest

5. Hansi Brand (Mrs. Jenő Brand)

6. Salom Offenbach (Sándor Offenbach)

7. Ernő Szilágyi

8. Joel Brand (Jenő Brand)

9. Edmund Veesenmayer SS-Standartenführer, Hitler's plenipotentiary in Hungary

10. Kurt Alexander Becher,
SS-Standartenführer

11. Franz Novak SS-Hauptsturmführer, "railway specialist" of Hungarian deportations

12. Adolf Eichmann SS-Obersturmführer,
organizer of the *Endlösung*

13. Group of Hungarian Jews on the ramp in Auschwitz-Birkenau, after arrival

14. Aerial photograph of the Auschwitz-Birkenau concentration camp complex, taken by the US Air Force on June 26, 1944. On the same day, the American Department of Defence declared that an air raid against the camp was "impossible".

15. A scene of deadly working conditions in the Mauthausen concentration camp

16. Zionist leaders in Colombus Street. From left to right: Ottó Komoly, Hansi Brand, Rezső Kasztner, Zvi Goldfarb, and Ferenc Révész

17. László Devecseri with his wife

18. Miklós Langer, one of the heroes of the "document war"

19. Carl Lutz, Swiss Vice-Consul in Budapest among the ruins
of the British Embassy, February 23, 1945

20. Jews of Budapest queue in front of the "Glass House" for Swiss protective papers

21. Gendarme Lieutenant Colonel Vitéz László Ferenczy,
conductor of Hungarian deportations

22. Hans Mauthner (János Mauthner), member of a Hungarian
industrial magnate family, interned to Vienna

23. Friedrich Born, International Red Cross representative in Budapest

24. Raoul Wallenberg as a young man

25. Raoul Wallenberg with his Hungarian co-workers

26. Jews arrested during an Arrow Cross raid in Teleki square

27. Miklós Schweiger, Becher's protégé and one of his testifiers

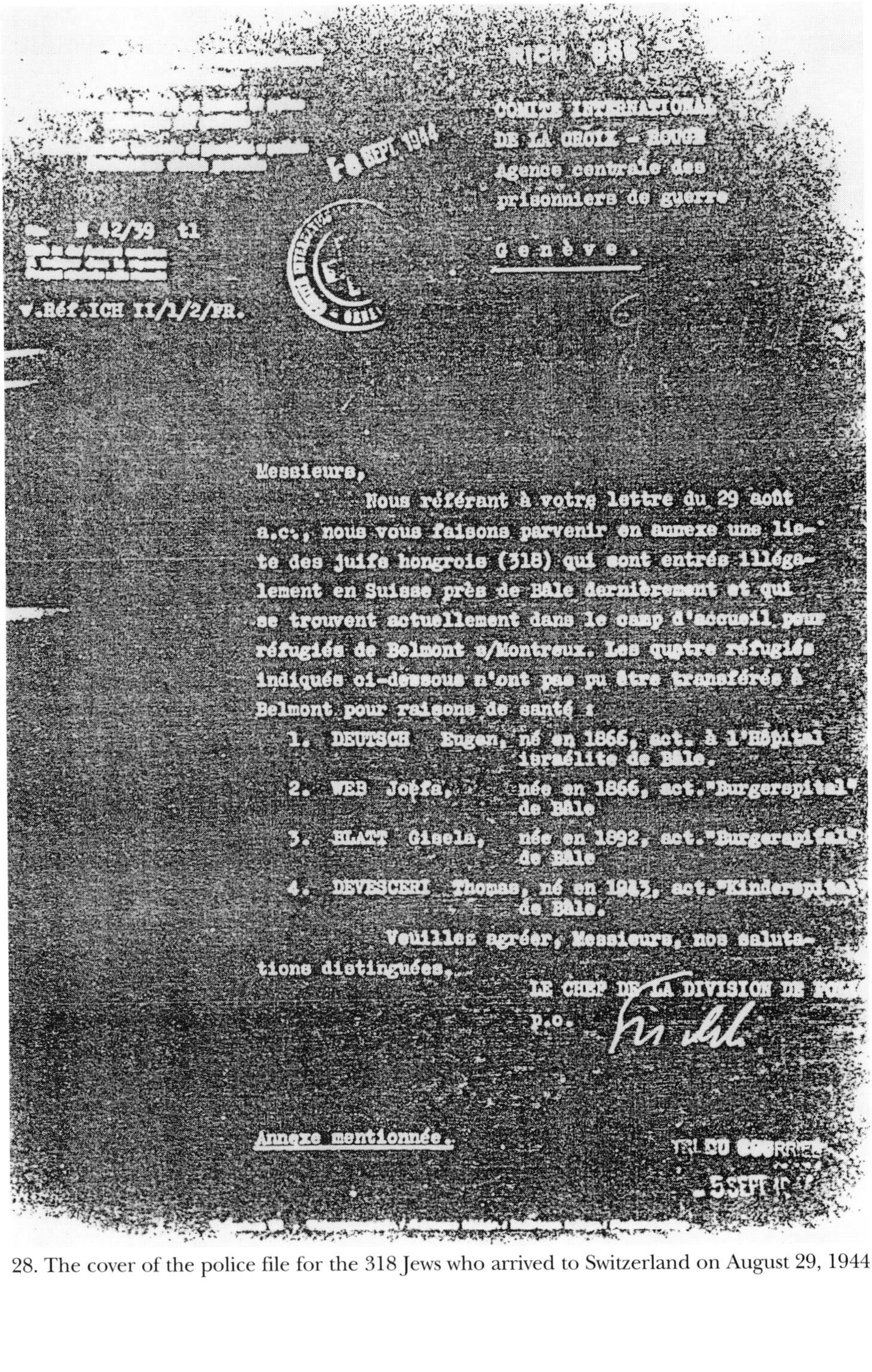

COMITÉ INTERNATIONAL
DE LA CROIX - ROUGE
Agence centrale des
prisonniers de guerre

G e n è v e.

N 42/39 t1

V.Réf.ICH II/1/2/FR.

Messieurs,

Nous référant à votre lettre du 29 août
a.c., nous vous faisons parvenir en annexe une lis-
te des juifs hongrois (318) qui sont entrés illéga-
lement en Suisse près de Bâle dernièrement et qui
se trouvent actuellement dans le camp d'accueil pour
réfugiés de Belmont s/Montreux. Les quatre réfugiés
indiqués ci-dessous n'ont pas pu être transférés à
Belmont pour raisons de santé :

1. DEUTSCH  Eugen, né en 1866, act. à l'Hôpital
              israélite de Bâle.

2. WEB Joffa,      née en 1866, act."Burgerspital"
              de Bâle

3. HLATT Gisela,   née en 1892, act."Burgerspital"
              de Bâle

4. DEVESCERI Thomas, né en 1943, act."Kinderspital"
              de Bâle.

Veuillez agréer, Messieurs, nos saluta-
tions distinguées,

LE CHEF DE LA DIVISION DE POLICE

P.O.

Annexe mentionnée.

28. The cover of the police file for the 318 Jews who arrived to Switzerland on August 29, 1944

Aus verschiedenen brieflichen Berichten aus Budapest vom
24.bis 28.Juli ,besonders aus einem Brief vom 28.Juli vom
Präsidenten der ungarischen zionistischen Organisation lässt
sich zusammenfassend das Problem der ungarischen Juden fol-
gendermassen charakterisieren:

Infolge der allgemeinen politischen Lage ( Attentat auf Hitler) und militärischen Lage spitzt sich der Gegensatz zwischen
den ungarischen verantwortlichen Stellen und den entsprechen-
den deutschen Behörden immer mehr zu.Die Ungarn versuchen,in
Hinsicht auf ihre Nachkriegsprobleme den katastrophalen Ein-
druck ihres Vorgehens gegen die Juden einigermassen zu ver-
wischen.Seit dem 10.Juli sind die Deportationen eingestellt
und deutsche Polizei bestärkt  von ungarischen Extremisten
versuchen,mit einigem Erfolg,den besorgten ungarischen Behörden,Juden zu entreissen und zu verschleppen.Auch in dieser
Haltung steckt ein gewisses Mass von Spiel,Berechnung und
Verstellung.Immerhin haben die ungarischen Stellen eine positive Haltung gegenüber dem Problem der etwa 40.000 Certifi-
cat-Inhaber bezogen.

Die schweizerische Gesandtschaft hat ein Büro eröffnet,das
in der Zusammensetzung und in der Funktion das Palästina-Amt
Ungarns vollständig ersetzt.Der jüdische Partner der schweiz.
Gesandtschaft ist Herr KRAUSZ,der zusammen mit den ungarischen
Stellen und der Schweizer Delegation auf regelmässige und
natürliche Art die Auswanderung vorbereitet.Die Listen werden
aufgestellt,deren Namen von den ungarischen und deutschen Behörden genehmigt sein müssen.Die Leute sollen in Zügen nach
CONSTANZA geführt werden,die Transit-Visen stehen bereit,
Schiffe werden durch die zionistische Stelle in ISTAMBUL
vorbereitet,das Kollektiv-Visa in Ungarn sei ebenfalls in
Vorbereitung,damit Gruppen von je 2000 Auswanderer in einer
Reise befördert werden können.Einige Tage vor der Abreise
sollen jedesmal die 2000 Interessenten in jüdischen Häusern
gesammelt werden.Die Transporte sollen von schweizer Beamten
begleitet werden.

Dieser Aktion steht in schroffen Gegensatz die Haltung der
Deutschen gegenüber.Das"Sondereinsatz-Kommando ",das von der
"rechten Hand " HIMMLER's autorisiert ist,hat mit anderen
jüdischen,auch zionistischen Gruppen Verhandlungen eingelei-

./.

tet,die folgendes Bild ergeben :

1.- Man ist über den Misserfolg der Mission JOEL's verstimmt
und misstrauisch geworden.

2.- Der Bedarf an Traktoren ist jedoch so gross,dass man den-
noch verhandlungsbereit ist.Um Zeit zu gewinnen,um die Bezie-
hungen mit der GESTAPO aufrecht zu erhalten,um Menschen zu
retten,haben einige Gruppen von Zionisten scheinbar die Nach-
folge JOEL's angetreten.Sie haben Folgendes der GESTAPO angeboten : Schafsfelle in der Slowakei ; Gold und Edelsteine in
Ungarn ; 300 Traktoren in der Schweiz.Dafür haben sie einen
Anfangskredit in Ungarn selbst von 3.000.000 sfrs aufgestellt
und einen von 2.000.000 sfrs bei S;M.in Aussicht gestellt.
Im Ganzen haben sie für 30.000.000 sfrs Waren angeboten,denn
durch ihren Raub in Ungarn seien die deutschen Verhandlungs-
partner einigermassen verwöhnt.

Jedoch interessieren sie die Traktoren fast ausschliesslich.
Die Tauschquote betrage : 1000 Juden pro 10 Traktoren.Der
den Unterhändlern in der Slowakei mitgeteilte Bericht,dass sich
in der Schweiz 300 Traktoren als mögliche Tauschobjekte be-
fänden,habe erlaubt,bis jetzt 17.000 Juden vor Auschwitz zu
retten,die sich aber noch in deutscher Hand befinden.Ein Teil
davon der Zug mit den 1200 Reisenden und ein anderer mit
1660 Reisenden befände sich ausserhalb Ungarns,vielleicht in
Bühenbelzen.Ueber den Verbleib der restlichen 14.000 besteht
den Briefen nach keine Klarheit.Die Berichte über B.B.stammen
anscheinend von slowakischen Freunden der Briefschreiber.
600 Juden befinden sich in Budapest selbst (Columbiastrasse 46)
"unter dem Schutze" der Deutschen.

Um Juden vor Auschwitz zu retten,verlangen die Deutschen Unter-
händler jetzt,da ihre Politik darin besteht,jetzt "unter dem
ungarischen Judentum die notwendigen Arbeitskräfte auszupumpen
und den Rest des für sie wertlosen Menschenmaterials für wert-
volle Ware zu verkaufen" mit dem Joint-Vertreter Dr.SCHWARZ
in LISBONNE zu verhandeln und die Lieferung von Traktoren ins
Werk zu setzen.Das Verhandlungsthema lautet : " Ohne Traktoren
keine Juden".

An Dr.SCHWARZ ging am 28.7.ein diesbezügliches Telegramm
zwecks Zusammenkunft gegen den 4-5-August zwischen dem GESTAPO-
Chef Ungarns,zweier Mitarbeiter aus Berlin,ISRAEL und DR.SCH.

Die ungarischen Zionisten kennen den abschlägigen Bescheid an
JOEL von Seiten Amerikas.Sie klammern aber ihre Hoffnung an

./.

29. Extract from a memorandum for the presidency of the International Red Cross,
August 6, 1944

30. The newspaper Független Magyarország (Independent Hungary)
on Kasztner, December 30, 1946. "Resister or traitor?"

# A NAGY EMBERVÁSÁR

A magyar zsidóság tragédiájának történetében ma már a legismertebb nevek egyike: dr Kasztner Rezső cionista erdélyi ujságiró, a Segitő és Mentési Bizottság (Waadat) budapesti meghizolja. Az ő szerepléséhez fűződött az a kisérlet: miként lehetne megmenteni a magyar zsidóságot a németek kezéből. Tömören: az a magyar zsidóságot a németektől. A nagyközönség annak idejéről hallgatott és tudott valamit. Tudta, hogy ilyen bizottság működik és annak látható feje: dr Kasztner Rezső és tudta azt, hogy akiknek sok pénze van: megmenekülhet a biztos gázhaláltól. Miként, hogyan: csak foszlányok jutottak el hozzá. A kisérletbe csak morzsák hallottak ki, igen csekélyre azokat a száma, akik valóban kisiklottak ezzel az ákcióval az SS halálos öleléséből.

A német hadsereg bukása és Hitler letünése után egyre sürübben sodródott a viln közepébe a Waadat akciója és dr Kasztner szerepe. Vádak és gyanúsitások sziszegése terelte egyre jobban a figyelmet feléje. Végül is a mult évi baseli cionista kongresszon a vádak nyilt formát öltöttek. Dr Kasztner Rezső erre elkészitette nagyszabású beszámolóját a nagy embervásárról és az egy kiküldött vizsgálóbizottság elé terjesztette. A 209 gépelt old las jelentés néhány példányban készült el. Ebből egy példány a "Haladás" birtokába jutott. Elolvastuk és ugy találtuk: ez nem maradhat bizalmas akta, hanem megköveteli a legszélesebb nyilvánosságot. Olyan drámai történet bontakozik ki ebből a munkából, amelyhez hasonló rig van a háború után keletkezett zsidó-jellegü irodalomban. Egészében is, részleteiben is rettenetes erejü dokumentum mi történhetett a XX. század közepén, földi lények mülivel, milyen aljassáz, kapzsiság, becstelenség kisérte a nemzeti szociali-st antiszemita irtó háborut, miként akarták árt lan tömegek sorsából, életéből, szenvedéséből és kétségbeeséséből a kulturvilág martalócai vagyont ba^rácsolni. Nem a szakvénnyá vált borzalmak és hulálnak kinjait beszéli el ez a könyv, hanem a zsákmányra éhes rabló SS-tisztek üzleti robantát, a vérrel és szivekkel üzött becstelen alkut, a legaláfóbb vásárt, amelyes az ó-kor rabszolgakereskedőinek rideg és lelketlen rendszere nem is eshe-tik egyazon megitélés alá.

A "Haladás" ezt a történetet a közönség elé tárja. Több folytatásban közlini fogjuk dr Kasztner Rezső beszámolóját. Azokat a részleteket, amik nagyjában ismeretesek, természetesen mellőzzük vagy rövid kivonatban adjuk, de mindazt, ami uj, jellemző és történelmi értékü kiveszük a német szövegből. Nem szivesen használunk bulvár stilust, de nincs megközelithőb jelző: szenzáciős és izgalmas könyv lapjai ütik ki egy szégyenteljes és fájdalmas história könnyét és gyászát elénk.

## BEVEZETÉ:

### I.

A budapesti Waadat Ezra we Hazolah (Segitő és Mentő Bizottsáġ) a továbbiakban röviden: Waadat, terjeszti be az alábbiakban jelentését a maga munkájáról: 1944 március 19-ig munkánkat főleg a lengyel, szlovák, jugoszláv zsidóság megmenteise foglalta le, Magyarország német megszállásával 'parkodásaink a magyar zsidó-ság védelmre terjedi ki; végül

dolgoztunk a német kézen levő maradványok megmentésén.

Magyarország német-megszállása 800.000 zsidó lélek haldoló itél tét jelentette. A viszonylagos szabad-ság, miben ezek a zsidók éltek és maga uz, hogy egyáltalában élnek, évek óta szálka volt a németek szemében. Most elhatározták, hogy ezt a csakmem érintetlen szigetet a elpusztitott európai zsidóság te-rületén, maradék nélkül felszámol-juk.

Mégis sikerült az ülés erejét Budapesten felfogni. A magyar zsidó-ság több mint egyharmada életben maradt. A lét körül vivott ellen-állásban Budapest bizonyult a leg-aktívabbnak és legsikeresebbnek.

Az alábbi beszámoló ennek a munkának legfontosbb fejezetét beszéli ti. A kívülálló számára sok minden paradoxnak, érthetetlennek tünhet fel, sőt hihet-ltennek fog lásze'ni. Őrült idők voltak. Mindaz, ami tör-tént, nekünk is, akik átéltük, meg-

foghatatlannak, kisértetiesnek tünik fel. Az emberi gondolkozás normá-lis mértékével nem is lehet felfogni.

A harcot is rendkívüli eszközök-kel és módszerekkel kellett meg-vivni.

A zsidó nyilvánosság még ma is aránylag keveset tud a mi akciónk-ról. Hiányos vagy elferdített hírek vezették félre.

A jelen beszámoló megpróbálko-zik vele, hogy a történtek áttekint-hető fejezetei a történelmi igaz-ságnak megfelelően feltárja. Fonto-sabb pontjában olyan tényeket gyüjt egybe, amit magunk éltünk át vagy ellenőrizhettünk.

### II.

Miként volt lehetséges zsidó éle-teket az SS kezéből kiragadni? A zsidó tragédia kényes fejezetéhez érünk el ezzel, amit alig ismernek és meg nem világítottak. Tény, hogy 1944 nyarától kezdve fokoza-tosan alábbhagyott a zsidóság to-tális kiírtása. Ez a hasadás a ná-cik politikai rendszerében, mely-ben az antiszemitizmus a feltétlen érvényes megváltozhatatlan cél maradt, Magyarország német meg-szállásával egyidejüleg és annak alkalmából következett be.

Hitler nem revidiálta álláspont-ját. A zsidóüldözéshen hozzáférhe-tetlenül megszállottságban tombolt: utolsó pillanatig ragaszkodott ahhoz, hogy minden zsidót ki kell irtani.

De 1944 közepétől Himmler, az SS mindenható feje, a totális halálos itélet végrehajtója egyre vontatot-

## 9. An Extraordinary Hostage: János Mauthner and the Deputy Chief of the Gestapo in Vienna

The SS profited immensely from the assets and property that it had "assumed" from the Weiss–Chorin–Mauthner–Kornfeld–Heinrich family. Those who had been sent to either Portugal or Switzerland were able to start new lives in those countries; the situation was, however, much different for those who had been taken to Vienna as hostages of the Reich.

The original motive for holding the hostages was to retain leverage over the activities of family members permitted to leave for neutral countries: namely, the five hostages would be forced to bear the consequences for any public display of opinion critical of the Reich, the Führer or the National Socialist system that fellow family members residing abroad dared to make. The twenty-seven-year-old János Mauthner was the first among the hostages to have direct contact with Dr. Karl Ebner, the deputy chief of the Vienna Gestapo who maintained authority over Jewish affairs in the city.

While the members of my family were placed under guard in railway carriages, I met with Dr. Ebner, the head of the Vienna Gestapo. My main objective during these discussions was to gain some sort of relief for my relatives during their stay in Vienna. Ebner, on the other hand, asked that we make it as easy as possible for him to watch over us. I am not sure whether Ebner knew who we were and what we were doing in Vienna, but my first impression of him was surprisingly good.[1]

[1] Magyar Államrendőrségi Államvédelmi Osztály, Népügyészi Kirendeltség [Hungarian State Police State Defense Division, People's Prosecutor Section] 3378/1947. ÁVO Nű. Sz., June 21, 1947, p. 3. Archives of the Ministry of the Interior, 1980. This document, which is the source of all quotes from Mauthner, seems to have been misplaced. The evidence, which first appeared on page 210 of *A Gestapo Magyarországon* [The Gestapo in Hungary], has been collected with the kind help of Gábor Baczoni.

The Gestapo governed the movements and everyday activities of the hostages during their stay in Hitzing, a pleasant residential suburb of Vienna. The Hungarian detainees were not permitted to visit public places or have social contacts; all of their telephone calls and correspondence were subject to secret-police censorship. Compliance with Gestapo regulations was, however, often left up to the hostages. Ebner paid little attention to them, delegating issues related to their oversight to his secretary, SS *Hauptsturmführer* Rudolf Wagner. After less that a month and a half of captivity, the energetic and self-assured János Mauthner took matters in his own hands:

> At the end of August, I heard from my friends that more and more Hungarian refugees had been arriving in Vienna; this gave me the idea of organizing a relief office for the large number of decent people who were among them and would be in need of assistance after arriving in the city. I first approached Kartal, the Hungarian consul-general, with this idea; I then informed Ebner, who again gave me the impression of being a surprisingly humanitarian and benevolent person.
>
> I don't know if his support of the racially and politically persecuted, which was very risky in Vienna at that time, was a product of genuine personal conviction or if he had simply anticipated the collapse of the Reich and was attempting to feather his cap. The reports I got on him from the president of the Vienna Jewish Community and the director of the Vienna Jewish Hospital were impeccable.[2] Without further investigation of his motives, I utilized his nearly unlimited power within the city of Vienna to promote my own objective of rescuing as many good Hungarian people as possible.
>
> The two leading officials at the Hungarian consulate (the consul-general, Dr. Kartal, and the vice-consul, Dr. Stephaich)[3] were honorable and not in the least right-wing Hungarians, who were prepared to support my endeavor in every way possible. With their help I was able to open my first office, which I called the Royal Hungarian Consulate General Relief Station (*Magyar Királyi Főkonzulátus Segélyhelye*).

---

[2] Gestapo officials had decided that it would be to their organization's advantage to permit a few Jewish organizations and institutions, such as these, to continue functioning.

[3] Both Pál Stephaich and Jenő Kartal had been assigned to the Hungarian consulate general in Vienna, which operated under the aegis of the Hungarian embassy in Berlin, in the months preceding Mauthner's arrival to the city—Stephaich in December 1943 and Kartal on March 19, 1944.

The genuine need for a relief office (*Fürsorgestelle*) such as established by Mauthner at 18 Panigl Gasse was quickly confirmed. An increasing number of refugees arrived from Hungary. Many of these desperate and confused people, families with half their members lost, frightened civil servants and others who had lost or abandoned all their possessions in Hungary, were in dire need of organized assistance, information and guidance. Mauthner lent his assistance as well, though all of this proved to be only temporary. Arriving to Vienna along with the "decent" Hungarian refugees was an increasing number of radical right-wing elements, whose suspicion, meddling and intense hatred soon subverted the operations of the relief office.

Naturally the work of the delegation fast became common knowledge. My activities were reported to the Gestapo countless times, but Ebner was always able to shield me. However, in January 1945, news of our work reached German officials who had the authority to place Ebner under arrest. I was interned in Znaim. A Swiss doctor arrived in Vienna immediately to take control over the delegation. A team of aides was soon sent from Switzerland to help the new director.

Mauthner made the above statements already in Budapest as a suspect during an interrogation that took place on June 20, 1947 at the State Defense Division of the Hungarian State Police (*Magyar Államrendőrség Államvédelmi Osztály*). He was probably unaware that an anonymous informant had filed a denunciation against him, thus placing him in the sights of the latest organization or repression, the Communist AVH, that had emerged in Hungary. The postcard addressed to the Political Police (Budapest, Andrássy Boulevard 60) reflected the "spirit of the new era." Informant XY concluded his denunciation of Mauthner with the following sentence: "I am writing as an anonymous member of the working class, because I'm too busy to present personal testimony."[4] The identity of this informant is still shrouded in obscurity. He definitely made life unpleasant for Mauthner, who was forced to endure an official inquiry into his wartime activities that lasted for nearly a year and a half.

---

[4] The text of the letter, full of spelling errors and conceived in a primitive manner, is as follows: "M. Weiss' grandson, János Mauthner, has arrived. He escaped with 47 others and the help of the SS—betraying the country!! I am surprised that the esteemed police haven't arrested him yet!!!! He lives, Vadász St. 12. He's carousing and squandering money. We request swift action ... With highest regards, XY." According to official records Mauthner lived at no. 3 Petőfi Square. He declared himself to have no assets or property and that he subsisted on money provided to him by his mother.

Mauthner's testimony accurately reflected the situation that prevailed in 1944 and 1945. Documents recently unearthed at the Geneva archives of the IRC confirm that the Gestapo's Viennese hostage transcended every boundary, providing Hungarian refugees with vital humanitarian assistance under increasingly menacing circumstances.

Mauthner had prior contacts with the International Red Cross. Following the German occupation of Hungary in March 1944, Jean de Bavier, the Budapest envoy of the IRC, helped Mauthner find refuge from the Gestapo, placing him under his personal protection at the Duna Palota Hotel. Though the deputy Gestapo chief Karl Ebner accorded to him freedom of movement in Vienna, Mauthner could not have undertaken his bold initiative without the aid of the increasingly influential IRC. On October 4, Mauthner held lengthy discussions with the German delegate of the IRC International Committee, Robert Schirmer.[5]

Schirmer offered IRC officials at the agency's headquarters in Geneva a detailed account of his acquaintance with the Hungarian hostage in Vienna and his relationship with Ebner. In a confidential report on the victims of National Socialist persecution submitted to Jean de Schwarzenberg, the head of the IRC department in charge of Jewish relief operations,[6] Schirmer wrote that Mauthner had obtained a permit that had enabled him to visit Hungarian deportees at labor camps in the vicinity of Vienna. Schirmer likewise stated in this report that Mauthner was also able to speak freely with Hungarian Jews who were performing forced labor in the city and that he had been providing critical assistance to refugees who had fled Hungary before the advancing Red Army.

Referring to the prospect of a growing wave of emigration to Austria from the east, János Mauthner advised Schirmer to establish civilian relocation camps for Hungarian refugees. According to Mauthner's plan, the IRC would then help the Hungarians at these camps to gain asylum in Switzerland. Schirmer responded with an allusion to Mauthner's previous collaboration with de Bavier and the Hungarian Red Cross. The German IRC envoy also suggested that Mauthner's plan should include shelter and protection for Jewish refugees, an undertaking that would require Ebner's support and cooperation.

Mauthner proposed several further actions that he considered to be of critical importance as well; among these was to arrange the meeting at the Swiss-

---

[5] Geneva archives of the IRC, G 59/2 155-10. 01.

[6] The IRC appointed the Austrian–Italian de Schwarzenberg to lead this department on December 15, 1942.

German border with an IRC committee member in order to provide him with detailed information on his refugee relief projects.

Mauthner informed Schirmer that Ebner was "well-disposed" toward IRC operations. Schirmer concluded that, based on Mauthner's description of his recent contact with officials of the Reich in Vienna, the time may have arrived to initiate an IRC inspection of a Jewish camp (labor camp) or concentration camp on the territory of what was formerly Austria. Schirmer subsequently submitted a request to IRC headquarters for further instructions with regard to Mauthner's proposals, attaching a signed, four-page outline of his plan.[7]

During this time, Mauthner attempted to help Géza Jünker get back on his feet after somehow obtaining the release of the sixty-one-year-old former factory manager from the Mauthausen concentration camp (no evidence indicating precisely how Mauthner was able to redeem Jünker has yet been discovered). Due to Jünker's impaired physical state, he was soon transferred to a hospital in Vienna, where János Mauthner often visited him. Mauthner also maintained close contacts with the staff at Dr. Emil Tuchmann's so-called Jewish hospital as well.[8]

Mauthner's plan was overly ambitious given the existing circumstances. It depended on the realization of several conditions, such as finding sufficient transportation, gaining permission to enter Switzerland, obtaining adequate supplies and provisions and securing all the requisite official permits and authorizations. IRC officials immediately reviewed Schirmer's memorandum and the attached outline of Mauthner's plan. On October 16, Carl J. Burckhardt, a member of the IRC International Committee, sent an urgent communiqué to the head of the Bern-based Justice and Police Authority, H. Rothmund. Burckhardt's communiqué, which described the growing stream of Hungarian refugees as "a very relevant problem," had a copy of Schirmer's memorandum attached to it.[9] Burckhardt also commented that the IRC did not wish to address the issues raised in Schirmer's memorandum without prior consultation with Swiss officials and that talks with Mauthner, or "if necessary with Dr. Ebner, would not be entirely useless."

Burckhardt considered the Swiss justice official's assessment of Mauthner's proposals to be "particularly valuable;" he therefore intended to send a Red

[7] This document specified the Hungarian hostages' Vienna address as Bossigasse 21a in district XIII. The building in which they stayed is still there.

[8] Based on testimony that Jünker provided to authorities at the State Defense Division of the Hungarian State Police on June 2, 1947.

[9] Geneva archives of the IRC, G 59/5-132.

Cross colleague to Bern for consultations. In the meantime the energetic Hungarian hostage paid a visit to the Swiss consulate in Vienna, presenting a copy of Schirmer's memorandum and introducing himself as a Red Cross employee. Mauthner indicated that the purpose of his visit was to inform diplomatic officials at the consulate of his proposal to find asylum for Hungarian refugees in Switzerland.

Burckhardt responded to Schirmer on October 27. The contents of Burckhardt's communiqué indicate that the IRC International Committee viewed the prospect of a visit to Jews languishing in German camps as a means of restoring the prestige of the Red Cross before international public opinion, which had accused the organization of passivity and indifference. Burckhardt recommended that Schirmer should "immediately arrange a visit to the camps ... insofar as this is deemed necessary."[10] However, the headquarters of the Red Cross in Geneva did not see cause to take any further action with regard to Mauthner's initiative and the potential for cooperation with Dr. Ebner.

The next existing communiqué, dated November 8, notified the IRC secretariat that "with reference to the Jewish camps in the vicinity of Vienna," Schirmer was, at that time, in Geneva. He would personally provide the agency with information regarding a long discussion that he had held with Dr. Karl Ebner, presumably in Vienna. On November 20, Schirmer traveled to Budapest, where he presumably evaluated the Hungarian situation.

During the second half of November, János Mauthner concentrated his efforts on rescue operations, primarily on obtaining visas and other travel documents. Letters from the German envoy in Switzerland to the interior ministry in Bern reveal that he also attempted to rescue relatives who had remained in Hungary. Mauthner helped Jews who had arrived to Austria without proper travel documents to continue toward their desired destination, exhibiting an uncommon degree of humanity. His work was facilitated through funds derived from the Hungarian state, international Jewish organizations and the IRC.

Mauthner sent away some people after having been informed of their political persuasions. He refused to provide assistance to refugees who had been active in extreme right-wing politics in Hungary, directing them to the consulate general for aid. He always stood firmly on the side of the persecuted and humiliated, a policy that was a source of increasing controversy.

[10] Ibid. G 59/2 13.

On December 21, Schirmer informed Schwarzenberg, from Berlin, that Mauthner's initiative had likely come to an end. Schirmer also declared that, after witnessing Mauthner's activities first-hand during his two-week visit to Vienna, he had deemed them to be effective and necessary: his relief office had provided assistance to many Hungarians and his selfless labors had received a positive response.

Mauthner, on the other hand, openly and vigorously opposed the Szálasi dictatorship and its supporters. It is for this reason that his activities were stopped. The authorities "expelled him from Vienna, interning him for an undetermined amount of time."[11]

According to Robert Schirmer, Mauthner also arranged for him to meet with Dr. Ebner. Ebner, in turn, put Schirmer in contact with officials responsible for Austrian (!) Jewish issues, "to the great benefit of the IRC."[12] Though Mauthner's operations had come to a close, Ebner "wanted adamantly to provide as much support as he possibly could for the relief work of the Geneva committee."

In February 1945, János Mauthner returned to Vienna, though he was subjected to strict limitations on his movements, and was not permitted to contact anybody. (He never again met with Ebner or his secretary). Mauthner nonetheless violated these Gestapo constraints. At the end of March, a member of Kurt Becher's staff informed him that, according to the German evacuation plan, the Hungarian hostages from the Weiss–Chorin–Authner–Korn-feld–Heinrich family being held in Vienna were soon to be transferred to the interior of the Reich. After discussing this prospect with his relatives, Mauthner decided to escape.

I brought along with me my friend Max Otting and his wife, who were also being held hostages under house arrest. Otting was the nephew of Count Stauffenberg[13] who tried to assassinate Hitler on July 20, 1944. I pro-

---

[11] Ibid. G 59/2 155-10. 01. Mauthner's internment probably lasted from December 10 to December 15.

[12] Through Ebner, IRC delegate Dr. Luc Thudichum was able to obtain permission to visit a Jewish labor camp or detachment, though there is no record of his ever having actually done so.

[13] Colonel Graf von Claus Schenk Stauffenberg (1907–1944) was one of the primary architects of the unsuccessful assassination attempt on Hitler that took place on July 20, 1944. He was executed in Berlin for his courageous act.

vided them with Red Cross documents and in their perilous company fled across the border into Switzerland.[14]

Mauthner lived in Switzerland until Easter of 1946. There he strengthened his network of connections, but he also took a keen interest in Hungary's historic political transformation and new democratic government. Mauthner returned home as soon as civilians began receiving permission to transit across the various occupation zones in Austria. This scion of one of the country's leading industrialist families arrived back to Hungary at an inauspicious time, since his pedigree had become undesirable in his homeland. By 1946, the political and economic struggle against "the plutocrats and the forces of reaction standing behind them" and the destruction of grand-bourgeois families had become an everyday reality in Budapest.

The series of attacks, building up into a campaign, was fully supported by the newspapers *Szabad Nép* [Free People] and *Népszava* [People's Word] as well as by *Ítélet* [Judgment], the bulletin providing information on the work of the People's Courts. At the end of 1946, the latter devoted three consecutive issues to a hostile and distorted presentation of "the first authentic evidence regarding the immense business transactions between the Gestapo and the Weiss, Chorin and Kornfeld families." All this played a part in János Mauthner's subsequent dismissal from his position at the Sigg Aluminum Company and his arrest at an informer's denunciation.

During the summer of 1947, at the time of the criminal proceedings against him at the State Defense Division in Budapest, Mauthner learned from a Swiss news report that Ebner had been arrested at the end of 1944. According to this report Ebner had been taken to Wiener Neustadt, where "a military tribunal sentenced him to be shot." Mauthner lent credence to this news, since Ebner had not been in contact with either him or the IRC since May of 1945. The former hostage reasoned that if Ebner were still alive, he would have certainly sought him as a witness to corroborate his wartime activities in support of refugees.

The deputy chief of the secret police had been "excluded" following the appointment of SS *Standartenführer* Rudolf Mildner as head of the Vienna Gestapo in January 1945. The new chief was one of Kaltenbrunner's confidants and took immediate action on his behalf. Ebner was quickly brought before an

---

[14] Magyar Államrendőrségi Államvédelmi Osztály, Népügyészi Kirendeltség [Hungarian State Police State Defense Division, People's Prosecutor Section]. 3378/1947. ÁVO. Nü. Sz. Witness interrogation report.

SS tribunal and charged with *defeatism*. One of the leading figures in the struggle against "ideological enemies" (*Weltanschauliche Gegner*, Referat II B, later IV B) and the anti-Jewish provisions (*Judenreferat* II B 4, later IV B 4) was condemned to death in March, though the sentence was not carried out.

The former *éminence grise* of the Vienna Gestapo sent Himmler a plea for clemency in which he contended that he had worked irreproachably and un-compromisingly in the service of the fatherland to resolve the Jewish question in the most Jewish of the German Reich's major cities. Ebner went on to claim that, during his mandate, Vienna had become free of Jews and that his devoted labor had provided the Reich's coffers with approximately one billion marks.[15]

All of this suggests that Ebner's relationship to Mauthner did not involve a glimmer of humanity after all. The facts indicate that Ebner's apparent compassion was the product not of a genuine desire to provide humanitarian support for the helpless and persecuted, but of a calculated survival strategy devised among high-ranking officers of the SS, SD and Gestapo. Ebner, just as his highest-ranking superior, SS Chief Heinrich Himmler, was taking "the times to come" into consideration, hoping to buy an "insurance policy" for the future. He wore his newfound humanitarianism as a life vest, designed to keep him afloat after the ship of National Socialism went down.

Ebner's calculations panned out well. In 1947 he was brought before an Austrian court, though the beleaguered Mauthner was unaware of this fact.[16] It was true (and he may or may not have told Mauthner about it) that in a calculated move, Ebner had provided support to some people whose lives were in jeopardy. Among them were the well-known actor Hans Moser, whose Jewish wife had got him into serious trouble. The couple served as key witnesses in Ebner's defense during his postwar trial.

The Mosers' testimony and the SS tribunal's death sentence tipped the scales of justice in Ebner's favor, sparing him from the hangman's noose in 1947.

---

[15] Wolfgang Neugebauer, *Der NS-Terrorapparat*. I. n. Emmerich Tálos–Ernst Hanisch–Wolfgant Neugebauer–Reinhard Sieder (Hg.): NS-Herrschaft in Österreich Wien öbv und hpt, 2000. p. 731.

[16] Ebner's court dossier can be found at the following location: DÖW, no. 8919.

# 10. In the Lion's Maw

## a. Those Left behind at the Bergen Camp

The 1,368 Hungarian "émigrés" left behind at Bergen-Belsen awaited their fates amid great doubt that Krumey would follow through with his promise to release them in the near future. Most of these captives wondered time and again if they could not have done something to avoid their plight. Many of them concluded that their fear of deportation had led them straight into the lion's maw; at an enormous cost, they had purchased their own deportation instead of liberation.

The privations were so extreme that they eagerly devoured the same daily gruel that they had pushed away in disgust just weeks before. They were forced to accommodate themselves to the oppressive atmosphere and living conditions at the camp.

In addition to the usual camp formalities, a large degree of autonomy dictated the daily routine of the "émigrés'" lives at the *Ungarnlager*. Kasztner's father-in-law, Dr. József Fischer, performed the functions of the *Lagerälteste* or *Ältester Jude* (the superior Jewish captive). Fischer wore a special armband to indicate his position, thus giving him authority to manage the common affairs of the deportees held at the Hungarian section of the camp. Fischer also designated fellow captives to serve as liaisons between him and the SS administrative secretaries at the camp.

The male captives at the camp were awakened at six o'clock in the morning, the women three-quarters of an hour later. After washing up, they tidied their living quarters, had a breakfast of unflavored tea and a slice of bread, topped variously with butter, jam, onions or nothing more than a little salt, and then went out for the hated morning roll call. Following this drawn-out daily ordeal, some of the captives were assigned the duty of cleaning up the camp grounds, which occasionally included fruitless attempts to exterminate fleas and other vermin. Most of the deportees were already awaiting their "lunch" by eleven o'clock, nibbling on any scraps of the dense, mud-colored bread that may have been left over from the morning meal.

The rations that arrived at noon consisted of a thin soup containing one or a mixture of the following vegetables: kohlrabi, cabbage, potatoes, squash, carrots, turnips and onion stems. For dinner, the Hungarian deportees received black coffee and a twice-weekly, half-liter portion of thick barley soup in which lucky souls occasionally uncovered a scrap of meat.[1] They were allowed a ten-minute shower twice per week.

The nerve-racking idleness, confinement and congestion led to an increasing number of heated conflicts among the ragged and emaciated crowd. By the beginning of fall, the lack of warm clothing and blankets had become universal and the rain fell almost continually. Mould covered the unheated, dank and drafty barracks everywhere.

The ordeals of life at the camp mounted from week to week. The women and girls had only cold water with which to wash. They pieced together pants from tattered blankets and various articles of warm clothing from unstitched knitted wear. The women at the camp also made clogs for the men, many of whose shoes had become worn out or had fallen apart. There was a chronic lack of water and medicines at the camp. Many of the deportees had developed painful carbuncles as a result of their vitamin-deficient diet. They tried to console each other and often themselves in the early autumn dark (most of the time the only light in the barracks was that of the emergency lamps above the doorway). The captives passed the time humming familiar tunes and trying to think hopeful thoughts of the future.

Some of the deportees noted sardonically that, in spite of all the misery and uncertainty, regardless of the terrifying air raids, *they could still consider themselves privileged*: they were not required to perform daily labor, nobody subjected them to physical mistreatment; in comparison to Bergen-Belsen's other contingents of prisoners, whose numbers were declining rapidly through attrition, the inmates of the *Ungarnlager* were undoubtedly in a much better shape.[2]

After having miraculously survived the horrors of a forced-labor battalion serving in the Ukraine as well as an almost equally horrible interlude at the Nagyvárad ghetto, the author and journalist Béla Zsolt also wound up at Bergen-Belsen. In the late fall of 1944, Zsolt witnessed the "reception" given to a group of Dutch Jews who had arrived to the camp, which he recorded for posterity along with other observations and impressions.

---

[1] Devecseri, pp. 22, 25.

[2] At the end of November 1944, there were approximately 15,000 captives being held at Bergen-Belsen.

They were privileged Dutch Jews. They paid thirty thousand Reichs-marks apiece not to be taken East, but to be kept at camps close to home instead. Now they were evacuated here, to this overcrowded menagerie, into this insane network of cages that begins 250 kilometers from here at Os-nabrück, into the wire-bound compartments in which the Germans have collected, and separated from one another, all the Jews from Europe, Amer-ica and Asia whom they still haven't got around to incinerating. Hamburg is here in the vicinity—Hagenbeck has surely taught Himmler that much. Naturally there are mostly European Jews here—Romanians, Greeks, Yugo-slavs, Bulgarians, French, English, Poles and Hungarians.

But even Jews from neutral Spain had a bloc in the camp—and the South Americans too.[3] Like us, these Jews hardly worked; at most they planted turnips and beets for the camp inmates in the little vegetable plots that ran between the barracks.

This camp is incomprehensible to a logical, sane mind—it's like a Ger-man *colportage* Utopia. If I were to suddenly distance myself from it and think through its origin and development, I could interpret it as nothing else but the manifestation of an insane people's evil and arbitrary collection ma-nia. And even now the number of Jews not yet incinerated is constantly dwindling outside the barbed wire in German Europe, this crazy collection mania has not subsided, but has ensured that the flow of incoming captives would continue unabated.

For lack of Jews, they started collecting other inferior races—mulattos and Negroes. One afternoon Hungarian words filtered through the wire toward us—Hungarian speech in a Gypsy intonation; musical Transdanubian Gyp-sies had been brought in with all their kit and kin. All were musicians, with their families. When the Russian advance had drawn near, they took to their heels and scampered across the border into Austria in the belief that the Hungarian and German gentlemen there would want them to fiddle sweet music into their ears just as they had in Kaposvár and Pécs. But somewhere along the way they fell into the hands of some mad racist, who had them crammed into boxcars and before they knew what had happened to them they found themselves trapped in the cage as well.[4]

---

[3] The Hungarian camp was adjoined on one side by the Dutch compartment, and on the other by the one in which Polish Jews with Argentine documents were being held.

[4] Béla Zsolt, *Kilenc koffer* [Nine Suitcases], (Magvető Könyvkiadó, 1980), pp. 390–391.

The deportees organized presentations and language lessons in order to break the monotony of life at the camp. They also arranged for tutoring and instruction of school-aged children. Poetry recitals and song concerts were held occasionally as well. Pál Klein, György Kovács and Béla Zsolt delivered well-attended lectures on history and other subjects. The actress Erzsi Palotay recited poetry on several occasions and the opera singers Dezső Ernster and Hanna Brandt sang various arias and songs.

The group also included the 51-year-old psychiatrist Lipot Szondi. His life in the camp is undocumented.[5]

Meanwhile the German camp authorities also permitted the deportees to send letters to their families in Hungary. Some even received responses and small sums of money in return. These parcels and messages represented signs of life from home. They proved that the residents of the star-marked houses had not been deported.[6] News of the Romanian turnabout and its consequences also reached the camp via this route. The deportees learned from a letter sent from Budapest that the people from the wealthiest Jewish families whom had been sent to Switzerland were living in hotels in Montreux.

The autumn Jewish holidays proved to be a crucial source of social cohesion and human dignity for the Hungarian deportees at Bergen-Belsen. The ceremonies and rituals surrounding these holidays were performed in an isolated corner of one of the barracks. Many of the deportees began to weep when the rabbi spoke of deliverance and migration to the Promised Land. (All religious rites were strictly forbidden at the camp.)

After that, many were overcome with feelings of defiance and self-defense. Waiting tensely for the war to end, a small group began to fabricate rudimentary weapons and occasionally exercised with them. They also tried to build of a stock of food, but because of the cold, they were forced to spend most of their time sitting on the bunk beds.[7]

The subsequent arrival from Auschwitz–Birkenau of young Jewish women from various regions of Hungary sent shock waves throughout the *Ungarnlager*. Their appearance was unsettling due to their *"heartbreaking condition, especially their dreadful mental and nervous state."* From these women, the

---

[5] After his release, Szondi lived in Switzerland, then went to the USA. The epoch-making instinct diagnosis system he worked out is named after him. He died in 1986 at the age of 93.

[6] Budapest Jews had been ordered to move into certain buildings that had been designated for their habitation by a Star of David to be displayed at the entry before midnight of July 24, 1944. See Szabolcs Szita, "A budapesti csillagos házak, gettók (1944–1945)" [The Star-marked Houses of Budapest (1944–1945)], *Remény* [Hope], vol. 5, no. 1, spring, 2002, pp. 29–36.

[7] Letter by Professor Alexander Barzel in Israel to the author.

residents of the Hungarian section of Bergen-Belsen learned of the horrors of the initial selection process at Auschwitz, of the mass slaughter that was taking place there and of the fate of the Hungarian Jews deported to the camp in Southeast Poland. According to the memoirs of Mrs. Emil Devecseri:

> They described in notes passed secretly into the kitchen how they had been brought here from the biggest part of the Birkenau camp in order to work. Their heads had been shaven. They were allowed one change of clothing and underwear. They had been separated from their children and parents. They find the accommodations and provisions here to be sumptuous compared with those at the place from which they came.[8]

The summoning of the chief representative of the Hungarian deportees, Dr. Fischer, to the headquarters of the camp commandant sent another surge of excitement through the *Ungarnlager*. There, two foreign men dressed in civilian clothing informed Dr. Fischer that the Hungarian Jews would be sent to Switzerland within a period of eight days. The subsequent passing of twelve days without any sign of their imminent release cast a pall over the deportees, though they had begun to receive filling and nutritious food of the sort that they had not seen since their arrival to the camp. (This had been part of a shipment of IRC rations that had arrived from Switzerland.)

On the morning of December 4, the inmates of the *Ungarnlager* were ordered to pack up immediately. They quickly threw their meager belongings together amid a scene of great noise, commotion and excitement. Then followed a nerve-racking period of waiting around that lasted a good day and a half before the final camp inspection was called. During this muster, the German slaveholders in charge of Bergen-Belsen instructed their "*reisefertig*"[9] Hungarian wards to tell people in Switzerland of the humane treatment they had received at the camp. *Provide the Germans with good propaganda!*

It was at this time that the deportees learned that not all of them would be released: the SS had decided to retain the Weiss and Kertész couples[10] as well as the members of Joel Brand's family for no given reason.

---

[8] Mrs. Devecseri's manuscript, pp. 29–30.

[9] Ready to travel.

[10] The SS command had discovered that these people had secretly established contact with their relatives arriving from Auschwitz. Five members of Brand's family were also retained.

## b. December 7; The Second Train to Switzerland

The second contingent of Hungarian deportees was permitted to travel to Switzerland on December 7 1944, via Bregenz and St. Margarethen. Of the 1,552 members of this group, 1,337 had been among the original set of "emigrants" who had left Budapest on June 30. The SS had released the others earlier, presumably in exchange for the payment of an exorbitant ransom.

Liberation from the Bergen-Belsen camp brought with it an unimaginable degree of joy and excitement. The memoirs of Béla Zsolt recount some of the noteworthy details surrounding this occasion:

> We roamed through Wasserkante, Western Prussia and Northeastern Bavaria for three and a half days straight—we engulfed a whole series of local feeder lines with the speed of an express train; some of these tracks had been laid just a half year earlier for strategic purposes and were not even shown on railway maps.
>
> We hardly saw a main or an urban route, and we sometimes strayed so far to the East that everybody on the train turned pale with fright. We began to believe the Dutch from the neighboring bloc, who after finding out about the order for our release, speculated that we were really being sent east to dig trenches and build fortifications before the oncoming Russians or to be vernichted.[11]
>
> The Dutch had been wasting away behind the barbed wire for more than three years and had seen and heard everything. However, we still could not believe that if the SS really wanted to get rid of us that they would have been distributing boxes full of canned food, pounds of butter and countless brick-shaped loaves of bread among us.
>
> The despondent Dutch, who hated us at the time of our departure from the camp, claimed that it was all just a trick, that the Germans had simply wanted to make the Swedish Red Cross officials who had arrived to Hannover believe that they were taking us to a safe place, that it was just because of the Swedes that they had given us the food and that was why we were being packed into passenger cars. Then they assured us that somewhere along the way there would be a small station, where the train would veer off to the right instead of the left, or the other way around, and that we would then get off at a platform and walk through a gate.

---

[11] To be annihilated.

That is to say, that everything would be as it had been up until that time, like in every camp, and that instead of going to Switzerland or Palestine we would disappear into thin air ... We believed them, yet we did not; but when the train turned toward the east near Berlin we really began to worry that we were again going to fall victim to German whimsy. But we simply could not believe that they were taking us to Auschwitz, because almost every day over the previous few weeks prisoners who had inadvertently remained alive had been arriving to Bergen-Belsen from precisely that and other hastily evacuated Polish camps along with sullen, tired-looking SS officials wearing a muddle of civilian clothing pulled out of some chaotic wardrobe at the last minute.

At the same time, we also knew by then that one did not necessarily have to go to Auschwitz or Treblinka to get the gas treatment in Germany—it could happen anywhere in the country and even in the middle of a big city. The gas trucks drove around the Reich just as like any other truck. As we sat there agonizing over the specter of an unexpected terminus, we suddenly arrived to a station close to Nuremberg just before dawn and moved from the sidetrack finally to a main rail line consisting of three pairs of tracks.[12]

After crossing the Swiss border, the dejected and tormented group took up residence in a military barracks in St. Gallen. The unaccustomed sound of friendly voices and the kind treatment they received surprised the liberated prisoners the most. The frail and sick—that is, almost everybody—were given special care and attention. Many with more severe ailments were sent on to the hospital for further treatment.

The ordeal of the concentration camps had numbed the senses of many of the Hungarian deportees to such a degree that they could express no feelings of joy at their regained freedom. Those who had recovered their enthusiasm for life more quickly gazed blissfully out the windows of the barracks at the stunning panorama that lay before them. Gradually, more and more of the deportees began to comprehend and enjoy their new circumstances, *their miraculous escape*. The members of the group of Hungarians that had arrived earlier also appeared. They brought the latest news, fine Swiss chocolate, apples, sardines and long since untasted pastries to the newly liberated deportees.

The benevolence, compassion and congeniality of the Red Cross nurses helped many of the Hungarian Jews to revive their strength and spirits. Sympa-

[12] Zsolt, pp. 382–383.

thetic locals furnished the tattered crowd with food, clothing and shoes. Mrs. Emil Devecseri noted that "at first it was a terrible feeling to line up again and take these donations, but I guess we got used to it."[13] The well-edited Swiss daily and weekly press, the mere availability of fresh information, was a source of particular delight.

Another mound of gifts awaited the children of the group at the local gymnasium following the celebration of Hanukkah, thanks primarily to the efforts of the Swiss FHD (*Frauen-Hilfsdienst*).[14]

On the other hand, most of the recently released captives still could not banish the distressing, even tormenting, question: what had become of their loved-ones? Would they ever see them again? News of the plight of Budapest Jews, further deportations from Hungary, and the horrors of the murderous marches westward provided fuel for this burning question.[15]

Following this short period of rest and regeneration, the assemblage was placed on a train—this time a comfortable Swiss passenger train with big windows—and taken to Montreux. Swiss locals again left them with gifts at several locations along the way.

They arrived via cog railway to the picturesque mountain resort, where they were housed, under armed guard, in an abandoned hotel. It was from this location—the Caux Esplanade refugee camp in Montreux—that Rezső Kasztner's father-in-law, the aforementioned Dr. Fischer, sent a letter of gratitude addressed to the Geneva-based office of the IRC presidency on December 19.

Introducing himself as the leader of the "refugees," József Fischer wrote that the 1352 Hungarians residing at Caux Esplanade were fully aware that their rescue had been helped and organized by the IRC.[16]

## c. Arrow Cross Terror and the Re-Filling of the *Ungarnlager*

On October 15, Regent Miklós Horthy had his long-delayed proclamation read on Hungarian radio in which he said he was asking for a cease-fire from the Allies, and that Hungary—in order to end the war as soon as possible—

---

[13] Devecseri, p. 59.

[14] Women's Relief Service.

[15] The Swiss press provided extensive coverage of these events. Many of the Hungarian deportees sought Swiss contacts that might be able to help them safeguard their loved-ones at home through provision of protective documents or in some other way.

[16] Geneva archives of the IRC, G 59/2/65-45.

would leave the German alliance. However, their ill-preparedness as well as a series of betrayals prevented his plans from being realized. The crucial role, once again through armed intervention—this time via the kidnapping of the regent's son—fell to the Germans. On the other hand, the Hungarian military leadership also took the side of the Germans. Its majority had actively supported the takeover of power by Hungarian radical, extreme right movements. The common purpose of these movements was the fullest possible deployment of Hungarian forces in the "joint ideological war," and the extension of military operations claiming increasing sacrifices.

By the help of Veesenmayer, a new government was formed, headed by Ferenc Szálasi, the leader of the Arrow Cross movement, a former staff major turned politician. He soon proclaimed himself "Nation Leader" (*Nemzetvezető*). The Hungarian Führer in fact made Hungary the last remaining satellite of the German Führer. By continuing the now senseless warfare, contrary to the interests of Hungary, he wrought enormous materiel and human losses upon the country which was already in flames from repeated bombing raids from the Allies as well as by artillery strikes from the advancing Soviet forces in its eastern regions.

Faithfully imitating the German practice, Szálasi's "Hungarist" government attributed a special role to government-directed terror and propaganda. His party set up a "Department of Jew Removal" headed by Count Miklós Serényi and later by István Kelecsényi. The mass arrests and deportations began anew. The *maestro of the deportations* (a nickname that Kasztner used frequently), SS *Obersturmbannführer* Adolf Eichmann, returned to Budapest immediately.[17] The *Sondereinsatzkommando* again assumed control over the fate of Budapest Jews who had been forced to move into the star-marked houses and of Jewish men still serving as labor conscripts in the Hungarian military.

Veesenmayer and Eichmann quickly summoned representatives of the government of Ferenc Szálasi for negotiations in which the Germans demanded an immediate "loan" of 50,000 Hungarian Jews.[18] In early November, armed guards consequently began driving groups of 2,000 to 4,000 Jews from the internment camp located at the Óbuda–Újlak Brick Factory toward the west-

---

[17] As Romania switched over to the allied side with the Soviets drawing closer, Eichmann had been engaged in re-location operations of ethnic Germans and Saxons in Bánát, Bácska, and Transylvania.

[18] The topic of these negotiations was not deportation, per se, but Hungary's "de-Jewification"—or, in the euphemistic language used by the negotiating partners, the "lending" to the Reich of the country's remaining Jews until the end of the war.

ern border of Hungary in order to work on construction of German military fortifications. SS officials led by *Obersturmbannführer* Rudolf Höss, the former commandant of Auschwitz, took custody over the lengthy processions of forced laborers at the Hungarian border town of Hegyeshalom. According to several sources, SS *Hauptsturmführer* Abromeit and Wisliceny occasionally appeared for this purpose as well.

The transit of these large groups of Jews comprised primarily of girls, women and elderly men, by foot, from Budapest to the Reich quickly turned into a series of horrible death marches. The spectacle of the bedraggled throngs trudging along the main road to Vienna and the corpses left behind in its wake was the source of widespread shock and consternation. Eichmann and his staff nevertheless continued the foot marches. Armed Arrow Cross irregulars, often with the full cooperation of the Budapest police, conducted manhunts throughout the capital in search of hideaway Jews in order to ensure that the Óbuda Brick Factory would remain filled to capacity.

On November 4, the Arrow Cross launched a forty-eight-hour national roundup. The Hungarian police and gendarmerie also went into action, arresting individuals whom the new régime considered unreliable. In the meantime, prisoners held in prisons, jails and internment camps were also sifted through. The selected captives—both men and women, many of them political detainees—were taken to the Star Fortress located along the banks of the Danube on the outskirts of Komárom. This fort had been designated as the main collection point for those whom had been singled out for deportation, including a large number of Gypsies and Gypsy families.

From November 16 onwards, a special German task force (*Der Befehlshaber der Sicherheitspolizei u.d. SD in Ungarn und Chef der Einsatzgruppe 6*) dispatched trainloads of Hungarians of nearly all social backgrounds to concentration camps in jam-packed boxcars. Deportation trains bearing the assembled prisoners departed from the Star Fortress on a weekly basis until the end of 1944, bound for Buchenwald, Ravensbrück and other concentration camps.[19]

Captives designated to perform forced labor were set aside in Komárom so as not to be included in "concentration camp transfers." (The file registration of these deportees was a unique phenomenon. Such records were not kept in connection with either the mass deportations from the provinces that had

---

[19] Szabolcs Szita, *A komáromi deportálás 1944 őszén* [The Komárom Deportation, Fall 1944], (Holocaust Dokumentációs Központ és Emlékgyűjtemény Közalapítvány: Budapest, 2002), pp. 8–11.

taken place during the summer or the transfer of prisoners at Hegyeshalom in November.) The printed forms containing the prisoners' personal records indicated that "detention is likely to last until the end of the war." A total of approximately 15,000 people were deported from Komárom.

From the end of October, several thousand Jewish men and women were forced to clear rubble and, at the behest of the Todt Organization, to build defense lines around Budapest in order to defend the city against the approaching Soviets. Those who managed to obtain some type of official document from the embassies of neutral states (most of which had a largely theoretical value only), were commonly referred to as "protected" Jews, awaiting their fate in the so-called "international ghetto."

The newly installed Hungarian government had designated a place for the rest of what remained of the tormented Hungarian Jewish community as well. Szálasi established six separate categories into which they were ranked. According to a November 17 decree, the majority were forced to move into the plank-fenced Jewish quarter located in the center of the city—the gates of which closed on December 10—where they were to remain until the conclusion of the war. (Even this walled ghetto was divided into four further sub-groups.) On the 29th, a "ghetto decree" was also issued by Interior Minister Gábor Vajna, which brought another wave of massive re-location from the Gentile population to the walled quarter. This was how the last Jewish ghetto in Europe was established.[20]

The Jewish Council was now transformed into a "Ghetto Council," faced with superhuman challenges under the leadership of Lajos Stöckler.

In the meantime, the Germans—still in need of "able-bodied Jews"—seemed never to be satisfied with the number of deportees. At their orders, armed Arrow Cross party activists conducted a new round of general inspections and random identity checks in Budapest on December 3 and 4. By that time, 35,000 to 42,000 Budapest Jews—mostly those who survived the terrible death marches that each claimed hundreds of victims—had been handed over to the SS at the Hungarian border town of Hegyeshalom or just across the frontier, in the Austrian village of Zurndorf.

---

[20] Located inside the ghetto walls were 243 residential buildings containing a total of 4,513 individual apartments. On January 2, 1945, there were 52,688 people, including 5,730 children, living in the ghetto; by January 8, this number had increased to 62,949, including 6,759 children. The population of the ghetto eventually surpassed the 70,000 mark. See Szabolcs Szita, "A zsidók üldöztetése Budapesten" [The Persecution of Jews in Budapest], *Holocaust Füzetek* [Holocaust Notebooks], no. 4 (Budapest, 1994), p. 62.

No documents indicating a motive for the wave of arrests that took place in early December have been discovered, though one may speculate that it was related to the evacuation of the *Ungarnlager* at Bergen-Belsen. It may be assumed that the machinations of Eichmann and associates again played a backstage role in this affair, though the "dirty work" was left entirely to the Hungarian Arrow Cross, which had become increasingly proficient at diverse methods of humiliating, tormenting and murdering Jews.

During the extensive manhunt that took place in Budapest in early December 1944, armed Arrow Cross militants, often in their late teens and early twenties, entered the Star-of David-marked "Jewish houses," and forced their inhabitants to line up in the courtyard. They made arbitrary arrests, picking out whomever they wanted, and took them to various collection points, primarily the Józsefváros train station and designated buildings on Teleki Square.[21] Arrow Cross identity checks became part of the daily routine at the so-called "protected houses,"[22] as well as in certain residential buildings whose inhabitants were Gentiles and even in inner city air-raid shelters. Arrow Cross activists used these identity checks as a pretext for indulging in their taste for looting, rape and brutality. The dimensions of the tragedy were growing day after day, detainees were taken after dark to the embankments of the Danube, where they were lined up and shot, their bodies floating down the river.

The prisoners assembled at Teleki Square, including groups of Jewish men from the forced-labor battalions, were soon taken to the nearest train station and loaded into boxcars. (The forced-labor conscripts had been taken from the Albrecht Military Base.)[23] Gendarmes escorted the train to Zurndorf, from where the deportees were taken to Bergen-Belsen.

Available data indicate that it took up to four days for the boxcars, containing sixty to seventy people each, to reach their destination. This journey, as well as the "reception" at the concentration camp, entailed several surprises for the deportees.

An unidentified man with a megaphone notified those who had been packed into boxcars at the Józsefváros train station that they were being kept

---

[21] The addresses of these residential buildings were Teleki Square 3, 4 and 10. Armed Arrow Cross activists and regular members of the Budapest police escorted Jews to these locations.

[22] These buildings—located on the Pest side of the Margaret Bridge in what was called the "little ghetto"—were run by various embassies of neutral countries (Sweden, Spain, Switzerland and the Vatican), and in some cases by the International Red Cross. Kinga Frojimovics–Géza Komoróczy–Viktória Pusztai–Andrea Strbik *Jewish Budapest* (CEU Press, 1999) p. 401.

[23] This was the name given to the still-existing barracks situated at the corner of what are now called Dózsa György Street and Lehel Avenue.

under close watch.[24] In order to pacify the deportees, he told them that they were not traveling to an unknown destination, but that they were soon going to be exchanged. Most of them had absolutely no inkling of the true motive behind this seemingly absurd interlude.

This information had been directed at a small segment of the deportees: among the approximately 4,000 Hungarian Jews awaiting departure in the boxcars *were the abducted protégés of the Rescue Committee*. The Germans had abruptly taken the latter away from the Columbus Street Jewish camp, where they had been waiting for more of the so-called "sample trains" that had departed the previous July to transport them to safety abroad.

The liquidation of the strongholds of the Rescue Committee took place according to well-established German pattern. (The Arrow Cross used the same pretext on several occasions as well.) The given "justification:" Jews had made sniper attacks at guards from inside the camp. Armed Arrow Cross irregulars and regular units of the police were therefore compelled to stamp out the "rebellion."

The Arrow Cross raid on the Columbus Street Jewish camp that took place on December 3 included beatings and some murders. Several days of Arrow Cross plundering of the camp furnishings as well as the personal belongings and food of the abducted residents provided a sordid epilogue to this incident.[25]

Postwar testimony indicated that armed Arrow Cross thugs had taken most of the stolen goods to a barracks housing the so-called "Legion of the Skull" located at the Radetzky military base in Buda.[26]

SS guards drove the 4,000 to 4,200 freezing and exhausted deportees into Bergen-Belsen *at the crack of a whip*. This reception and the appalling conditions at the camp offered the fresh arrivals no cause for optimism.

[24] According to DEGOB report no. 641, this person was a representative of the International Red Cross.

[25] According to Kasztner, the original motive for the raid had been to obtain provisions from the camp's food warehouse. Subsequent events were to prove that there was more at stake. Kasztner also asserted that residents of the camp had shot and killed two Arrow Cross fighters during the raid, though there is no evidence to corroborate this claim. The Arrow Cross purportedly killed the Jewish camp superintendent, a man by the name of Muskovics, as well as a certain Dr. Rafael and his seventeen-year-old son in retribution. *Der Bericht*, p. 144. The gunfire that preceded the raid was likely nothing more than an Arrow Cross intimidation tactic. Kasztner alludes to the existence of a small arsenal on the camp grounds, though without indicating its possible purpose or function. Jenő Lévai's embellished history of this event cites fifteen dead and Kasztner's alleged order to hide weapons at the camp, an act that would have been totally foreign to the established methods of the Rescue Committee. See *Jewish Fate*, p. 364.

[26] TH A-1089. Two interrogation reports were prepared in May 1945. The building in question stands to this day on Bem Square in Budapest's second district.

The guards led the Hungarian deportees to the evacuated *Ungarnlager,* where they were to serve as *exchange prisoners.* Under this status, the new inhabitants of the Hungarian section of Bergen-Belsen were obliged to do no work beyond routine cleaning and maintenance, were permitted to retain their personal belongings, and were not required to have their heads shaven or to wear the "camp stripes."

A Jewish man from Szeged served as the representative of the repopulated *Ungarnlager.* In addition to the daily camp rations, the Hungarian prisoners received occasional IRC aid packages, which were divided into six or seven parts before distribution. These parcels typically contained supplementary food, sweets and cigarettes.[27] Roll call—*Appell*—was held less frequent, sometimes only twice per week.

A simple glance into the adjacent section of the camp, where SS guards continually brutalized gaunt inmates amid growing piles of withered corpses, provided the new inhabitants of the *Ungarnlager* with proof of their privileged status. According to the established "order," prisoners in this part of the camp were starved, beaten to death or worked to the point of collapse. As late as December, an undetermined number of Hungarian labor conscripts were also placed in this dismal sector of Bergen-Belsen.

The Jewish families that had been deported from the Great Hungarian Plain also wound up at the *Ungarnlager* during the final months of the war. Within a short period of time, these deportees came to comprise approximately half the population of the section of the camp designated specifically for Hungarians.

Though existing documentation is contradictory, it is clear that a portion of the Jews deported to Bergen-Belsen in December 1944 were sent on to work at an airplane factory located in the vicinity of Leipzig, at Raghun, either later that month or in February 1945. Those left behind at the concentration camp could do nothing more than wait and search for signs of hope on the horizon. Some found solace in the spreading rumor that "they were going to be taken to Switzerland in exchange for medicine."

---

[27] Information based on DEGOB report no. 25 and an account given by Mrs. József Reiner on June 22, 1945. According to the latter, the new representative of the *Ungarnlager* was Simon Fischer. Along with the daily quota of black coffee and soup or vegetable stew, the most recent deportees received thirty dkg (approximately ten ounces) of bread and twice-weekly supplementary rations. Symptoms of starvation became widespread beginning in the spring of 1945, when daily rations underwent a continual reduction until the Allied liberation of the camp.

At the beginning of April 1945, Camp Commandant Kramer sent three trainloads of prisoners under his charge to Theresienstadt. The first transport departed on April 7 carrying 2,679 people, including an unknown number of Hungarians.[28] 1,712 deportees registered at the *Ungarnlager* were sent on the second of the three trains, which departed April 9. The trip lasted twelve days, during which time the train was the target of a heavy British–American air attack. By the time they reached Theresienstadt, only 1,584 of the deportees were still alive.

On April 10, a total of 2,400 prisoners from fifteen countries, including at least 400 from Hungary, were herded into the boxcars. (Most of the latter had arrived with their families from the Strasshof labor camp.) The brutality of the SS guards, the catastrophic lack of food and water, typhus and general debility exacted a heavy toll en route to Theresienstadt. Repeated strafing from Allied airplanes during the entire length of the 500-kilometer trip drove some of the closely confined passengers insane.

Those who were still alive could do no more than mutter; they could barely move for lack of strength. Among them lay the corpses of fellow passengers who had died along the way—some days beforehand, others just recently. The living were simply too weak to remove and bury them, although even had they had the strength to do so, the SS escorts would simply not open the doors of the locked boxcars.[29]

Soviet forces liberated the survivors in the vicinity of Tröblitz on April 23.

Records show that of the 2,400 passengers who departed on the third train from Bergen-Belsen on the 10th April, 565 died by June 21. Of the victims, 51.7 % were men and 48.3 % women. The following table further classifies the victims according to age:[30]

---

[28] Benjamin, p. 92. The Americans liberated the passengers of this train in the village of Farsleben, near Magdeburg, on April 13. After recuperating from their ordeal, the Hungarians in this group straggled back home beginning in September.

[29] László Kovács, "Ungarnlager–Bergen-Belsen és ami utána következik" [*Ungarnlager–Bergen-Belsen* and its Aftermath], *Remény* [Hope], vol. 5, no. 1, spring 2002, p. 60. More than 400 men, women and children died in an epidemic during the first eight weeks following liberation. The last Hungarian deportee to die was the forty-one-year-old Ilona Sólyom, on June 21, 1945. Ibid.

[30] László Kovács, *Tanú vagyok* [I Am a Witness], (Szabolcs-Szatmár-Bereg Archives Publications II, communiqués, 32: Nyíregyháza, 2004), p. 221.

| Age in Years | Percentage of Total Victims |
|---|---|
| 1 to 14 | 4.3 |
| 15 to 20 | 4.6 |
| 21 to 30 | 7.8 |
| 31 to 50 | 44.9 |
| 51 to 60 | 22.1 |
| 60 + | 16.3 |

## d. Subsequent Negotiations in Switzerland

Kurt Becher maintained his contacts with the Zionists even after the extreme right-wing takeover in Hungary. During the Szálasi dictatorship, Becher accorded several small favors to his Jewish negotiating partners, which did not represent a departure from the prevailing tactics of the SS. In his meetings with Kaszter and his partners he continued to conceal and manipulate the intentions of the SS regarding newer deportations. Though he promised to use his influence with high-ranking Nazi officials in Berlin in order to promote some Zionist objectives, Becher also made ominous references to "wartime constraints." In effect, Becher resisted any move designed to prevent a new round of deportations.

Becher cooperated, for the most part, with Eichmann; in fact, he occasionally outdid the maestro of the deportations. The aggressive side of Becher's character manifested itself in his propensity for blackmail and thinly disguised self-enrichment. He worked hard to consummate the various SS "deals," which entailed increasing exploitation of Hungary. Official SS terminology deemed such maneuvers to be "evacuation" operations.

On October 23, 1944, Becher was appointed chief of the Budapest "evacuation unit" for the SS, a position (*Sonderbeauftragte*)[31] from which he was able to indulge in his above-mentioned predilection for wealth and extortion. Exploiting the deepening plight of Budapest Jewry, Becher exerted increasing pressure on Saly Mayer, often through Kasztner, to arrange a meeting between him and representatives of the Roosevelt administration.

Jewish organizations in Palestine informed British officials that what remained of the Hungarian Jewish community was in mortal danger. Though he lacked any real leverage over Allied military procedures, the president of the

---

[31] Special representative. His stated duty was to "oversee evacuation measures on the territory of Hungary."

Jewish Agency, Chaim Weizmann, repeatedly called upon the British to *send back* Joel Brand from Palestine, and to bomb the concentration camps and the railways that led to them. In response, Weizmann received nothing but delaying promises and empty words.

Officers operating under Eichmann's command were in the process of preparing plans to deport Budapest Jews to the Reich on foot when Weizmann received a letter from Churchill's secretary, John Martin. "We can assure you that both His Majesty's government and that of the Soviet Union are aware of the danger of further persecution taking place in Hungary and will do everything within their power to prevent it."[32]

The new emergency prompted Kasztner to again seek succor in Switzerland, informing Mayer on several occasions that the continued operations of the Rescue Committee and the fate of Budapest Jews depended completely on the disposition of the SS. With the help of American diplomatic officials, Kasztner was eventually able to convince Swiss authorities to issue a visa to Becher.

The SS officer traveled to Switzerland in order to meet with McClelland, the envoy of the War Refugee Board (WRB) council in Switzerland. Becher quickly realized that his negotiating partners were merely playing for time and that he should not expect the various international Jewish organizations to agree to send the Reich its desired war materiel. However, the military situation along the European fronts and Becher's personal security demanded that he maintain his hard-won contacts with the Joint and the WRB.

Becher met with McClelland in the city of St. Gallen on November 2. During their talks at the Walhalla Hotel, Becher declared that the partisan uprising in Slovakia had prompted the Germans to resume the deportations in that country; he also referred to the impending "labor deployment" of able-bodied Budapest Jews to the Reich. Becher informed McClelland that he was willing to negotiate the release of more Jews from Hungary. Finally, the SS officer urged McClelland to arrange for the delivery of previously specified supplies, in exchange for which the Germans would be willing to treat certain categories of Jews held in the Reich as *privileged foreigners or prisoners of war.*[33]

---

[32] This letter was sent following Martin's visit to Moscow, on October 30, 1944. Hausner, p. 487.

[33] These negotiations gave rise to a legend that Kurt Becher had played a role in Himmler's order to halt the gassing of prisoners at Birkenau. The motive for this command was actually based on Germany's need to "deploy" all available sources of labor at its disposal with the rapidly advancing Soviet army drawing close to the borders of the Reich. Under these circumstances, the Germans did not feel the need to maintain the full extermination capacity of this

The talks resumed the following evening at the Savoy Hotel in Zurich, both parties *incognito*. (It is still not clear whether the WRB envoy undertook these negotiations in an official capacity or independently.) At the end of the two-hour meeting, McClelland declared that he would sanction the depositing of twenty million Swiss francs as ransom money in an SS bank account. According to McClelland, the Joint would remit the specified sum of money, though the Germans would be responsible for procurement of the equipment and supplies in question. The WRB envoy would arrange for official Swiss permission to export the latter to the Reich if the Germans showed concrete signs of holding up their end of the deal.

Lending weight to McClelland's claim was an authorization bearing the signature of United States Secretary of State Cordell Hull for the deposit five million dollars in a frozen Swiss bank account. (This amounted to twenty-one million Swiss francs at the existing exchange rate.) However, the transfer and deposit of the money did not necessarily mean that the Germans would have access to it; these funds were appropriated to cover the cost of materiel and equipment stipulated in the deal, which, however, the Germans would not be able to procure in Switzerland.

In any case, one of Becher's closest associates, SS Major Herbert Kettlitz, received permission to remain in Switzerland to arrange for the purchase of the commodities. For his part, Becher was able to report to Berlin the following facts of vital importance: the Joint was willing to pay for the release of Jews; and their concessions on the Jewish question had facilitated contacts with the Western powers after all. In light of the failure of Joel Brand's mission the previous May, the negotiations between Becher and McClelland made it seem as if the Americans had revised their earlier, unyielding, position.

Kasztner and his associates found in the outcome of the negotiations reason to hope that Himmler and his entourage might be prepared to compromise, even if the stipulated compensation was tardy or nullified altogether. Due to the constantly deteriorating situation on the battlefield, leading SS officials, including Becher and his staff, were adamant about maintaining a hand in the negotiations, which might provide them with a means of vindication after the war.

Kasztner and Mayer also attempted to reach agreement with Becher and Kettlitz on concrete issues pertaining to the status of Hungarian Jews. Becher remained firm in his insistence that able-bodied Jewish men and women be

---

camp. Dismantling of crematorium II began on November 25 and that of crematorium III (as well as the gas chambers contained within them) soon thereafter.

required to leave Budapest, because they were liable to turn against the Germans if Allied troops reached the city. As a goodwill gesture, Becher agreed to petition his superiors to exempt Jewish men under the age of sixteen and over the age of fifty, Jewish women under the age of sixteen and over the age of forty and invalids from this obligation.

Becher returned from Switzerland on November 6. Until that date, he and Kettlitz had been moving about the country comfortably, settling *financial issues of an unknown nature*. They also fulfilled instructions that they had received from their SS superiors. The hiding of expropriated Jewish assets which Becher and Kettlitz had presumably been engaged in was made possible by the protective shroud of Swiss bank secrecy, which remained intact for decades after the war had ended.

Becher was presented with a new opportunity barely one week later, on November 14. This was the date on which Nazi and Arrow Cross officials signed an agreement regarding the "evacuation" of assets and property from Hungary, in reality a German vehicle for achieving the vast and rapid destruction and emptying of the Hungarian economy, for which Becher served as a primary activating force.[34]

Kasztner's situation became more difficult following the negotiations. He again concluded that, for the Americans and the Swiss, the prospect of paying a ransom for Hungarian Jews represented nothing more than opportunity to engage in tactical maneuvering. Though they repeatedly employed humanitarian catchphrases, the American and Swiss negotiators seemed as if they could not truly comprehend the mortal threat that afflicted Jews in Budapest and the SS concentration camps. Kasztner concluded that the outcome and future of the negotiations would depend, to a large degree, on precisely what information Becher presented to Himmler, and how he chose to present it.

The fact that the Szálasi government had no interest in the survival of the Budapest Jewish community simply exacerbated the situation. Arrow Cross officials had proclaimed that they would create a "Jew-free" Hungary, an aspiration that manifested itself in the régime's refusal to put a stop to the atrocities that had become commonplace on the streets and squares of Budapest.

---

[34] For more information on Becher's role in this process, see Kádár–Vági, pp. 208–211. In the opinion of these authors, twenty to twenty-five percent of the assets and property removed from Hungary had originally belonged to Jews.

This gave rise to a paradoxical situation in which the Zionists looked to Becher, and even Himmler, for a modicum of protection against Eichmann and his Arrow Cross accomplices. In the negotiations regarding the future of Budapest Jewry, the Zionists believed that their best chance for success probably lay in the vindication-seeking Himmler, the omnipotent SS overlord who retained ultimate decision-making and executive authority with regard to the liberation of Jews residing in the territories under German occupation.

On the 28th, Kasztner again traveled to the border of Switzerland. The Germans had ordered him to do so following the arrival of "bad news": Kettlitz had sent Becher a telegram informing him that the deposit of twenty million Swiss francs had been cancelled and that subsequent negotiations regarding the transport of goods and materiel to the Reich had ended in failure.[35]

The news was passed on to Eichmann, who immediately summoned Kasztner to his headquarters. In the presence of Becher, Eichmann shrieked that the final deadline for the deposit would be December 2 and that if the money did not arrive he would have all the Jews remaining in Budapest "liquidated." Similarly difficult problems confronted Kasztner after he had arrived to the German–Swiss border: the new United States secretary of state, Edward Stettinius,[36] rejected any further negotiations with the Germans. At the same time, he rescinded his predecessor's offer to appropriate a sum of five million dollars for rescue operations.

Saly Mayer declared that they had detected no change in the posture of the Germans in light of the most recent developments. He also contended that any agreement or fulfillment of prior arrangements would be futile. In a private meeting with Mayer on December 1, Kasztner depicted the plight of Budapest Jews, the new wave of persecution and the consequences of the establishment of the inner-city ghetto. He also underscored his opinion that breaking off negotiations with the SS might seal the fate for the 150,000 Jews who continued to reside in Budapest and could still have a chance.

During subsequent talks with the two SS officers[37] who had arrived with Kasztner, Mayer expounded in great detail upon the reasons for the Allied refusal to remit the previously stipulated sum of money. The IRC official

---

[35] Kettlitz was expelled from Switzerland on the 27th.

[36] Stettinius' stance vis-à-vis the negotiations had undergone a transformation: as deputy secretary of state, he had supported them. Stettinius declared that, since the proposal had originated from the highest echelons, it would be advantageous to "let the Germans believe that we are taking it seriously." Information based on the protocol of the conference of June 7, 1944. See Hausner, p. 358.

[37] Kettlitz and a new negotiator, SS *Hauptsturmführer* Erich Krell.

then offered to deposit four million Swiss francs that he had at his disposal in the closed account. Kasztner and the two SS officers then became involved in a lengthy debate, after which they came to an agreement: they would not report the most recent setback to Becher, from whom this news would likely pass straight up the chain of command to Himmler, earning them all a certain date with a firing squad. Of course, transmitting false information might also cost them their lives, but at least it would offer them a slim chance of survival.

The SS officers accepted Kasztner's reasoning, sending an embellished account of the latest developments to their superiors in Budapest in which they claimed that a deposit of 5 million Swiss francs was forthcoming. According to this telegram, the delay in the evacuation of the *Ungarnlager* at Bergen-Belsen had prompted the Allies to withhold three-quarters of the expected sum of the deposit.

The Germans yielded: within days, the SS ordered the immediate evacuation of the *Ungarnlager.* Becher allegedly informed Kasztner via telegram that the lives of Jews in the Budapest ghetto would be spared. However, Becher warned that "the situation would become untenable" if the further fifteen million Swiss francs were not transferred in the near future.

On December 8, Becher again urged Kasztner to expedite the depositing of the money. This time Kasztner did not return to Hungary, electing to remain in Switzerland instead. On December 15, Saly Mayer arrived in Switzerland for a meeting with the Hungarian Zionist leader, who persuaded the head of the European division of the Joint that the twenty million francs demanded by the SS must be transferred to the specified account *in such a way as to make it inaccessible* to the Germans.

Saly Mayer then took action after all. According to documents recently discovered at the Swiss *Bundesarchiv,* between November 28 and December 21, 1944, Mayer paid the Luzern-based Th. Willy Company 207,600 Swiss francs for shipment of sixteen tractors.[38]

An antecedent to this transaction had taken place in July, when the *Warenvermittlungskontor GmbH Budapest*—a Becher-controlled front company for the SS—ordered forty tractors at the price of 17,300 francs per unit from the same tractor factory. Mayer agreed to pay the bill for this consignment in exchange for the liberation of the "selected" Hungarian Jews. Payment for the

---

[38] On January 7, the WRB authorized the Joint to remit five million dollars to Mayer. This money was to be allocated only with the permission of the WRB. For information regarding subsequent negotiations see Bauer, pp. 362–364.

tractors was delayed until late November, when the number of units was re-duced from forty to sixteen.

The Germans never took possession of the tractors, which were eventually shipped out of Switzerland.[39]

## e. The Rescue Committee in Budapest, Winter 1944

As previously mentioned, Kasztner did not return to Budapest in Decem-ber, choosing instead to remain in Switzerland. In his absence, Biss maintained the Zionists' contacts with Becher and Eichmann. Endre Biss was the Rescue Committee's financial secretary, though he also worked to protect those living in the star-marked houses as well.

As the military front drew closer to Budapest—Soviet artillery began the shelling of Budapest on December 8—the members of the Rescue Committee concluded that the fate of the city's Jews was almost entirely in the hands of the Germans. Those living in the vastly overcrowded ghetto were easy prey for the Arrow Cross, which only the Germans could prevent from unleashing its thugs upon the Jews. The European experience that the SS was, in general, not in the habit of leaving Jews behind alive made the situation even worse.

Kasztner urged the Germans to provide the Allies with evidence of their credibility by sparing the Budapest Jewish community. Becher allegedly took Kasztner's advice into consideration, requesting further orders on the issue from Berlin. On December 8, as has been mentioned, Becher sent Kasztner a telegram to Switzerland, promising that the Budapest ghetto would be spared. Though, for lack of documentation, his claim cannot be declared a sham, it is highly unlikely that the SS ever intervened on behalf of Jews residing in the Budapest ghetto. The legend of German clemency toward Budapest Jews was later supplemented with that of Himmler's personal intervention on their be-half, without any supporting evidence whatsoever.

Although, in 1947, Kasztner repeatedly referred to Becher as the *savior of the Budapest ghetto*, this assertion does not conform in the least to the estab-lished facts. Nor can it be an incident that the "savior" himself failed to re-member it when he was interrogated.

During the final weeks of 1944, Szálasi's deeply anti-Semitic minister, Emil Kovarcz, and armed Arrow Cross thugs indeed began making plans to liqui-

---

[39] Sebastian Speich, Fred David, Shraga Elam, Anton Ladner, *Die Schweiz am Pranger. Banke, Bosse und die Nazis Ueberreuter* (Frankfurt, 1997), p. 112.

date the Budapest ghetto. A number of reported liquidation plans circulated in the city, causing a great deal of anxiety and unrest. The eventual rescue of the Jews in the Budapest ghetto was due to the valiant efforts of several Hungarians as well as the arrival of Soviet troops and not in the least to any intervention on the part of Becher.[40]

The SS Reich commander raised the issue of Hungarian Jewry and the Budapest ghetto during later negotiations with representatives of international organizations working to protect European Jews. On April 19, the self-seeking Himmler held secret talks with the Swedish industrialist Norbert Mazur, who was serving as an official envoy of the World Jewish Congress. During this meeting, Himmler suggested that his actions vis-à-vis the Jews had been received with "ingratitude." The commander-in-chief of the SS then described the concessions that he had granted to Hungarian Jews: "I spared 450,000 Hungarian Jews and what kind of thanks did they show for it? In Budapest they shot at our troops."[41] In fact, Himmler's alleged "mercy" was a nothing more than a big lie, just as was the story of the sniper fire from the ghetto.

Several members of the Rescue Committee assisted the International Red Cross during the Szálasi era. (The IRC served as a front organization for the Zionists.) A separate division of the IRC, the so-called "section A," functioned at the organization's inner-city headquarters on Mérleg Street. Ottó Komoly was the director of this section, which organized relief operations and handled other Jewish-related matters, which had become increasingly difficult and complex with each passing day.[42] Komoly put together a staff of 250. Those working at the Economic section included Hansi Brand, Zoltán Weiner and several young Zionists, such as János Sampias and Imre Benkő (aka Ernő Teichmann).[43] Amid the growing atmosphere of chaos, preservation of Red

[40] In 1946, Kasztner recalled that he had asked Becher to intervene on January 11, 1945, in order to prevent the last-minute liquidation of Jews confined in the Budapest ghetto. Becher's alleged response to Kasztner's request was "don't worry, I have already talked to Himmler about this. He rejects any kind of retaliation." See *Der Bericht*, p. 132 and pp. 144–145. For a more recent study of Becher's alleged role as "savior of the ghetto," see the following work: József Szekeres, *A pesti gettók 1945. januári megmentése* [The January 1945 Rescue of the Budapest Ghetto], (Budapest Főváros Levéltára: Budapest, 1997), pp. 87–89.

[41] *Der Bericht*, pp. 181–182. At the end of December, a Nazi doctor in the town of Gmünd spoke of the alleged attack from inside the Budapest ghetto. According to his allegation, which was likely based on a newspaper report, the Jews "threw boiling oil from windows onto our fighting troops." *Holocaust Füzetek*, no. 4, 1994, p. 67.

[42] Funding for assistance to persecuted Jews arrived from the Joint via the IRC.

[43] Reminiscences by several people unanimously emphasize the merits of Hansi Brand in financial management, Weiner in the purchasing of food and equipment, and of Rudolf Weisz in managing the transportation.

Cross prerogatives, maintenance of up-to-date records and distribution of IRC protective documentation was a vital service to Hungarian Jews. At the same time, IRC employment and documents certifying it provided freedom of movement, a great advantage.

The personnel of Section A devoted much of its time and effort to safeguarding homes that had been established for Jewish children. In December, Hungarian authorities repeatedly demanded that these institutions be dissolved and their diminutive wards be immediately transferred to the central ghetto. The Budapest embassies of neutral European states assisted the Section A in postponing the relocation of the children residing in the hospices to the Budapest ghetto. Ottó Komoly twice met with the secretary of the Swedish embassy, Raoul Wallenberg, first in the middle of November, then again on December 7, on the latter occasion in the company of several trusted colleagues.

The menace to the children grew commensurately with the thirst for blood of armed Arrow Cross thugs. When Section A workers perceived a direct threat to one of the children's homes, groups of armed Zionist youths wearing the uniforms of the so-called "auxiliary armed forces" (known by their Hungarian-language acronym as KISKA) were sent in commandeered military trucks to collect the threatened children.[44] Section A also helped to obtain, deliver, and distribute food for these youngsters.

Arrow Cross irregulars ran amuck throughout Budapest—not even the orphanages were safe from their brutality. Beginning on December 12, these institutions were the target of continual harassment. In some instances, orphanages were evacuated without warning; in others, Arrow Cross activists threatened, manhandled and even killed the adult attendants. Most of the children's homes did, however, make it through until the end of the war unscathed. Approximately thirty such institutions existed in January 1945, providing shelter for 3,000 to 4,000 children and 1,000 to 1,200 adults—numbers that grew temporarily during the nightly Arrow Cross raids and roundups.

Thus, Ottó Komoly oversaw the nourishment and protection of nearly 6,000 people from his Mérleg Street office.[45] He was in grave danger himself. Authorities took Komoly into custody several times in spite of the fact that his identity papers bore the authenticating signature of Foreign Minister Gábor

---

[44] Personal recollections of this event are contained in *A halál árnyékában* [In the Shadow of Death].

[45] There was also a Section B, which was engaged in child-welfare operations on territory that lay outside the IRC's protective jurisdiction. The Catholic Holy Cross Association and the Protestant Good Shepherd Committee worked closely with this department.

Kemény; though he was released on each of these occasions, several of his staff members were confined indefinitely to the ghetto.[46]

The Arrow Cross reign of terror prompted the manager of the nearby Ritz Hotel to ask Komoly to move into his establishment so that he could place the coveted sign indicating IRC protection at the entryway. The Zionist leader accepted this offer, taking up residence in the hotel on December 28. On the first day of 1945, two courteous police officers arrived to Komoly's office, politely requesting that he come along with them for "an important meeting." Komoly then disappeared without a trace. Presumably, the Arrow Cross did away with him somewhere.

Arthur Weisz, the head of the Glass House in Vadász Street, suffered a similar fate at about this same time: Weisz, who maintained at least 3,000 Jews under his protection, reluctantly left the IRC sanctuary established at his enterprise after an Arrow Cross militia officer had given him his word that he would come to no harm; Weisz' credence in the soldier's word of honor cost him his life.[47]

As a consequence of Kurt Becher's Hungarian end game, Lipót Aschner, a prominent industrialist, was able was pay his way out of the concentration camp where he was being held. (Aschner arrived from Oberlanzdorf to Mauthausen on May 5 in frail physical condition, though in a solid frame of mind.) Becher presented the Zurich subsidiary of the Budapest-based Tungsram Company[48] with an initial proposal of one million Swiss francs in exchange for the release of the firm's managing director. In the end, the SS officer agreed to set Aschner free for the reduced price of 100,000 Swiss francs. On December 18, the Germans transported Aschner from Mauthuasen to Switzerland.[49]

Paul Holzach took delivery of the ransom on behalf of the Intercommerz A. G. Becher, using the code name Vorrat Linde, or Auxiliary Linden, orchestrated this transaction. In May 1945, Holzach transferred this money to an account belonging to a tractor factory in Luzern. This smokescreen worked perfectly. Becher continued to manipulate this money, with the shameful consent of Swiss officials, well into the 1950s.[50]

---

[46] Ibid., p. 211.

[47] For more detail on the tragic deaths of these two men see Tschuy, pp. 267–268.

[48] The Tungsram Company was the holder of several international patents and was the primary Hungarian manufacturer of light bulbs.

[49] Becher made a similar offer for the release of Leo Goldberger, who was also being held at Mauthausen. However, Goldberger's family, which had gone into hiding and was already struggling with financial difficulties, could not raise the required ransom money.

[50] Shrage Elam uncovered documentation pertaining to this affair during research conducted in Switzerland during the 1990s. See *Die Schweiz am Pragner*, pp. 111–123.

# 11. Spring 1945

## a. Jewish "Family Camps," Late April and Early May 1945

The exceptional lack of original documentation, much of which was purposely destroyed, pertaining to the Jews from the Great Hungarian Plain who had been rescued from deportation to Auschwitz–Birkenau, has left researchers with a mere rough outline of their final weeks of captivity. According to one available source, only 6,000 of them were left behind, while the rest were taken to Bergen-Belsen and Theresienstadt.[1]

From the outset, the SS had regarded these deportees as a trade commodity, though they never did serve as a source of large-scale profit or an underpinning for the Europa Plan and other grandiloquent-sounding schemes as the Germans had hoped they would.[2] More than one-third of these Jews ended up in a concentration camp, perhaps precisely for this reason. Those whom had been sent to Bergen-Belsen apparently enjoyed some privileges, such an exemption from forced labor. There is no data regarding the camp status of those sent to Theresienstadt and Mauthausen.

Several peculiar factors shaped their destiny. After he had been placed under arrest in the summer of 1945, Judenkommando officer Siegfried Seidl claimed that Krumey often consulted with Rezső Kasztner in his capacity as a representative of the Joint. Recently discovered documents at the Geneva archives of the International Red Cross confirm Seidl's assertion.

In 1945, five large transports of Jews arrived to the Terezin defensive fortifications, where they took up residence in the stronghold's artillery casemates. A majority of the total of 1,073 deportees who had arrived to the improvised camp on March 8 was likely from Hungary. On April 15, authorities at the camp registered the arrival of seventy-seven more captives from Amstetten.

---

[1] DÖW 17142.

[2] Besides the Hungarians, two other "exchange groups" were released from Bergen-Belsen: at the end of June 1944, 222 Jews were permitted to leave for Palestine; at the end of January 1945, 136 captives were sent to Switzerland.

The total number of deportees to arrive to the camp from the annexed territories of Austria eventually reached 1,512;[3] of these, the majority—1,150—were listed as Hungarian Jews. Records denoting the release of 1,138 Hungarians from the camp suggest that twelve of the original 1,150 deportees died in captivity.[4] Incomplete data indicate that the latter had arrived from forty-one Jewish camps—thirty-seven in Upper Austria, three in Vienna and one in Styria.[5]

From 2,000 to 2,500 forced laborers remained at the Strasshof camp.[6] (Due to lack of documentation, it is not known how many deportees arrived from the so-called "family camps.") Heavy Allied bombing postponed the scheduled March 21 departure for Theresienstadt. The captives packed into the boxcars were left with virtually no food or water. Five days later, the American air force conducted bombing raids on trains loaded with military equipment and supplies at the Strasshof station. During this attack, the explosion of a car full of gunpowder showered the "Jewish train" with a hail of splinters, immediately killing sixty-four passengers, whose corpses were subsequently buried in a mass grave in Strasshof.[7]

A group of one hundred Hungarian deportees who had suffered wounds of various severity during the attack was immediately transported to the previously mentioned Jewish hospital in Vienna for treatment.[8] Local residents extricated the remaining captives, some of whom went voluntarily to the bug-infested "transit camp" in the vicinity, while Ukrainian Waffen SS troops brutally forced the rest back into the damaged boxcars.

There is little evidence regarding the rest. What is certain is that the Ukrainian camp guards fled before the advancing Soviet army on April 9 and 10.

Because of the heavy siege of Vienna, the daily shelling and bombing, the breakdown of law and order and the stoppage of work and production, most of the Hungarian slave laborers working in Vienna went underground, hiding out in the most diverse locations. Many solitary deportees attempted to escape in order to avert the threat of being taken farther. Amid the uncertainty of these

---

[3] *Totenbuch Theresienstadt. Herausgeber: Mary Steinhauser und DÖW*, (Vienna, 1971), pp. 21–22.

[4] Karel Lagus and Josef Polák, *Mesto za mřížemi*, (Prague, 1964), pp. 343, 350.

[5] *Magyarok az SS ausztriai lágerbirodalmában* [Hungarians in the Austrian SS Camps], p. 249.

[6] DÖW 17142. In his testimony of August 8, 1945, Seidl indicated that 2,000 captives had been left behind; according to Kasztner, there were 2,500. *Der Bericht*, p. 168.

[7] Eleonore Lappin, "Die Rolle der Waffen SS beim Zwangsarbeitseinsatz ungarischer Juden im Gau Steiermark und bei den Todesmärschen ins KZ Mauthausen (1944/1945)," *DÖW Jahrbuch 2004*, (Lit Verlag: Münster, 2004), pp. 102–103.

[8] *Der Bericht*, p. 168.

dire circumstances, many Jewish deportees received life-sustaining aid and support from the local population. An outstanding instance of such benevolence occurred at the suburban Oberleitner estate, though many such notable cases occurred in the center city as well.

Hungarian forced laborers working in the Gau Niederdonau region received evacuation orders between April 17 and 19. Those residing in the northern part of this district were instructed to congregate in the city of Gmünd. Several groups of deportees were started off without receiving specific orders regarding their subsequent destination. These assemblages simply wandered from place to place, which was not a rare phenomenon during those times of pervasive chaos and disorder. Other deportees found themselves adrift after scheduled trains did not arrive or they could not find their appointed relocation camp.

Three "Strasshof People" working in Gmünd—Dr. Lipót Fisch from Kiskunfélegyháza, Dr. György Újhelyi from Tótkomlós; and Piroska Pollák—managed to evade the April 19 evacuation to Theresienstadt. With help from Austrian civilians in the vicinity of Nondorf, these people found shelter at Johann Weissensteiner's Hochenesch tannery, where they remained in hiding until the end of the war. Dr. Artur Lanc and a certain Dr. Krisch, himself on the run from the Gestapo, provided the Hungarian escapees with the most concrete assistance.[9]

During the second half of April, Nazi authorities paid much less attention to the "Strasshof People" than to Jewish trench diggers. There is little information available regarding their movements at this time; however, it is known that many of them removed their Stars of David from their clothing, and sought refuge at various locations, often at abandoned homesteads or in the woods. SS motor patrols, stray Wehrmacht sub-units looking for a hiding place and hostile local residents posed the greatest threat to the Strasshof deportees as they drifted about the Austrian countryside. At the same time, the randomly encountered humanity of individual Austrians was a source of solace and sustenance to the wandering Hungarians.

The final days of the war saw several instances of tragedy for the Hungarians. On April 13, seventy-six deportees from Szeged and Debrecen were murdered by Ernst Burian and six SS troopers using bazookas, hand grenades and machine guns in Göstling a.d. Ybbs. The youngest of the victims were two- and four-years old, and the oldest: eighty-six-year-old Hanni Schiffmann and sev-

---

[9] DÖW E 20164, Joanna Nittergerg, "Gemeindezentrum im Zeichen der Begegnung," *Illustrierte Neue Welt,* January, 1987.

enty-seven-year-old Jenő Németh. These people had been scheduled to depart for Amstetten the very next day.[10]

On the 15th, motorized SS murdered between ninety and one hundred Hungarian Jews in the community of Randegg in much the same way. Merciless killers belonging to the Leibstandarte "Adolf Hitler" shot forty-two Hungarian Jews in a quarry near Sulzbach.[11] (These deportees had been doing forced labor in Weissenbach a.d. Triesting.) The names of seventeen natives of Szeged who had been among the latter victims were made public after the exhumation of their remains from a mass grave discovered at the quarry in 1947.[12]

Another contingent of forced laborers from Szeged were butchered by members of the so-called "civil-defense police" (Schutzpolizei) at Nikolsburg (known today as Miklolov). Four of the civil-defense officers rousted the group of thirteen women and eight men from their barracks late at night and drove them to a nearby hill, where they were mowed down with machine guns.[13]

Later in 1945, the unidentified remains of fifteen Hungarian deportees were exhumed near Thenneberg bei Altenmarkt (like Sulzbach, located in the Pottenstein district of Lower Austria). The Viennese Jewish community reburied these corpses at the new Jewish cemetery located in the Austrian capital.

A further thirty-four deportees were murdered by the SS on April 15 at the Stangental Cement Plant near Lilienfeld, at the foot of the Limestone Alps. A dozen SS troopers went on a killing spree just to the north of Ybbs a.d. Donau, in the village of Persenbeug, between midnight of May 2 and dawn of May 3. After murdering four groups of Hungarian forced laborers, comprising a total of 223 people, the Germans doused the bodies with gasoline and ignited them, producing a fire that was still burning the next day. The names of all but nine of the victims are known. On April 26, 1964, those killed at Persenbeug were given an honorary reburial at the St. Pölten Jewish cemetery.

Hungarian Jews were the target of lethal SS assaults even as they headed toward home, on foot, via the Austrian roadways. The number of deportees killed during the arduous trek back to Hungary is at least 500. Sixteen of them,

---

[10] DÖW 12876., 17142., E 18241. Josef Buchinger, *Das Ende des 1000 Jährigen Reiches*, Vol. II (Vienna, 1972), p. 225.

[11] Buchinger, vol. I, p. 136.

[12] *Délmagyarország*, November 29, 1946.

[13] Ibid., November 6, 1946. See Szabolcs Szita, *Utak a pokolból. Magyar deportáltak az annektált Ausztriában* [Roads from Hell. Hungarian Deportees in Annexed Austria], (Metalon Manger Iroda Kft., 1991), p. 179.

natives of Debrecen, survived this peril. They were hidden by inhabitants of the village of Rohr at a hideout between Höllental and Piestingtal.[14]

Scholarly investigation of the deportation of Jews from Hungary in 1944 indicates that losses among deportees held at Strasshof were proportionally much lower than those among provincial Jews deported to Auschwitz–Birkenau or forced laborers working on military fortifications along the frontier of the Reich. In August 1945, authorities registered the return from captivity in the Reich of 6,885 Jews from Transdanubia and 25,485 Jews from the Great Hungarian Plain. Of those deportees who had returned from Strasshof, 8,419 were from Debrecen, 6,554 from Szeged, 2,711 from Szolnok, 1,984 from Karcag and 1,247 from Kiskőrös.[15]

## b. The Fate of the Rescue Committee's Swiss Charges

According to Kasztner, immediately following Germany's capitulation, American officials began pressing for the prompt relocation of the Hungarian deportees liberated from Bergen-Belsen to an UNRRA[16] camp located in the African city of Philippeville. This was due to a previous obligation to the Swiss, undertaken by the Americans.

The Hungarian Jews in question voiced strong opposition to their proposed resettlement in Africa. Dr. Dezső Hermann[17] sent letters of protest in the name of his fellow concentration-camp survivors to the new president of the United States, Harry S. Truman, British Prime Minister Winston Churchill and several officials of the UNRRA. Though the impact of the letters is unknown, Swiss authorities fortunately decided to scrap this resettlement plan.

In the meantime, an increasing number of children from this group of Hungarian deportees were placed in so-called "aliyah shelters" maintained by Swiss Zionist organizations, primarily Ichud and Ha-Shomer Ha-tzair. Jewish children from Hungary were placed alongside those from Belgium, France and Poland at one such institution located on the picturesque banks of Lake Vierwaldstätter near the village of Weggis.

---

[14] Buchinger, vol. I, p. 103.

[15] *Roads from Hell*, p. 181.

[16] Acronym for the United Nations Relief and Rehabilitation Agency.

[17] Dr. Fischer had been permitted to leave the camp established for the deportees. Hermann became his successor as "camp president," serving his constituents with dedication and zeal.

In May, following Algiers, the Italian city of Bari emerged as another possible location for the resettlement of the Hungarian Jews who had recently been liberated from SS captivity, though this plan was also abandoned. The American-administered, Switzerland-based UNRRA then announced that these deportees would be relocated, on or before June 4, to Tunisia, where they would await the arrival of their official certificates. This scheme again raised the ire of the Hungarian camp survivors, whose vehement expressions of disapproval and resistance, both active and passive, to the plan temporarily strained their relations with Swiss authorities. Hermann was eventually forced by the Swiss to relinquish his position, and was replaced by the more diplomatic Dr. Dezső Weisz.

As a consequence of their above-mentioned fractiousness, Hermann and his associates were separated from their fellows, and the Hungarians were divided into two groups. The ailyah group of 700 ready to immigrate to Palestine subsequently received immigration certificates.

In August, this group, with Dr. József Fischer as their leader, traveled to Haifa Palestine in a closed group. Thus, after a long delay and many trials they saw their old dream, the aliyah come true. We have no evidence as to what happened to the other group (which returned to Hungary).

A few of them, such as Mr. Devecseri and his family, chose to remain in Switzerland. This was by no means easy; permission to settle in Switzerland required finding local sponsors and significant capital.

Approximately 180 of the Rescue Committee protégés who had remained in Switzerland prepared to return to Hungary at the end of July. According to an existing register, 171 people from this group arrived to Budapest on August 6.[18] The Swiss authorities accountable for the safe return of the camp survivors received an acknowledgment from the Deportee Welfare Committee (known by its Hungarian-language acronym, DEGOB) in Budapest indicating that it had assumed responsibility for the repatriated deportees and their belongings.

The register indicates that the eighty Jews in this group who had originated from the northern part of Transylvania that had reverted to Romanian rule after the war were thereafter to be considered citizens of Romania. Of these, the oldest repatriate of declared Romanian nationality had been born in 1874, the oldest of declared Hungarian nationality in 1875; the youngest of declared Romanian nationality was five years old, the youngest declared Hungarian nationality, two years old.

---

[18] Information from the Geneva archives of the IRC, G 59/5-138.

This contingent of concentration-camp survivors had departed St. Margare-then on the afternoon of July 28 in five Sauer automobiles and four Chevrolet trucks. According to an official Swiss report on the journey prepared on September 2, they traveled via Munich and Salzburg to Wels, arriving there on August 2. The convoy then passed into the Soviet occupation at the town of St. Valentin two days later. From there they were taken to Vienna, then on to the Hungarian capital. The Swiss official who wrote the report, Pierre Santschi, indicated that the DEGOB moved the repatriates into temporary housing on Ajtósi Dürer Street in the Zugló district of Budapest.

The convoy returned from Hungary with passengers as well, taking seventy-one people—French, Belgians and Dutch—to Bregenz and 134 Italians to Innsbruck. An additional thirty-three Italians were picked up in Vienna and taken to Innsbruck along with their compatriots.[19]

---

[19] Ibid.

# 12. The Bonds Survive

## a. Kasztner, Becher and the Others

Kasztner left Switzerland at the end of December. His destination was supposed to be Budapest, but he only got as far as Vienna due to the Soviet siege of the Hungarian capital. He lived in Vienna from 29 December 1944 to March 28, 1945. As was his custom, Kasztner led a restless life, traveling frequently.

In Vienna, he used a German passport. He saw Becher on December 30. Becher arranged for him to live at the Grand Hotel and put him in touch with Dr. Ebner as well. The deputy Gestapo chief instructed Kasztner to reduce his social contacts to a bare minimum and not to reveal to anyone that he was a Jew (it was not displayed in his passport either).

On January 3, 1945, Kasztner visited the Jewish hospital located at 16 Malzgasse, where he purportedly had his first encounter with the Hungarian Jews whom Eichmann had "put on ice" in Vienna. After that, he devoted an increasing amount of his time and energy acting in their interest.

Kasztner held more talks with his established SS contacts; with Becher, now promoted, who had just established a local branch office of the Manfréd Weiss Enterprises, and with Wisliceny, who continually attempted to deflect blame for the extermination of Hungarian Jews onto his superiors, particularly Eichmann. It was indicative of the changed environment that the latter, a formerly zealous supporter of the deportations, had also seen the light and *turned into a rescuer of Jews.* According to Wisliceny, he had assisted Red Cross organizations that had been present during the transfer of Hungarian deportees at Hegyeshalom. In fact, Wisliceny claimed, he had arranged for sick and otherwise incapacitated Jews who had arrived to the Reich to be sent back to a treatment and convalescence center that he had established in the Transdanubian city of Mosonmagyaróvár. According to Wisliceny, this act of benevolence brought him into a serious conflict with his commanding officer, who threatened to have him court-martialed.[1]

Wisliceny alleged that he had done everything within his power to safeguard a distinguished leader of the Slovak Jewish community, Gizi Fleischmann, as well. However, a fellow officer transferred to Hungary from France, SS *Hauptsturmführer* Alois Brunner ("he was of the worst sort"), blindly followed Eichmann's orders, and dispatched the head of the Slovak Rescue Committee to Auschwitz.[2]

Kasztner also visited Krumey's Vienna offices, where he learned that the treatment of Hungarian forced laborers working in Ostmark was "strict, though fair." Krumey also informed Kasztner that their labor had been profitable. The SS officer went on to claim that all the forced laborers had access to medical care, though interment of the dead sometimes presented problems; the latter was, apparently, due to the intransigence of the Viennese Jewish community (!), which insisted on charging 150 Reichsmarks per burial (increasingly frequent because of the air raids), while he could pay no more than fifty.[3] Krumey was taken aback: how could an organization that operated under his oversight, at his mercy, dare to charge that much?

On January 22, Kasztner traveled to Bratislava with Krumey and a Red Cross envoy named Thudichum. He met with another Red Cross official, Georges Dunant, at the Swiss consulate located in that city. During talks with Kasztner, these IRC officials agreed to furnish the Hungarian forced laborers at Strasshof with clothing and footwear, and to provide the Jewish hospital with a "large quantity" of lacking medication, both at Red Cross expense.[4]

---

[1] *Der Bericht*, p. 150. Kasztner apparently got carried away in the prevailing drift, claiming that he had sent two Jewish doctors to the border with medicine. The evidence precludes the possibility of any such direct Jewish assistance.

[2] Through his cunning manipulation of the Bratislava Rescue Committee, Brunner managed to deport 8,000 Slovak Jews to Auschwitz–Birkenau and a further 4,000 Slovak Jews to Sachsenhausen and Theresienstadt between September 30, 1944 and March 31, 1945. See Andor Sas, *A szlovákiai zsidók üldözése 1939–1945* [The Persecution of Slovak Jews, 1939–1945], (Kalligram Könyvkiadó: Bratislava, 1993), p. 17. It was characteristic of SS deceit that even as Himmler and his closest associates were holding negotiations regarding the mass redemption of Jews, they were dispatching deportation trains to the death camps.

[3] Ibid., p. 152. Kasztner later remarked that this must have been due to the manipulations of the Jewish desk of the Vienna Gestapo, which maintained tense relations with Krumey's SS squadron.

[4] Dr. Thudichum's version of this episode seems to be the most reliable. His memorandum of February 12, 1945, indicates that only a few shipments of the stipulated relief ever reached their destination: "In spite of our efforts, we have achieved practically nothing up to this point." See Arieh Ben-Tov, p. 223.

During his stay in Bratislava, Kasztner met secretly with Dr. Juraj Révész, one of the leaders of a group of some 2,000 Bratislava Jews (including 250 children) who were hiding in the city. During this meeting, Révész informed Kasztner that some Hungarian Jews who had escaped from the procession of forced laborers marching toward Hegyeshalom had also found refuge in the city, though they were in great danger of being recaptured. (Kasztner later also held talks with Weissmandel at a hideout located outside the city.) On the 24th, Kasztner traveled back to Vienna to see Becher again, who was in the city to oversee the evacuation of "commodities, equipment and machinery of military value" from Western Hungary and their redistribution and reinstallation in the Reich.

The Swiss connection also remained intact. According to Kasztner, negotiations took place on January 31 and February 11. In the meantime, the situation changed because Himmler's need for Becher's services had diminished. Now the omnipotent SS overlord himself took the initiative, meeting with several representatives of neutral states in order to discuss "the Jewish issue."[5] As a result of these negotiations, Himmler authorized the release of 1,200 Jews who had been languishing at Theresienstadt, sending them to Switzerland.[6] As a further "conciliatory gesture," he also permitted the IRC to send food to several concentration camps.[7]

Meanwhile, Kasztner had been lobbying international relief organizations to send warm clothing to the Hungarian Jews at Strasshof. However, promised Swiss financial assistance for this, and other, relief did not materialize before the end of the winter.[8]

As spring (and the Reich's defeat in the war) was approaching, the attitude of SS officers changed rapidly. Eichmann's deputy, SS *Obersturmbannführer* Krumey, decided to "turn over a new leaf" once and for all. At the beginning of March, staff officers at Krumey's Vienna headquarters obtained a list of Hungarian Jews who were doing forced labor on the Reich's border fortifications, thus providing their superior with an opportunity to perform more "good deeds." According to Kasztner, Krumey was preparing to have several

---

[5] Among the people with whom Himmler met beginning in November 1944 were Jean Marie Musy, a former member of the governing council of the Swiss Confederation and Count Folke Bernadotte, the nephew of the king of Sweden.

[6] Müller-Tupath, p. 201.

[7] A larger quantity of IRC parcels arrived to Mauthausen in April, and with some regularity after that. *Magyarok az SS ausztriai lágerbirodalmában* [Hungarians in the Austrian SS Camps], p. 166.

[8] For example, distribution of 2,000 pairs of shoes to camp inmates did not take place until March 13.

hundred Jewish trench diggers sent to Vienna for a week of rest and recuperation.[9]

In light of the mercilessness of the *Baulleitung* (Construction Management) run by special Nazi party commissioners, the incessant brutality of the German guards, the relentless physical exertions and the hideous spectacle of mass death to which these forced laborers were subjected day after day, Krumey's alleged "care" amounted to nothing more than a barefaced lie, one of many. Indeed, the customary National Socialist notion of rest and relaxation for these Jewish trench diggers had them lying dead in a lime pit.

Kasztner's visit to Bratislava had produced an unintended meeting as well. In the middle of March, while having coffee at the Carlton Hotel, he ran across Gendarme Lieutenant-Colonel László Ferenczy, who, after recognizing the Zionist leader, wanted to arrest him on the spot for espionage on behalf of the Jews and Americans. Though Kasztner's German passport saved him then, Gestapo agents sent by *Hauptsturmführer* Alois Brunner soon broke into his hotel room, delivering him into the custody of the Bratislava SS. Kasztner was released only after the intervention of Becher's Bratislava contacts.[10]

At the beginning of April, Becher was given another special assignment by Himmler (references to this episode, in regard to which no primary documentation is known to exist, are contradictory). He was allegedly appointed: "extraordinary Reich concentration camp commissioner" (*Reichssonderkommissar für sämtliche deutsche Konzentrationslager*). If Becher did, indeed, receive this authority from Himmler, its true implications subsequently became inextricably entangled in the vast web of lies and deceit that the SS spun at the end of the war.[11] (There is no evidence that Becher ever took any concrete measures in this capacity, a topic that he refused to discuss even years after the war had ended.) It is clear, however, that Becher's primary objective in the spring of 1945 was to solidify his grounds for postwar vindication through acts of "Jewish rescue."

On the 10th, Becher and Kasztner visited Bergen-Belsen. (Several sources indicate that he invited Kasztner, whom he had disguised in an SS uniform. According to these sources, the two had established a genuine personal friend-

[9] *Der Bericht,* p. 163. The allegation had not a grain of truth to it; it is in complete contradiction the hard facts of the labor of trench-diggers in the border regions.

[10] Ibid., p. 167. SS *Obersturmbannführer* Vitezka, the head of the Bratislava SD, ordered Kasztner's release.

[11] According to the authors of the *Personen-Lexikon der NSDAP,* in 1945 he was Himmler's commissoner (Beauftrãger), with an unspecified authority, for "negotiations with Jewish places" (Vehabndlungen mit jüdischen Stellen).

ship and "were very attached to one another.") The two toured the camp, witnessing first-hand the appalling sight of mass starvation and death. Both of the men left the camp in a state of shock after seeing, with their own eyes, the large heaps of emaciated corpses awaiting disposal.

According to Becher, by the time he and Kasztner visited Bergen-Belsen, there was no longer anything that could be done for the prisoners at the camp—"it was *too late* to do anything constructive for them."[12]

On the 16th—once again together—they visited Theresienstadt. This was also the last time they saw one of Eichmann's deputies, SS *Sturmbannführer* Günther.

Kasztner and Becher parted company in Berlin. The SS officer then continued his tour of the Reich's concentration camp network at Mauthausen, in the vicinity of Linz, where he again found somebody whom he could exploit to his own advantage. At the conclusion of his visit, Becher instructed the camp commandant to relieve a forty-year-old prisoner named Schweiger, registration number 79,500, from his daily forced-labor duty at Mauthausen's infamous quarry.[13] The self-vindicating SS officer later ordered Schweiger's release from the notorious death camp.[14]

Becher informed Schweiger that his removal from Mauthausen had been "a personal gift to Dr. Kasztner." Schweiger was then taken to the hills above Weissenbach, where Becher's staff officers provided him with food and shelter. During subsequent meetings at this location, Becher referred to Schweiger by his first name, nearly pampering the former *häftling*, up to then a mere number. After several days, the SS officer instructed Schweiger to write him an *apologia*, which he showed to the Americans immediately after his capture on May 12.[15]

Before being taken prisoner, Becher entrusted Schweiger with a portion of "the property of the Jewish people" that had been in his possession, which consisted primarily of cash, gold and jewels. According to Kasztner, Becher

---

[12] Müller-Tupath, p. 222

[13] *Magyarok az SS ausztriai lágerbirodalmában* [Hungarians in the Austrian SS Camps], pp. 71-72.

[14] Several sources indicate that Schweiger left Mauthausen on May 5, though this date is clearly inaccurate: on May 3, the front had already reached the vicinity of the camp, which American troops liberated on May 5. Ibid., p. 167.

[15] This letter listed Becher's alleged Jewish-rescue activities and Jewish personal contacts. Schweiger, as a prisoner at Mauthausen, could not possibly have been aware of the information contained in his letter even had it been factual. The integral text of this document is contained in Müller-Tupath, pp. 175-176.

had made the lawyer *Herr Doktor Schweiger* the trustee of a significant share of the assets that the Budapest Rescue Committee had turned over to the Germans, amounting to a net worth of several hundred thousand dollars.[16]

However, the Americans' rapid advance into the Reich dashed Becher's carefully conceived plan; in the end, Schweiger delivered the money and valuables that the SS *Standartenführer* had given to him to an agent of the American Intelligence Corps in the vicinity of Bad Ischl.

## b. The Kasztner Report

In December 1946, Kasztner attended the convention of the World Zionist Organization in Basel. Even before the proceedings began, delegates denounced Kasztner for his alleged collaboration with the Germans.

Others probed Kasztner's handling of the enormous sums of money and assets that had been put under his discretion during the war years. What had happened to the funds that he had received from the various international Jewish organizations? What had become of the property and assets that Hungarian Jews had rendered to him? Delegates at the congress elected to establish an international committee to investigate Kasztner's financial dealings. This panel conducted several hearings on this issue, in the course of which Kasztner presented it with a detailed report of his wartime activities, fiscal and otherwise.[17]

Stenciled copies of Kasztner's account, entitled "Report of the Budapest Jewish Rescue Committee, 1942–1945" (*Der Bericht des jüdischen Rettungskomitees aus Budapest, 1942–1945*) were circulated to all members of the investigative committee.[18] (The identity of the organization, if any, delegating Kasztner to the convention, is unknown. It is certain that he was not listed among the thirteen delegates whom the various Zionist bodies functioning in Hungary had sent to the meeting.)[19]

The 190-page typewritten report was divided into thirteen sections marked by Roman numerals. In the introduction, Kasztner declares that until the German occupation of Hungary on March 19, 1944, when he turned his attention toward

---

[16] *Der Bericht*, p. 183.

[17] *Haladás*, December 25, 1946.

[18] Kasztner's report was first published fifteen years later, in Germany, under the following title: *Der Kasztner-Bericht über Eichmanns Menschenhandel in Ungarn* with a preface by Professor Carlo Schmidt, (Kindler Verlag: Munich, 1961).

[19] The list of Zionist delegates from Hungary is contained in Emed, p. 107.

the protection of Hungarian Jews, his Rescue Committee activities had mainly involved providing various forms of assistance to Polish, Slovak and Yugoslav refugees. Eventually, his efforts became focused almost entirely on rescuing Budapest Jews languishing under the threat of deportation to one of the Reich's network of concentration camps, an endeavor whose exceptional complexity and lethal implications necessitated recourse to extraordinary methods.

The first section of Kasztner's report is divided into seven chapters of various lengths, comprising a total of 147 pages, in which the veteran Zionist recounts the history of wartime Jewish rescue operations. The initial chapter depicts the permutations in the status of Hungarian Jews, the progression of the war and the arrival of Polish and Slovak refugees as they occurred in the year of 1943. This section of the report also outlines the Rescue Committee's array of domestic and foreign connections, which reached as far as the Warsaw ghetto.

Chapter II essentially outlines the major events and developments that occurred during the first two months of the German occupation, such as the emergence of the Rescue Committee's distinct Hungarian, Swiss and German "lines," explains why the Hungarian Jews did not rebel, and also describes the psychological preparations and eventual implementation of the initial sequence of deportations from Hungary. This chapter also discusses the failure of the Brand mission.

The brief third chapter elaborates upon the various German intrigues that took place at this time. The report describes the process of secret negotiations, their progress, eventual exposure and subsequent depiction as a Zionist plot. Details surrounding the "privileged" camp and the first group of emigrants to leave for Palestine are also included in this section of the report. Chapter IV treats the preparations for the deportation of Budapest Jews, the uprising in Slovakia, and the consequent surge in the intensity of German persecution of Jews in that country as well as various other events that took place during the summer of 1944. The chapter concludes with a brief account of the first group of 318 Hungarian Jews released from Bergen-Belsen as a result of the negotiations.

In Chapter V, consisting of a mere fifteen pages, Kasztner recounts the negotiations that took place on the Swiss border, and other significant events taking place in the first month of that fall, notably the various IRC measures aimed at protection of Hungarian Jews, particularly children. The main topics covered in the sixth chapter, twice as long, are as follows: Szálasi's mid-October rise to power; the activities of the Budapest embassies of the neutral European states during the Arrow Cross reign of terror; the raids of Arrow Cross terror brigades on the so-called "protected houses" that had been established by those embassies in the capital; and the death march of forced laborers to the

Reich via Hegyeshalom. This chapter also touches upon a new fantasy rescue plan that emerged at this time, according to which Jews would have been exchanged for *Volksdeutche* (ethnic Germans).

The seventh chapter, the last of those constituting the first section of the report, begins with a description of the circumstances surrounding the departure of the second group of Hungarian Jews for asylum in Switzerland, continues with a portrayal of the Budapest ghetto, in connection with which the author recounts the legend of Becher's alleged intercession on behalf of the thousands of Jews confined to this zone in the center city, and concludes with an account of Ottó Komoly's death. Kasztner leaves the reader of his report with the impression that he wrote this chapter based on rumor and hearsay.

The second section of the report is nearly forty pages long. Kasztner again embellishes Becher's role in Jewish rescue operations, also describing events that took place in the weeks preceding the collapse of Hitler's Reich. Kasztner repeatedly dealt with the destiny of the "Strasshof" deportees as well as that of Hungarian Jews at Bergen-Belsen and Theresienstadt. The chapter also touches upon the final days before the Soviet occupation of Berlin.

Rezső Kasztner's report, which also includes a number of references of a personal nature, concludes with copies of a number of letters significant from the viewpoint of Kasztner's activities.

The *Kasztner Bericht* is still considered to be an authoritative summary of the remarkable battle for Jewish self-preservation waged against the Gestapo and the SS. It represents an important primary source for research pertaining to the period and the events regardless of the author's proclivity for exaggeration and self-vindicating analysis. Kasztner's partiality for conclusions that justify his own actions and overriding personal ambition are palpable throughout the text. There are occasional manifestations of the author's propensity for self-aggrandizement as well.

In sum, the report suggests clearly that Kasztner, Komoly and their associates were most often compelled to choose the lesser evil. Had they proven less adept at making tough decisions under volatile conditions, they may not have succeeded in saving a single life. Kasztner was keenly aware that he was taking part in an extraordinarily high-stakes game. (Kasztner wrote that he felt as if he had been "playing roulette with Eichmann, for human lives." He knew that he might well draw the bullet and that "moreover, the loser was going to be branded a traitor.")[20]

---

[20] Gideon Hausner, p. 217.

The *Kasztner Bericht* also makes it clear that, during the dangerous times following the German occupation of Hungary, the members of the Rescue Committee *were themselves captives and victims of the SS and the Reich's merciless extermination machinery.*

## c. Kurt Becher, Savior of the Jews

Kasztner's relationship with Becher exhibited a curious developmental curve following the capitulation of Hitler's Third Reich. In 1945, the Zionist leader gave testimony regarding his wartime activities to an American board of inquiry. In his deposition, Kasztner referred to the high-ranking SS officers who had taken part in earlier committee hearings, including Becher, as *war criminals,* who began *searching for alibis* once they recognized that Germany was going to lose the war.

Kasztner's portrayal of Becher underwent a sudden transformation in January 1946. According to this new depiction, the SS officer had shown a genuine humaneness toward Jews, even persuading Himmler to stop the extermination machinery. On August 4, 1947, Kasztner again presented a war-crimes tribunal with sworn statements pertaining to the case of Becher, then a prisoner. The trial had not yet begun, so the Zionist leader's deposition was largely preventive by nature. For reasons unknown, Kasztner again made several false and exaggerated claims.

Kasztner's postwar testimony has not stood the test of time. Of Becher, he declared, for example, that "he had the courage to make a stand against the extermination plans." Enlisting the SS colonel's alleged merits at length, Kasztner was ready to twist certain facts to suit his subjective version of Jewish rescue operations. He claimed that his direct personal experiences with Becher had convinced him of his honorable intentions and goodwill. Emphasizing the personal rapport that he had established with Becher, Kasztner insisted that *"under the circumstances, he did everything he possibly could have to save innocent people from the crazed butchery of the Nazi leaders."*

Kasztner claimed that Becher had been behind the release of Jewish prisoners from Bergen-Belsen, Theresienstadt and the Neungamme camp located in the vicinity of Hamburg. Another of his unfounded assertions was that Becher had worked to prevent the implementation of Kaltenbrunner's order to liquidate concentration-camp inmates, thus saving 33,000 Jews at Mauthausen and 17,000 more at Plausenburg from an excruciating death in the gas chambers "at the last minute."

The facts: the number of prisoners in Mauthausen at the end of April may be estimated at 70,000. The decisive factor in their survival was the rapid taking of the camp by American troops and the disintegration and fleeing of the guards.[21] In the final days the SS wanted to kill the inmates of the Ebensee subcamp all together. That act of mass murder was prevented not by those at the top of the SS hierarchy but by the information and organized resistance of the prisoners.

Kasztner urged Allied judicial authorities handling Becher's case to bear in mind the exculpatory testimony he had given in regard to the former SS officer "to the greatest possible degree." After concluding his sworn statement, Kasztner declared that he had testified not only on his own behalf,[22] but in the name of the World Jewish Association and World Jewish Congress as well.

Thanks to Rezső Kasztner's diligent efforts, in August 1947, the former high-ranking SS officer was again able to portray himself *as a rescuer of Jews.*

Kurt Becher was released from Allied detention in December of that year, though he subsequently became the target of "de-Nazification" procedures at Nuremberg. Kasztner again *intervened personally* in the defense of Becher and other former SS officers with whom he had maintained contact during the war. Among the latter was Hermann Krumey, the so-called "writing-desk murderer," who was considered responsible for the deaths of three million Jews.[23]

In 1948, Becher returned to his hometown of Hamburg, where he continued to bask in the aura of his alleged Jewish-rescue activities. Until Saly Mayer's death in 1950, the former SS officer regularly received *"aid" packages.* Existing vouchers indicate that these parcels had come from the Swiss Society for the Promotion of Jewish Emigration.

---

[21] *Magyarok az SS ausztriai lágerbirodalmában* (Hungarians in the Austrian SS Camps), p. 217.

[22] Kasztner signed his deposition as the former president of the Hungarian Zionist Association, 1942 to 1945.

[23] Elam, pp. 68–69. Kasztner traveled to Nuremberg with the backing of the Executive Committee of the Jewish Agency. The former Zionist leader's covert attempt to regain possession of at least a large portion of the Jewish property and assets he had yielded to the Germans in compensation for the release of captive Jews certainly played a role in his changed attitude toward former SS officers such as Krumey. Former SS General Jüttner's assistance to Kasztner in this endeavor prompted the latter to express a favorable opinion of him as well. (During a subsequent meeting in Geneva, Kasztner informed Chaim Pozner of this motive for his change of heart with regard to these German officers.) In 1995, the Israeli historian Shoshana Eshoni-Beri published documents proving that various Jewish organizations, including the Jewish Agency and the Jewish World Congress, had covered the cost of Kasztner's trip to Nuremberg. Ibid., pp. 70, 73.

Becher proceeded cautiously down his new career path. In the late 1940s, the former SS colonel purchased a small company called the *Firma Albert Johann Meyer*. This concern conducted trade in Eastern Europe in the 1950s, importing honey and paprika from Hungary, for example.[24] Later on, his business grew rapidly. His company continued to make inroads into the Hungarian market, establishing profitable trade links with the Hungarian state monopoly foreign-trade company Monimpex. Becher's Hungarian imports centered on distinctive national food products, such as salami and paprika, and alcoholic beverages, such as apricot brandy and fine wines. The former SS officer evidently considered his prior activities in Hungary—his extortion, his plunder, the several millions of dollars worth of material damage he did to the Hungarian economy in less than a half year of SS duty in the country—to be *a strictly private matter.*

Becher's business flourished. His entire family soon became involved in the company's wholesale import trade. By the middle of the 1980's, most of the enormous granaries situated at the Hamburg harbor had become part of the Becher family enterprise. The Bechers also owned other storage facilities located throughout the world—in Frankfurt, Munich, Berlin, Antwerp, Paris, London, New York and São Paulo. However, after learning of Kurt Becher's Nazi past, Dutch officials politely declined the family's request to build a warehouse in The Netherlands.

Former SS Colonel Becher retired from the family business in July 1987, at the age of seventy-eight.

## d. Kasztner's Subsequent Activities, the Jerusalem Trial

Rezső Kasztner returned to Switzerland on April 15. The following day, a banquet was held in his honor at which the Jews who had arrived to safety aboard the *Musterzug*—the "sample train"—celebrated him as their savior. On May 8, the day of Germany's surrender, Kasztner sent a telegram trumpeting his accomplishments to Tel Aviv under the rubric "mission accomplished."

Kasztner again visited the Hungarian refugees residing in Switzerland, who paid tribute to his wartime services at a "festive rally." One of those in attendance later remembered that "he had many shocking things to say about the inhuman devastation ... inflicted by the Germans and Hungarians, to which

---

[24] Becher had already established commercial contacts with Agrimpex by 1949.

ninety percent of our fellow European Jews fell victim." Even decades after the war, the elderly woman who wrote the above lines, like many Jews who lived through the Holocaust, still had not come to grips with the implications of her survival: "We feel like we are unable to bear the weight of our immense pain and grief. Our spirits have been shattered—we just cannot comprehend how and why it happened to be precisely us who survived, just a precious few among so many."[25]

On September 13, Kasztner, then in London, issued a lengthy written summary of his personal observations regarding the attempted extermination of the Hungarian Jewry, again highlighting his own rescue and relief efforts. This treatise contains numerous embellishments: among his wartime accomplishments, Kasztner lists not only the rescue of the Budapest Jewish community, but also the partial survival of German concentration-camp inmates, their escaping full extermination.[26]

Serving as a representative of the Joint, Kasztner spent most of the subsequent months in Vienna, where he helped to organize relief efforts aimed at Jews who had survived deportation.[27] There is no evidence indicating that he returned to Hungary: in 1946, he lived in Zurich; in 1947 he represented the interests of the Jewish World Congress in Genoa.

In 1946, the newspaper *Haladás* published the first detailed account of the "Kasztner operation" to appear in Hungary.[28] This report described Kasztner's wartime Jewish rescue activities as well as the nature of the accusations that had been leveled at him following the war, most notably at the Zionist World Congress in Basel. According to the *Haladás* reporter, the principle charge against Kasztner had been that *"he had collaborated with the Germans and that he could not account for much of the enormous sum of money and assets that he had received from Jews in Hungary and across the world."* The article also mentioned that an international fact-finding committee had been established to investigate Kasztner's financial dealings, as well as the 200-page report that the Zionist leader had prepared in his own defense.

The *Haladás* report concluded that Kasztner had done everything within his power to save "as many Jews as possible." Furthermore, the article stated

---

[25] Devecseri, pp. 95–96.

[26] The integral text of this document is contained in *The Destruction*, vol. II, pp. 907–921.

[27] Between 1945 and 1952, the Joint provided "stateless" European Jews with 342 million dollars in financial assistance and helped to expedite their emigration to Palestine.

[28] *Haladás*, December 25, 1946.

that "his good faith is beyond doubt," an assertion that the ongoing investigation would most likely reconfirm. It was the same newspaper that, beginning on March 6, 1947, published a series of articles under the title "The Grand Trade in Humans," which contained an abridged translation of Kasztner's *Bericht.*

The introduction to the serial maintained that "whispers and false accusations" had focused attention on Kasztner, who had consequently produced his "shockingly powerful" report, which demanded the most extensive publicity possible. The author of the introduction contended that the vile financial dealings of SS officers serving in Budapest at the end of the war "went beyond the cold and heartless commerce carried on by ancient slave traders." The eighteen-part *Haladás* series on Kasztner concluded on July 10. The editors of the newspaper indicated that its readers had taken a keen interest in the translation of Kasztner's vast discourse.[29]

Some light should be thrown on the nearly forgotten figure of Joel Brand as well. Brand was living in Israel at the end of the war. As shock from the wartime devastation began to subside, more and more people concluded that Brand had acquitted himself with tremendous courage in the face of mortal danger. He was widely acclaimed for his natural intelligence and the sacrifices he had made in the interest of Hungarian Jews. Brand served as a witness during Eichmann's postwar trial in Jerusalem, though heart problems plagued him throughout the proceedings. He was close to cardiac arrest.

For many years after the war, Brand insisted upon the seriousness of the SS commodities-for-Jews trade initiative, code-named *Blut gegen Waren,* which he had transmitted to the Allies in 1944. He saw his mission as one of historic significance, underscoring his belief that the Allies made a grave mistake when they rejected the SS "exchange proposal." Toward the end of his life, however, after reconsidering several aspects of his mission, Brand came to realize that he had been merely a tool of one of Heinrich Himmler's survival maneuvers. What the Reich SS chief and his officers serving in Budapest really wanted was to somehow drive a wedge between the Allied powers, giving rise perhaps to a new, anti-Soviet, coalition. Brand ended his life in grave illness, at the age of 58.

Dr. Rezső Kasztner settled in Palestine with his family before the proclamation of the State of Israel. He worked as the director of the Hungarian-language section of the Jewish Agency's radio station, the editor of the newspa-

---

[29] *Haladás,* March 13, 1947.

per *Új Kelet* and, in the early 1950s, the press secretary at the government ministry of commerce and industry.[30] Kasztner also took part in partisan Israeli politics, though he never held an elected office.

It has been suggested he would have been wiser to stay out of the limelight following his emigration to Palestine. Kasztner was presumably aware of this himself, though to have withdrawn from public life would have been incompatible with his restless and gregarious nature. He was incapable of remaining silent in the shadows of the almost immeasurable catastrophe, the terrible destruction wrought on the Jews of Europe.

He was celebrated by many as a savior of European Jews. He himself lived in the conviction that he had made history in the recent past. He became a prominent and influential member of the governing Mapai Party.[31] However, Kasztner was never able to get rid of the cloud of burning questions and rumors that hung over him in a society that was still reeling from the catastrophic personal losses suffered during the war. (Adding to the controversy was the fact that, at the same time, those who had performed individual acts of true heroism, *without the safeguard of de facto immunity from Nazi persecution*, were hardly mentioned at all). Accusations of treason and collaboration followed Kasztner wherever he went. By 1953, more and more Jews, in particular the survivors of the Kolozsvár ghetto,[32] began to place public blame on Kasztner for the deaths of their families and loved-ones at the hands of the Nazis, and demanded justice in an increasingly loud voice.

A scandal had long been brewing. This volatile concoction steeped in the trauma of the Holocaust was finally touched off by a Mizrachi-oriented orthodox Jew named Malkiel Gruenwald, who disseminated a crude, mimeo-

---

[30] "He was a charming person and a fantastic journalist, a genuine European intellectual and a committed Zionist," his one time colleague, journalist Yosef Lapid (Tamás Lampel) wrote in *Új Kelet* on 16 December 1966, on the occasion of the inauguration of the Kasztner memorial Park in Haifa.

[31] The Mapai Party espoused a policy of negotiation with the British. The advocates of a more confrontational approach to relations with the occupational authority considered such talks to be tantamount to "collaboration." On several occasions, militantly anti-British organizations and political parties attempted to draw a tactical parallel between the policies of the Mapai Party and Kasztner's wartime bargaining with the Germans.

[32] During the trial, it became clear that Kasztner had alerted Jewish leaders in Kolozsvár to the impending catastrophe. As a result of Kasztner's warning, several of the passengers on the *Musterzug*, including Dr. Fischer and other prominent Kolozsvár Jews who had been apprised of the manner in which Jews were being killed at Auschwitz, refused to take showers during their journey. Hansi Brand confirmed that the leaders of the Kolozsvár Jewish community were aware of the extermination of Polish Jews.

graphed tract denouncing Kasztner for alleged collaboration with the Nazis.[33] A Zionist court of honor convened to examine Gruenwald's charges and consequently exonerated Kasztner, declaring the allegations to be "unfounded" and "without substance."[34] This verdict did not, however, stem the avalanche of incrimination directed at Kasztner that Gruenwald's pamphlet had set in motion.

Due in part to his status as a party and government functionary, Kasztner was compelled to initiate legal proceedings against Gruenwald, charging him with slander. Kasztner's libel suit came to trial in January 1954, entailing months of hearings that served to revive in vivid detail almost the full story of the tragic devastation of Hungarian Jewry a decade earlier. The Israeli press provided extensive coverage of this trial, which took place in a Jerusalem district courtroom, recounting with precision all the arguments and counterarguments presented during the proceedings.

The court's reexamination of Kurt Becher's activities during the last two years of the war and the exaggerated, unfounded and vainglorious statements that Kasztner made in the former SS colonel's defense, were undoubtedly harmful to the plaintiff's cause. The situation became ever tenser, and Kasztner found himself in a trap: his personal sentiments almost unconsciously impelled him to treat Becher's alleged "heroism" as a fact, though he had no supporting documentation to corroborate his claims to that effect.

According to Kasztner, Becher had been behind Himmler's orders to suspend the deportation of Budapest Jews in August 1944 and to halt the mass execution of Jews held at Nazi concentration camps two months later. Kasztner also testified, again without providing any substantiating evidence, that Becher had played a role in the decision of the SS high command in Budapest to discontinue the forced marching of Jews held at the Óbuda Brick Factory to the Reich in order to construct border fortifications; the former Hungarian Zionist leader likewise claimed that Becher had helped to save the 85,000 Jews amassed in the Budapest ghetto and had prevented the extermination of thousands of others held at various concentration camps.

Kurt Becher himself had taken a much more cautious approach earlier, during questioning connected to the Nuremberg Trials. Though he did present his alleged Jewish-rescue credentials in the course of the proceedings, Becher

[33] "Levelek a Mizrachi tagjainak" [Letters to the Members of Mizrachi]. Hebrew-language newsletter, no. 17, 1953.

[34] Gruenwald was an elderly, pathologically mendacious and defamatory underground journalist.

apparently did not, at that time, recollect having played any part in the effort to save the Jews crowded into the Budapest ghetto in 1944. (Indeed, he played none.) He also all but denied having been appointed "Special Reich Concentration Camp Commissioner" during the final weeks of the war. Becher was presumably aware that this "extraordinary" commission would have made him liable to prosecution for the ordinary, everyday atrocities that the SS had committed during the period of his command.

Kasztner, on the other hand, became entangled in his own, reckless statements during the legal proceedings he had initiated. His self-assured boasting often made a travesty of the courtroom. Kasztner spun a web of unfounded statements and twisted facts in which he himself eventually became trapped. He attempted to extricate himself by glossing over the exonerating testimony that he had previously made in Becher's defense. (As was previously mentioned, in May 1948, Kasztner also made exculpatory statements on behalf of Eichmann's former deputy, Hermann Krumey.)[35] However, evidence presented to the court on behalf of the defendant worked against Kasztner.[36]

Gruenwald's attorney, Shmuel Tamir,[37] deftly pinned the charge of collaboration with the Nazis around Kasztner's neck. The counsel for the defense convincingly argued that the former Hungarian Zionist leader's suppression of Nazi intentions to deport and exterminate Hungarian Jews had made him an accessory to the death of hundreds of thousands of his compatriots. Tamir contended that Kasztner had done all this in order to save a few thousand prominent Hungarian Jews, including his friends and family members.

Justice Benjamin Halevi largely concurred with Tamir's arguments, delivering a scathing opinion in regard to the activities of Kasztner and his associates on June 22, 1955. Halevi's severe and unfounded pronouncement, colored by the prevailing political climate, reverberates to this day: "Kasztner sold his soul to Satan."

---

[35] Kasztner's testimony was of great benefit to Hermann Aloys Max Krumey, who was finally brought to justice more than two decades after war had ended. In August 1969, Krumey and another officer in his unit, Otto Heinrich Hunsche, were finally sent to prison for the crimes they had committed—Krumey for life and Hunsche for twelve years. *Die westdeutschen Strafverfahren wegen nationalsozialistischer Tötungsverbrechen, 1945–1997*, (K.G. Saur Verlag: München, 1998), p. 170. Becher had been called to the stand as a witness at the trials of both Krumey and Hunsche.

[36] Such was the letter he had written to Finance Minister Eliezer Kaplan on June 26, 1948. In this missive, Kasztner boasted that Becher's release from postwar detention in Nuremberg had been the direct result of his personal intervention on behalf of the former SS officer.

[37] Tamir was an extremely aggressive, demagogic and talented lawyer as well as a vociferous partisan of Begin's opposition Herut Party.

However, the Gruenwald trial actually demonstrated that, even given the grave moral complexities of dealing with the devil, it was possible, even compelling, to have confronted Halevi's Satan. But Kasztner—not for the first time—was left to his own devices. Many of the survivors, too, continued to point attacks and accusations at Kasztner, making him a scapegoat for their own omissions. In retrospection, from a distance of several decades, it emerges clearly from certain undertones and particular emphases characterizing the trial that Kasztner's condemnation served as an attack upon the then governing political group as well.

Judge Halevi's verdict had been predicated upon a churning morass of un-healed war wounds and political upheaval. Kasztner and the prosecuting attor-ney filed an immediate appeal with the Israeli Supreme Court. One week fol-lowing Justice Halevi's verdict, the Sharett government collapsed because one of the parties in its ruling coalition abstained from a vote of confidence per-taining to the comportment of the cabinet in connection with the Kasztner trial.

Kasztner's appeal entailed several more months of questioning and cross-examination, which were punctuated by scandals and misconduct of various consequence. The Israeli Supreme Court delivered its definitive verdict in the case on January 15 and 17, 1958. Chief Justice Agragat declared "God forbid us to regard Kasztner as guilty." The sentence of the lower court was annulled by the five-member body, and Kasztner was exonerated from the charge of collaboration with the Germans. Gruenwald was condemned to a one-year, suspended prison sentence for libel.

However, Kasztner did not live to witness this turn of events. He died on March 12, 1957 in Tel Aviv, ten days after having been mortally wounded by assassins' guns.

## e. Becher's Single Interview

In the decades following the war, several attempts were made to bring Becher to justice for the acts he had committed during the war. In the 1960s, a Munich tribunal accused Becher of having participated in the massacre of Jews while serving with an SS cavalry unit operating in the Pripet swamps during the summer and fall of 1941. These legal proceedings implicating the entire staff of which he had been a member were suspended *due to insufficient evidence.*

A court in Braunschweig later resumed the same inquiry, convicting one of the commanding officers from Becher's former SS cavalry unit in 1964, on the charges outlined above. Becher was called to testify again in the case of Franz Magill, who was subsequently sentenced to five years in prison.[38] In sworn statements, Becher indicated that his failing memory prevented his recollection of the incident in question. The former SS colonel claimed that he was unaware of any planned and organized massacre of Jews.

Kurt Becher's name surfaced during Adolf Eichmann's 1961 trial in Jerusalem as well. Eichmann's attorney wanted to call Becher to the witness stand in his client's defense, but Becher refused to travel to Israel for the proceedings. He did appear before a Bremen court to respond to the defense attorney's questions, though the Jerusalem Supreme Court later repudiated this testimony. The same body surely would have done likewise in regard to Becher's frequently stated claim that he had "saved the lives of thousands of Jews."[39]

In May 1982, a Bremen court formally charged Becher with murder for the last time. The proceedings were discontinued in November of the same year, again "for lack of evidence."

Kurt Alexander Becher consented to be interviewed on Israeli television in 1994, the one and only time he was ever to do so. On December 22 of that year, Becher appeared on the program *Fact*, answering questions posed to him by journalist Ilana Dayan. During this interview, Becher discussed his activities as a high-ranking SS officer during the Second World War, touching upon Kasztner's role in Jewish rescue operations and his Jerusalem trial as well. Becher, who claimed to have learned of the proceedings from a German newspaper, declared that he considered the accusations leveled at Kasztner to have been a criminal act against a man who deserved to have a *monument raised in his honor* in Israel for the unparalleled services he had rendered to the Jewish people during the final years of the war. Kasztner was the only one who—in the prevailing circumstances—achieved any real success in the interest of the Jews.

The former SS *Standartenführer* went on to claim that Kasztner had elected to stand up for him deliberately, because he had become "one-hundred percent" convinced of his integrity and good faith. In response to one question, Becher added that the Hungarian Zionist leader had not taken a single penny from funds he had collected for passengers on the train bound for Switzerland

---

[38] The 2nd SS Kavallerie regiment wreaked havoc in the region of Davidgrodek, Janow and Luniniec in 1941, massacring at least 4,500 Jews from the Pinsk ghetto. In addition to Magill, Walter Dunschot and Hans Walter Nenntwich were also given prison sentences of four and a half and four years respectively.

[39] Karla Müller-Tupath, p. 10.

in 1944. Moreover, Kasztner had never given him any money either during or after the war.

In conclusion, Dayan asked the eighty-six-year-old Becher if he regretted anything that he had done during the war. In response, the former SS officer stated that he had carried out his duties as a soldier to the best of his ability; these obligations, which he had performed "with dignity and out of true conviction," had not placed him in a position to do anything about the "Jewish issue." What he did, *he did entirely out of conviction, on the grounds of humanity*.[40]

---

[40] Ibid., p. 225.

# Epilogue

This volume has been the product of extensive research into wartime Jewish rescue operations in Budapest. An examination of the facts and data that emerged during this research indicates that the Germans conducted an active trade in human beings pursuant to their execution of the *Endlösung*. This commerce in human lives became an essential element of the operations of Hitler's "knightly order," the black-clad SS, and constituted and integral part of the implementation of Nazi interests.

During the final years of the war, the SS high command recognized the potential financial profit to be gained through expropriation—"Aryanization"—of the property and assets of Jews corollary to the *Endlösung*. This campaign of plunder entailed both the extortion of wealth from prosperous Jewish families facing the threat of deportation as well as the collection of ransom from the kin of Jews already being held at concentration camps. In either case, the immunity gained through such remuneration *was regarded as only temporary respite,* and was treated according to diverse viewpoints in their circles.

From the summer of 1944 on, exploitation of this abundant source of financial profit became the chief objective of high-ranking SS officers. As a by-product of this quest for riches, these ravenous prosecutors of the *Endlösung*, who had been responsible for the gassing of millions of Jews at Nazi concentration camps, hoped to *wrap themselves in sheep's clothing.* In order to achieve this end, they initiated contacts with "world Jewry" in order to expedite a more or less open trade in humans. Members of the SS high command hoped that, in this way, they might make it appear as if they had attempted to rescue Jews from the very ravages that they, as Hitler's loyal henchmen, had been inflicting upon them. Himmler and his inner circle perceived yet another potential benefit to the trade in humans: the opening of a rift in the Allied coalition lined up against the Reich and Germany's possible subsequent realignment into an anti-Soviet bloc.

This volume, within its confines, depicts a unique series of events that took place during the final year of the Second World War in connection with the struggle to preserve human life. Following Germany's occupation of Hungary, the various elements of the Nazi security apparatus made easy prey of Hungarian Jews, multitudes of whom the SS deported to their deaths at Auschwitz-Birkenau. A small group of Zionist leaders constituting the Budapest Jewish Relief and Rescue Committee, undertook negotiations with these pitiless mass-murderers with the intent of redeeming Jewish lives in exchange for financial compensation.

Ottó Komoly, Dr. Rezső Kasztner and their associates, with off-stage support from the largely underground Zionist movement, thereby became an acting party to the SS' human trade operation. These men courageously ran both the intended and unintended risks of dealing with the persecutors of their people. They wanted to save Jewish lives *at any cost*, lives that meant nothing to the fanatic architects of the genocide and apparently too little to the Western democracies to warrant their undertaking vigorous action to preserve them.

By the middle of 1944, Kasztner had become the primary yet increasingly lonely figure associated with this buyout strategy. Kasztner's aptitudes and personality obviously predestined him for a public role but he was not content with that. He wanted to be the *redeemer* of the Jews. He became entangled in negotiations and situations from which there was no escape. Though he knew his own life was continuously at risk, he elected to take another roll of the dice time after time. He played the game through to its conclusion, organizing, traveling, negotiating, promising, and bluffing. Kasztner attained his objectives, then disavowed them. He saved thousands, while abandoning others for reasons unknown.

Some considered Kasztner to be conceited, while others thought him to be straightforward and congenial. In an everyday sense, he was simply a man whose abomination of what he saw taking place around him compelled him to undertake a complex mission to rectify matters as much as possible. This mission entailed many objectionable duties: Kasztner's discharge eventually forced him into the morally compromising position of German protégé, an inglorious designation that followed him for the rest of his life.

Many aspects of Dr. Rezső Kasztner's wartime activities, particularly his involvement in the human trade, are contradictory. He continues to be a controversial figure to this day: some consider him to have been a servile Nazi lackey, even a scapegoat for the Jewish genocide who merits consignment to the trash heap of history; others view him as a heroic rescuer of Jews, a leader of Jewish resistance to German persecution who deserves to have a statue or memorial erected in his honor.

That Kasztner was a dedicated Zionist is irrefutable. The establishment of a
new Jewish homeland—Eretz Israel—was one of his life's main objectives. After
the war had ended, this ambition thrust him into awkward situations from
which he again emerged, in the eyes of many, as a morally tainted defender of
Nazis. Kasztner's restless nature led him into the deepest recesses of political
life, where spirits born of his wartime commerce with the perpetrators of the
genocide continued to haunt him.

The primary SS negotiating partners of the Budapest Zionists had been
Adolf Eichmann and Kurt Becher. These two members of the Nazi terror
apparatus personified the two primary objectives of the SS in 1944–1945—
completion of the Endlösung and gaining profit, financial and tactical, through
human trade. As described in the pages of this monograph, the two SS officers
approached these objectives from divergent angles and bear varying degrees of
responsibility for their execution. In light of the large existing corpus of histori-
ography dealing with Eichmann and Auschwitz, this book has focused on the
extortion and survival strategies practiced by the lesser known of the two, SS
Standartenführer (a rank attained during the final weeks of the war) Kurt
Becher.

Becher was a cold, calculating, cynical and cunning military careerist. He
was always on the lookout for potential sources of material gain. Becher, contrary to Eichmann, saw his position as a high-ranking SS officer as a vehicle for
personal enrichment. Though no expert in the field of either economics or
diplomacy, the SS Standartenführer nonetheless achieved considerable success
in both.

During the final episode of the war, Becher behaved with brazenness indicative of his pragmatic character. With the war coming to an end, Becher discovered a possible route of escape from under the rubble of the crumbling Reich:
the man who had, until then, served diligently as a persecutor and plunderer of
Jews, assumed the mantle of a rescuer of Jews. In the persons of Kasztner and
Schweiger, the man once described as the SS Reichsführer's "most humble
Becher" had shrewdly identified those negotiating partners who could help
him avoid being held accountable for his persecution of Hungarian Jews and
plunder of the Hungarian economy.

Becher very rarely exposed himself to personal risk, continually taking cover
behind his rank and the powers that be in Berlin, particularly Himmler.

The Book of Fate held good tidings for Kurt Becher. The great self-
preservationist was to live eighty-six years. In August 1995, Becher died an
extremely wealthy man in the northern German port city of Bremen.

Kasztner (similarly to Brand), on the other hand, put everything on the line—his life, his reputation, his family, and sometimes much more than would have been reasonable. He frequently found himself abandoned. In Switzerland, instead of genuine support, he got little more than insincere, temporizing and vacant promises; from the Joint he received only ambiguous messages; and from the various Zionist organizations in Palestine, merely reassuring words.

Kasztner dared to expose himself to crossfire in the no-man's land separating discordant alternatives. He knew that those who ventured to defy the all-powerful Germans perished; however, he was also aware that those who acquiesced were frequently liquidated as well. Kasztner had, therefore, staked out this middle ground from which, transcending all forms of counterfeit morality and starry-eyed romanticism, he was able to coordinate some measure of resistance to the insatiable murderers.

It followed from Kasztner's missionary zeal, personal vanity and the increasingly precarious footing from which he conducted his unyielding struggle on behalf of Hungarian Jewry and his Zionist colleagues that he reached the point where he would be a defender of Nazis and, following the war, providing testimony, however reluctant, in the defense of several SS officers. It is for these reasons that many people came to view him as an accomplice to the collective subjugation and mass obliteration of Hungarian Jewry—*a Jewish scapegoat.*

Beginning in the early 1940s, the constituent members and external benefactors of the Budapest Jewish Relief and Rescue Committee, with Dr. Rezső Kasztner and Ottó Komoly in the lead, undertook a diligent and forthright effort to rescue and otherwise assist persecuted Jews; until the German occupation of Hungary, they worked in cooperation with fellow Zionists Joel and Hansi Brand, Sámuel Springmann and others, to relieve the plight of thousands of Jews who had taken refuge in and around the capital city.

From the early summer of 1944 on, they were engaged in saving life for an enormous counter value. Their self-sacrificing efforts had a great part in helping a *large number of Hungarian Jewish children and occasionally entire families* who had been deported to the territory of annexed Austria to survive what, for six million other Jews, was the terminal catastrophe of the Holocaust. None of them gained any personal profit from their actions. And Ottó Komoly paid with his life for his endeavor to rescue Jewish children.

Eichmann ultimately paid the supreme penalty for his war crimes in 1963; however, many of his fellow SS officers, to the deep chagrin of many, were never to be held accountable for their misdeeds.

On the other side, Kasztner met his end in March 1957, after being gunned down by radical Jewish nationalists. Joel Brand died a nervous wreck in 1964.

*Endlösung* and human trade: this was a complex and contradictory story lasting until 1945, involving ruthless, fanatical executioners as well as desperate men and women fighting to save the lives of others. Though some of the culprits for these crimes were punished for their actions after May 1945, the justice served was inconsistent and incomplete.

# Index